Lyn Ofrane

Stephen P. Cohen, the president of the Institute for Middle East Peace and Development, has lectured at Yale and elsewhere.

Also by Stephen P. Cohen

The Idea of Pakistan

BEYOND AMERICA'S GRASP

BEYOND AMERICA'S GRASP

A Century of Failed Diplomacy
in the Middle East

STEPHEN P. COHEN

PICADOR

FARRAR, STRAUS AND GIROUX / NEW YORK

www.picadorusa.com

Picador® is a U.S. registered trademark and is used by Farrar, Straus and Giroux under license from Pan Books Limited.

For information on Picador Reading Group Guides, please contact Picador.
E-mail: readinggroupguides@picadorusa.com

Designed by Abby Kagan

The Library of Congress has cataloged the Farrar, Straus and Giroux edition as follows:

Cohen, Stephen P., 1945–
    Beyond America's grasp : a century of failed diplomacy in the Middle East / Stephen P. Cohen.— 1st ed.
      p. cm.
    ISBN 978-0-374-28124-3
    1. United States—Foreign relations—Middle East. 2. Middle East—Foreign relations—United States. 3. United States—Foreign relations—20th century. 4. United States—Foreign relations—21st century. I. Title.

    DS63.2.U5C57 2009
    327.7305609'04—dc22

                      2009011519

Picador ISBN 978-0-312-65544-0

First published in the United States by Farrar, Straus and Giroux

First Picador Edition: November 2010

10 9 8 7 6 5 4 3 2 1

For Elaine

CONTENTS

Right after the 1967 Six-Day War, I set out to educate myself about the Zionist conflict with the Arabs in Palestine, and soon I immersed myself in years of direct conversation with Arabs and Israelis, beginning in Egypt, Israel, Jordan, Lebanon, and Syria, and eventually extending from Morocco, Algeria, and Tunisia through Iraq to Saudi Arabia, Kuwait, the Gulf Emirates, and down to Yemen.

I was determined to allow myself the opportunity to be educated not only in the library and by the analyses emerging from Western scholars, but also to a greater part by imbibing the perceptions, beliefs, and perspectives of the peoples of the region—Arab and Israeli, Mashreq and Maghreb, and those from the Arabian Peninsula and the Arab Gulf.

I have spent nearly forty years traveling, sojourning, and visiting in countries throughout the Middle East, talking with and especially listening to intellectuals, businesspeople, political leaders, parliamentarians, journalists, writers, and students and other young people. I have convened many meetings of Arabs and Americans, Arabs and Israelis, and, more recently, Jewish, Islamic, and Christian leaders and religious scholars.

I was fortunate enough to have outstanding teachers, such as Dr. Osama El-Baz, the senior political adviser to Egypt's presidents Sadat and Mubarak; Dr. Boutros Boutros-Ghali, who went from being dean at Cairo University to minister of state for foreign affairs of Egypt during the peace process years from 1978 to 1982, and then became secretary-general of the United Nations; Shimon Peres and Yitzhak Rabin, prime ministers of Israel, and Moshe Dayan, then foreign minister of Israel; King Hussein of Jordan and Crown Prince Hassan of Jordan (as he then was); Hani al Hassan, political adviser to Chairman Yasser Arafat, and who, together with Said Kamal, was the first official PLO interlocutor with Israeli officials; and Said Kamal himself, who has been my longtime friend and colleague and who became PLO ambassador to Egypt and later assistant secretary-general of the Arab League.

I have walked the corridors of power in Washington and the Middle East, and I have trudged through the mean and dusty streets of the powerless, the dispossessed, the underground, and the angry. I have lived the highs of helping to broker peace agreements through my conversations with President Sadat of Egypt, Prime Minister Peres of Israel, and King Hussein of Jordan, and of making many exciting discoveries with Palestinian leaders such as Abu Mazen and, of course, the enigmatic, charismatic, and maddeningly erratic Yasser Arafat. I remember Arafat at his best in meetings I held with him and his confidants Abu Iyad and Abu Jihad, when he broke taboos by beginning to talk to, recognize, and seek peace with Israel; and I still shudder at the memory of him at his worst, trash-talking about Jerusalem and unable to make the decision to say yes to Bill Clinton before the roof fell in on Arafat, Barak, and the whole peace process.

I have listened to people whose detestation for each other seemed bottomless, and I have tried to reach under the mountain of anger, resentment, and contempt to find a core of hope for a better future. When Ehud Barak was crushed by Ariel Sharon in the election of January 2001, and Bill Clinton left office with many pardons but no apologies for his failures in the Middle East, I feared that the violence this time would sink all of my hopes and my work of forty years, and even risk the lives of the many good people I had worked with and trusted.

The more one hopes, the harder the fall. For this reason, many people engaged with Israeli-Palestinian affairs turn to cynicism as a defense against their disappointment. Only the gradual, persistent development of a trusting relationship with individuals deeply rooted in the different sides of the conflict can overcome the temptation of cynicism in the long run. With these trusted relations, one can see and experience oneself how people from the different parties share the pain and disappointment that accompany reversals in the peace process. They live in it when it gets worse and when it improves, and they do not escape from its intensity. And they are always in touch with its victims.

Despite my determination to focus on the people of the Middle East, I gradually came to understand how essential the role of the United States was to the troubled identities of the region, and to the troublesome and dangerous conflict that has continuously smoldered, and sometimes erupted in flames, for almost a century.

This book is the product of these intense experiences and of extensive scholarly research that lasted from my days as a graduate student and then assistant professor at Harvard University in the late sixties and early seventies, through my time teaching these issues at the City University of New York Graduate Center, at Princeton University, at Lehigh University, at the Hebrew University of Jerusalem, at the Jewish Theological Seminary of America, and, most recently, at Yale University. I was also deeply influenced by my experiences lecturing at Cairo's Al-Ahram Center for Political and Strategic Studies, at the Palestinian Research Center in Beirut and Palestine, and at institutions in Jordan, Syria, and Israel.

In December 1976 I was invited to Al-Ahram Center for Political and Strategic Studies, which shared offices with Egypt's leading newspaper, *Al-Ahram Daily*. Instead of the planned one-hour discussion, the Egyptian intellectuals, writers, and government officials present grilled me for four and a half hours with penetrating questions about Israeli society and how it would respond to a hypothetical Egyptian peace initiative. I learned more about Egypt and Arab politics from those questions than I could ever have learned in the stacks of Widener Library. After those many hours in which, as my father used to tell me, I talked my heart out, I was utterly exhausted. Little did I know that answering such questions to Arab interlocutors throughout the region would become a core of my life's vocation. The questions came with underlying hope for peace and often with great hostility toward Israel and toward the United States. But I knew from that first experience that answering those questions, however intentioned by the questioner, was the essential precondition for any change in a positive direction toward peace in the region.

BEYOND AMERICA'S GRASP

PROLOGUE: THE UNITED STATES IN THE MIDDLE EAST

THE UNITED STATES TAKES THE STAGE AS A WORLD POWER

When President Wilson went to Paris in 1919, the world was to discover an important limit of American presidential power. The separation of powers in the United States meant that congressional views on foreign policy could not be ignored in negotiations with the United States. If the party in control in Congress was not the party of the president, congressional leadership could prevent the president from implementing his foreign policy. This remains a very difficult lesson for many foreign leaders to learn and understand. After World War I, whether or not Wilson fully understood this congressional power, he certainly had not prepared the ground for the Republican leadership to follow his innovative direction at the Paris Peace Conference.

Wilson came to Paris much clearer on the philosophy he would carry to the conference than on the military facts on the ground or on the very explicit imperial demands of Britain and France. American idealism in foreign policy was well represented by Wilson's declaration of the Fourteen Points, including the insistence on "open covenants openly arrived at," rather than the secretive diplomacy in which France and Britain specialized. Wilson also spoke for the self-determination of small peoples under colonial control. Most of all, he stood for the idea of the League of Nations, which he saw as the path to open negotiations among the powers of the world and to collective security. Wilson's most important advocacy for an American interest in foreign policy was the primacy he gave to open navigation of the world's seas. He was less precise and less knowledgeable about the working ways of the great powers and of the life of the peoples of the now defunct Austro-Hungarian and Ottoman empires. Sadly, his advisers were unable to fill in all the details. Moreover, Wilson had not built any substantial support for his approach to American policy among members of the majority Republican Party in Congress. Nor could he predict that his own physical vulnerability to ill health would stop him in his tracks. This combination of factors meant that Wilson went to Paris with exaggerated expectations of his ability to influence the other participants and departed with deflated outcomes and a new recognition that the United States did not yet have the necessary power or wealth, or the internal policy unity, to prevail over the entrenched intentions of the European powers.

While in Europe, Wilson expanded his public popularity, but that adulation could not make up for his limited influence with the key leaders he was about to face in negotiations. He was able to persuade them to form the League of Nations, but he could not win on the primary issue: the nature of peace with Germany. As to the future of the Ottoman Empire, he could not overcome the imperial plans of Britain and France. The best he could do on this issue was adopt an idea from Jan Smuts of South Africa: to replace direct imperial control with the institution of a mandate system. But even on the issue of mandates, Wilson could not be fully convincing, because his own American government would not accept a mandate over Armenia, even though the Christian Armenians had suffered terrible massacres. This upset the American people, but not enough to assume this new kind of overseas responsibility.

KING-CRANE COMMISSION

In the days before he left Paris, President Wilson hoped to convince friends in France and Britain that the future of Palestine and Syria could be decided by close consultation with the peoples involved. For this purpose he proposed a tripartite delegation of the United States, France, and Britain, which would go to the region to hear what the people there actually wanted for their future. The French refused to choose a delegation until the British fully withdrew from Damascus and recognized French rights over that territory. The British were not willing to form a delegation unless it was agreed that all considerations would begin from the point of who had military control over the areas to be discussed. Realizing that these British and French conditions were never going to be met, Wilson dispatched his delegation to the region on its own. This commission, which came to be known as the King-Crane Commission, is notable for the wide gap it showed between the perceptions within certain elements of American civil society and the policies of the U.S. government. For example, Henry Churchill King and Charles R. Crane found strong opposition to any French mandate in Syria, but the United States did not have the standing to cancel the secret Sykes-Picot Agreement between Britain and France, which gave France the upper hand on the future of that country. King, president of Oberlin College, was a Protestant theologian, and Crane was a wealthy Chicago businessman with strong Arabist commitments.

The two Americans fulfilled their responsibilities with careful attention and persistence. They interviewed the local people in Syria (including Palestine) and were determined to base their recommendations on what these indigenous residents desired. By the time they submitted their findings, President Wilson had departed from Paris, and their report sat on the shelf, too little and too late to have any impact on actual policy making.

Their King-Crane Commission Report demonstrates one set of attitudes that American civil society had maintained toward the Ottoman Empire. However, it does not grapple with the three factors that actually determined the disposition of these territories. First, the

United States never endorsed the peace conference at Versailles. Second, the British and French had overpowering interests in the conference's outcome, which were directly contrary to the desires of the indigenous Arab peoples, as reported by King and Crane. Third, Woodrow Wilson had already endorsed the Balfour Declaration, which pledged Britain to help establish a Jewish homeland in Palestine. King and Crane had found near unanimous opposition to the Zionist idea among local Arabs.

King's strong Protestant attachment to the Holy Land has continued to be a significant element in American public attitudes toward the Middle East, and Crane's business interests were able to express themselves through the support of an early U.S. search for oil in the Arabian Peninsula. However, the strategic interests of both the United States and its allies in the region would continue to dominate decision making, though that strategic perspective came to include strong support for the eventual Jewish state in the late forties, and since then, and strong emphasis on America's interests in the oil resources of the region. Official negotiations over these territories took place after the Paris Peace Conference had concluded, in San Remo, Italy, in 1922.

U.S. BUSINESS PRECEDES ITS GOVERNMENT INTO OIL POWER IN THE ARAB/PERSIAN GULF

Before World War I, the British had discovered oil in Persia (later to be called Iran) and staked their claim on it by creating the Anglo-Persian Oil Company, which later became the Anglo-Iranian Oil Company. This oil became the basis for British Petroleum, BP. The United States did not compete with the British for control of Iranian oil, but American businesses insisted that their government demand equal treatment for oil purchase by U.S. companies intending to operate in the region. However, the Iranian government of the 1920s wanted U.S. business to play a wider role. Iran sought advice from the American private sector on its oil price negotiations with Britain and on ideas about oil profit sharing with the British. The Iranian government went further still by engaging American businessmen in the general planning of the Iranian economy. Thus a positive niche for American-Iranian business relations had been established since the 1920s. But this private-sector niche was sacrificed by the Eisenhower coup against the Iranian leader Mossadegh in 1953, which undermined the trust and replaced it with the deep suspicion that an American on Iranian soil was up to no good.

Within a few years, U.S. geologists uncovered Saudi Arabian oil, the great mother lode of all petroleum resources. American oil business interests pushed the United States to establish a consulate in Saudi Arabia and to enter negotiations with King Ibn Saud, which led to the creation of Aramco, the Arab-American oil company. A number of leading American oil interests banded together to gain access to the greatest oil resources in history. This agreement with Ibn Saud assured American oil giants of their leadership among all oil distributors.

In the preparations for World War II, the United States realized that it needed more oil than was being pumped in America. Roosevelt sent his trusted aide Harry Hopkins to reach an agreement for Saudi oil to sustain the Allies in their military effort throughout the war. The United States also established a major forward supply base in Egypt, for military equipment and other items needed for the war. In this way, Egypt and Saudi Arabia became two pillars of American national security, which they have remained ever since. With this in mind, President Franklin Roosevelt, though infirm and in his last months of life, decided that his meetings in Yalta with Churchill and Stalin required him to begin planning for the postwar world. He stopped on his way home for meetings with key leaders of the Middle East and Africa. His yacht carried him to the Great Bitter Lake, in Egypt's Sinai Desert, south of the Suez Canal, where he met with King Farouk of Egypt, King Ibn Saud of Saudi Arabia, and Emperor Haile Selassie of Ethiopia. The critical meeting was with King Ibn Saud, and it was a complex and difficult one. The positive outcome was an understanding of the strategic partnership between the two nations. The United States would provide a security umbrella for Saudi Arabia against any non-American foreign influence, especially from the Soviet Union. In return, the Saudis assured the United States and, through it, the soon-to-be-created NATO alliance of a reliable source of energy at reasonable prices to help implement what was to become the Marshall Plan for the reconstruction of Europe, and to ensure American postwar leadership through NATO and through tremendous U.S. economic growth. The problematic part of the meeting between Roosevelt and Ibn Saud was their direct discussion of the future of the Middle East. They failed to reach any agreement on the disposition of Jewish war refugees, a responsibility Roosevelt had himself neglected during the military phases of the war but felt he could no longer postpone. Ibn Saud, of course, could not violate Arab expectations by accepting more Jews in Palestine. Roosevelt, by this time, had accepted the Zionist goal of creating a Jewish state in Palestine, and this, too, was anathema to King Ibn Saud. Remarkably, these two great leaders did not allow this powerful issue of Palestine to undermine their fundamental bilateral strategic agreement.

This Roosevelt–Ibn Saud meeting demonstrated that the United States, by its victory in World War II, had become the most important international player in what would turn into the Israeli-Palestinian conflict and the Israel–Arab states conflict. It also demonstrated that as powerful as the United States was, it could not smother the profound Arab feelings of rejection of a Jewish state. Nor could the Arabs prevail over the American awareness of the necessity, after World War II and the Holocaust, of creating a Jewish state. Despite the strategic significance of the United States to the Arabs going into the cold war, and the strategic significance of the Arabs to the United States by geography and oil resources, neither could move the other. This historic standoff was to continue until the Egyptian president Sadat's peace initiative of traveling to Jerusalem in 1978 and Crown Prince Abdullah's peace initiative leading up to the Arab summit in Beirut in 2002. Roosevelt and Ibn Saud had, in this one intense meeting, resolved the American-Saudi alliance through the cold war, but the Arab-Israeli conflict required many more iterations of struggle and negotiation. It still requires one more on Israeli-Palestinian peace and a regional treaty between Israel and the key Arab states, which can be brought about only by the next great encounter between a U.S. president and a Saudi king, an encounter that would not be allowed to end without an agreement on the future of the Jewish state and the Palestinian people.

The United States under Harry Truman was faced with historic decisions on the partition of Palestine and on the recognition of the state of Israel, as soon as it was declared in May 1948. To carry out these decisions, Truman had to overrule the opposition of the State Department Arabists, which reflected the opposition to a Jewish state from countries such as Saudi Arabia and Egypt. Truman did decide that the United States would join with Britain and France to observe the Tripartite Agreement, a negotiated settlement to refuse arms supplies to either side of any conflict that ensued.

Though the U.S.–Middle East story begins in earnest with President Wilson, the Middle East policies of Britain had many years earlier set the stage on which America would become a leading actor. Our purpose here is not to review British imperial history in the Middle East but—as we turn our attention to specific countries with which the United States has played an important role, especially from World War II onward—to explain some basics of the table as set by the British and the French. Ever since the creation of the Anglo-Persian Oil Company, the British and the Persians tried again and again to reach agreement on a fair division between them of the profits to be made from oil sales. It was the failure of direct negotiations between the Anglo-Persian Oil Company and the Iranian government to reach a long-term understanding that opened the way for the United States to become involved in the core issues affecting the British relationship with Iran and Iran's relationship with its primary natural resource. Somehow the Iranians were able to see the United States as an honest broker in the British negotiations with Iran. In the 1920s the United States could advise without having a major stake in the dispute. But in the 1930s there were changes to the equation: if in the 1920s the United States gained entry as advisers, in the 1930s they became concessionaires. As oil played a more and more prominent role in the industrial development of the United States and Europe and in the strategic planning of World War II, Iran and its oil gained greater strategic importance. It was pressure placed by U.S. oil companies on their government and the great strategic threats emerging in the 1930s that combined to make the struggles over oil-rich countries so intense.

FROM WILSON TO TRUMAN, THE UNITED STATES ENTERS THE ISRAELI-ARAB CONFLICT

Another dimension of American civil society and private-sector impact on U.S. government policy is exemplified by the history of the struggle over the creation of a Jewish homeland and eventually the existence and security of a Jewish state. The idea of a Jewish state grew into existence in the late nineteenth century, through Jewish thinkers in Western Europe such as Theodor Herzl, who lived in Vienna. Herzl was motivated to propose the idea of a Jewish homeland by his disappointing experiences watching the Dreyfus trial in Paris, which shattered his hopes that the Enlightenment and the ideas of equality that had emerged from the French Revolution would allow Jews to become equal citizens in modern Europe. Still, it was in Eastern Europe, where the masses of Jews lived, that the idea of a Jewish state began to have wide popular appeal. Chaim Weizmann, a Russian Jew, first became a Zionist diplomat in continental Europe at the time when he tried to overcome opposition by the Ottoman Empire to Jewish settlement in Palestine and in the Sinai Desert.

With the outbreak of World War I, the central diplomatic scene of Zionist efforts moved to Britain, which was leading the Allied war effort. Weizmann realized that his intense personal diplomacy in Britain nonetheless required some equivalent effort in the United States. The Zionist movement in America was at that time weak, but Louis Brandeis, who had been appointed by Wilson to the Supreme Court, the first Jew ever to hold that high a position, was unabashedly Zionist, and he considered advocacy for Zionism as fully consistent with his American patriotism. Although he played only a minor role in the story of the Balfour Declaration, which was after all primarily a British story, Brandeis did provide timely assistance to Weizmann's efforts with the British cabinet, passing on to Weizmann the critical information regarding Wilson's sympathy concerning the idea of a Jewish homeland. This helped prompt the British cabinet to approve the Balfour Declaration at a critical moment in the summer of 1917. At that time the British were desperate to encourage the United States to enter the war and were very worried about how to prevent Russia from dropping out of it. Given the lack of reliable scientific analysis of Jewish opinion in either Russia or America, it seemed to the British that supporting the Zionist cause could help in both cases, and could preempt the implementation of the rumored idea of Germany's becoming the new sponsor of Zionist diplomatic aspirations. This stereotyped exaggeration of Jewish power over either American or Russian decisions is a powerful example of the unintended benefits to Jews that sometimes comes from the anti-Semitic imagination.

Woodrow Wilson's semi-entry into the Middle East created an ambiguous legacy for his successors, persisting until today. Wilson brought to his thinking about the transition of Ottoman lands from their colonial status a strong American idealism that aroused powerful hopes that the United States, as it rose to world power, would bring about a change in world politics that would liberate many oppressed peoples. However, this idealism was not matched by an equivalent commitment to action. Wilson's benevolent view of how victory in World War I should be free both of punishment of the losers and of the extension of imperial ambitions was not the one he had shared with a broad consensus of the American people. After returning from the Paris Peace Conference, Wilson began to face the Republican congressional rejection of his ideas for the League of Nations and for collective security. He was determined to go over the heads of Congress directly to the American people. He started his amazing, exhausting series of speeches, traveling from state to state and city to city, until his human frailty overwhelmed his superhuman idealism.

Wilson had left Paris before the ultimate decisions were made about the succession to the Ottoman Empire. He was right that he had to rescue his peace leadership ideas in America, but he ignored his inability to fulfill the promises implied in his Fourteen Points speech made before entering the war, the speech that had ignited so much hope in the Arab world that America was going to champion their self-determination after the war. It is not that he could have done it, even if he had stayed longer in Europe, but that by making this great promise and not fulfilling it, he initiated the problematic American reputation of speaking with idealism about the future of others while acting in service of American self-interest.

If we see the Paris Peace Conference as a great struggle between Wilsonian ideals of a new world order after the war versus the continuation of the British and French struggle for power against Germany as the great land and economic power of Europe, it seems that Wilson's ideas were defeated until Franklin Roosevelt, George Marshall, and Dwight Eisenhower, in alliance with the Russian Red army, crushed Germany more fully in World War II. This unconditional surrender of Germany put an end to the great wars of Europe. Only then could a consensus emerge to forge a world organization made up of all the combatants, this time including the United States. However, the joining of American, British, and Russian forces in the conquering of Berlin also set the stage for the cold war, which dominated world politics for the next forty-five years. This shift of power from Britain and France and their empires to the United States signaled an end to the colonial domination of the Middle East and Africa. The United States has continued to try to control the politics of the Middle East with its values and with power exerted from a distance, and even from within the region itself, but it still has not instilled in its people sufficient understanding and empathy for that world and its culture and religions to be able to maintain that singular impact on life in the region and the values of its peoples.

CHAPTER 1

WILSON SEARCHES FOR LEADERSHIP

W hat is the role of the United States in the Middle East? How is that role perceived around the world? The difficulty of these questions goes back to the very origins of the United States and to how the Founding Fathers understood the idea of a republic. Their concept of a republic was shaped in contradistinction to an empire, as a construct that had grown out of the struggle for independence from Britain. At the same time, a parallel, but no less pervasive, view was emerging in America. In this view, the United States was a potential world power on par with Britain, that would take her rightful place in civilizing the world. The continuing tension between these disparate national self-perceptions manifested itself in the sometimes confused role the United States played in the seminal period following World War I.

The first hundred years of American foreign policy focused on staying disentangled from the internecine battles of the Great Powers of Europe and their competition for empire. A major reason for America's remaining out of the race to colonize was its desire to ensure that its economic development would not be impeded by the policies of other governments. Because much of America's early economic development was linked to Britain, the maintenance of proper credit and trade relations with the motherland was essential for American growth and prosperity. It was not in the best interest of the fledgling American economy to clash with Britain over imperial aspirations. And so it was that the British model of international relations was the model that America both emulated and rejected. For example, it was the British model of naval power that set the American course for its own military expansion after the devastation of the Civil War; but it was the British model of empire, rejected by most in the United States, that was seen by President Woodrow Wilson as a reason to maintain a healthy distance from Britain and its goals in World War I.

These conflicting attitudes toward Britain as role model emerged as the sharp distinction between the two American presidents who led the United States into its modern international role at the beginning of the twentieth century: Theodore Roosevelt was the first American imperial president; Woodrow Wilson the first American anti-imperial president.

Roosevelt bestrode the world as a great hunter, a man on safari. He wanted the United States to itself be a Great Power and to reinforce the role of Britain in the world by playing an equivalent role in new areas of special interest, such as the Western Hemisphere and in East Asia. He saw these regions as the keys to the economic future of the United States as a Pacific economic powerhouse. This led to America's leading role in the construction of the Panama Canal and its dominance of the Canal for a hundred years. Wilson, on the other hand, traveled to Europe as a peacemaker, struggling to manage the transition from theoretician to practical negotiator. The differences between the two men led to very different views on how the United States should see World War I and the peace negotiations that followed it. Even from his deathbed in a New York hospital, "Theodore Roosevelt issued a statement repudiating the Wilson Fourteen Points, and calling upon Britain, as a victor in war, to claim whatever spoils it felt entitled to,"[1] while at the same moment Wilson was attempting to convince Britain of the virtues of a "peace without victory."

The Roosevelt-Wilson contrast is the context in which America's involvement in the world has to be understood. Wilson wanted open agreements arrived at only to replace the Great Power competition, including its politics of secret alliances and compacts. Not unlike Roosevelt, Wilson also saw a unique role for the United States, but for him its uniqueness needed to be expressed in nonimperial forms and in ways that enhanced the United States as a Great Power seeking peace and cooperation rather than military advantage or projection of power. The tension between these different approaches to America's role in the world has never been resolved; they both continue to find expression in the debate on U.S. foreign policy, and especially foreign policy toward the Middle East.

AMERICAN PREPARATIONS FOR THE END OF WORLD WAR I

Wilson was unprepared to be a wartime president. He had been elected on domestic issues and was well prepared with his internal agenda, but had never really focused on the broader world. As that world descended into the Great War in 1914, Wilson began to focus his imagination on America's entering the scene of world politics after its long quiescence spent consolidating its nationhood and building its economic strength. Wilson did not see America as a new player who would tip the European balance of power. Rather, he envisioned the United States as a transforming phenomenon, a new and nobler kind of Great Power: a nation that was strong and wealthy and yet, for all that, did not pursue control of the world system. His dream was of a United States as the power that would use its influence to bring an end to this Great War and then to all wars, to resolve the conflicts started by others, and to bring about a world economy based on a truly global free trade system. Most of all, Wilson's United States would launch a new world order guided by an international organization that would abolish the system of secret covenants covertly negotiated that had led to antagonistic alliances of world powers, and had deluded them into believing they could successfully wage war against other powers without suffering unacceptable losses.

In this lofty but grandiose self-image of the United States, Wilson was initiating a pattern that would play itself out again and again over the next century. He drew on the best ideals flowing from America's democratic and constitutional origins and created a distinctly American image of what was right and what was best, and then projected that image onto the world, all the while justifying the use of force to spread those ideals and to muscle others into adopting and complying with them. The result for Wilson and his successors has been deep disappointment at not having been able to realize this idealized image so admired by still-colonized peoples. Instead, America has engendered disillusion, mistrust, and even intense resentment in other nations. The best intentions have curdled into sour expectations. America's attempts at making the world mirror American ideals and aspirations have been received by the world as invitations to lie upon a very well appointed Procrustean bed.

Wilson did not adequately assess the intensity of opposition in his own country to putting American power and wealth to such an altruistic use. The idea of collective security implicitly entailed the threat that the United States would be drawn into wars not of its own choosing and generated by others. Wilson was thinking of a smaller and more homogeneous world than that in which the United States finds itself in the twenty-first century. He did not imagine an America that would choose to enter precisely the conflicts involving control of non-European countries that he saw as the legacy of empires and colonies, a legacy he abhorred. He certainly did not envision the United States deeply engaged in conflicts involving the states that emerged out of the Ottoman Empire after the end of World War I.

However, Wilson did venture boldly into that colonial world with his strong rhetorical support for the concept of national self-determination for subjected peoples that would eventually come to undermine the stability of the imperial order that prevailed in his time. In doing so, he accelerated the launch of an international concept that heightened expectation of change in the world system, particularly among colonized and imperially controlled peoples, who believed their time of independence was approaching and passionately expected their impending freedom to be championed by the United States.

Wilson knew very little of the details of life and governance in those new post-Ottoman Middle Eastern countries. Even his advisers were not especially knowledgeable about those lands or the challenges they faced as they emerged from the ruins of the Ottoman Empire.

For three long, bloody years Wilson kept America out of World War I, despite persistent pressure from Britain and France and from pro-British elements within the United States. America's active merchant marine and banking support were essential to keeping the Triple Entente afloat during those difficult years. Wilson's efforts to stay out of the war were grounded in his view that the conflict was essentially about the old politics of European power struggles and thus did not merit the involvement of the United States. He believed his role would emerge at the end of the war, in the form of his serving as a mediator and peacemaker. As early as 1916, Wilson was corresponding with the leaders of Great Britain and France to offer himself in that capacity. He hoped to fashion a peace settlement that would represent a major departure from the status quo in world affairs and prevent future massive wars. "At a time when militarism was becoming the prevailing mood, [Wilson] had spoken in the noblest tradition of Western Liberalism,"[2] calling for a just peace for all parties. By the time the Americans were drawn into the war by the Germans, Wilson had long been preparing for the peace.

Wilson's formulation of the postwar world entailed three major initiatives. The first was his policy of "a peace without victory." Throughout 1917–18, almost everywhere Wilson spoke he enunciated his ideas about a proper peace settlement at the end of the war. He was convinced that if the Germans were humiliated by the conclusion of the war and its postwar settlement, Germany would, before long, engage in yet another war with Britain and France, and the cycle would not be broken. His ideas further involved support for self-determination to meet the national aspirations of the subjugated peoples of the nonvictorious empires. In a speech delivered on July 4,

1918, Wilson set out his vision of the peace settlement with particular anti-imperial eloquence:

> The settlement of every question, whether of territory, of sovereignty, of economic arrangement, or of political relationship, [should be] upon the basis of the free acceptance of that settlement by the people immediately concerned, and not upon the basis of the material interest or advantage of any other nation or people which may desire a different settlement for the sake of its own exterior influence or mastery.[3]

Wilson's idea of the way peace should be approached was a departure from the historical course of conquest and annexation. He tried to establish from the beginning that the United States was going to the Paris Peace Conference as an arbiter, not to seek territorial aggrandizement. He hoped to convince the other Great Powers to engage in the conference on the same premise, but their human and economic losses were too great to allow such farsightedness. As I discuss later, Wilson's expectations were continually frustrated by the Allied Powers' attempts to undermine his vision of a just peace.

In order to reach his stated ends of a peace without victory, Wilson had drafted what have become known as his Fourteen Points. The Fourteen Points were delivered on January 8, 1918, to a joint session of Congress, and they included such ideas as open covenants, openly arrived at; adjustment of colonial claims based on the interests of the local populations; and autonomous development for the peoples of the Austro-Hungarian and Ottoman empires.[4] But for Wilson, the most crucial section of his speech was the last, in which he called for the creation of a general association of nations. This association, to be called the League of Nations, was intended to be an international body that would be responsible for the application of the peace settlement and the maintenance of a new world order. Wilson saw the League as the most promising means of forestalling another international war, and so he became entirely focused on it. Throughout the Peace Conference in Paris, Wilson pushed tirelessly for the creation of the League, and in an almost single-minded way became determined to implement it.

The third part of Wilson's preparations for the peace conference took the form of an advisory council. In order to prepare himself for his time in Paris, he drew upon his career in academia. He had his closest adviser, Colonel Edward House, create the "Inquiry," an agglomeration of scholars brought together to study and prepare reports on various areas of the world. "The Inquiry provided the earliest precedent of use by the United States government of numerous scholars whose special talents were directed toward the shaping of American Foreign Policy."[5] The scholars were arranged by area, studying Africa, Austria-Hungary, the Balkans, the Far East, Italy, Latin America, the Pacific Islands, Russia, Western Asia, Western Europe, economics, diplomatic history, and cartography.[6] The members of the Inquiry worked for months before the peace conference, and many accompanied Wilson to serve as his advisers in Paris.

All of Wilson's preparation combined to establish a new framework for peacemaking and diplomacy that he saw as a beacon of light for oppressed peoples around the world. His ideas of self-determination and independence "kindle[d] the fire of extreme nationalism in the newly created states of Eastern Europe"[7] as well as throughout the fallen Ottoman Empire. Minorities in all corners of the globe heard in Wilson's words the promise of an end to imperialism and an opportunity for independence. They anticipated an imminent change in the tide of Great Power politics.

What is striking is that it appears that when he was drafting his Fourteen Points, Wilson did not know much about the Ottoman Empire, nor did he ever truly realize what an impact his ideas had on the people of that region. At this time very few, if any, Americans studied the modern Middle East, and so the "expert" who was to be Wilson's guide, William Westermann, actually knew very little about the region or its people. His specialty was the Middle East of the Byzantine period.[8]

Ironically, it was to the people of the Ottoman Empire that President Wilson became a hero. Even though it was not the primary focus of Wilson's commitment to self-determination, it was in the Ottoman Empire that an idealistic image of the United States and its perceived goals in international relations was to have its biggest impact by its stark contrast with the imperial goals of Europe. While the Great Powers were seen as the contrivers of confidentially negotiated agreements arrived at over the heads of the people to be governed, Wilson was seen as the advocate for independence for Ottoman Arab lands and peoples and for governance emerging primarily from their own desires and aspirations, not from those of colonialist powers.

But by the end of the Paris Peace Conference, the hopes of the Ottoman peoples were crushed. When Wilson left the conference in June of 1919, owing both to mounting domestic pressure to return to America after a full six months abroad and to concerns about his health, the future of the Ottoman Empire had barely been discussed, and had certainly not been decided. It had become clear that Wilson was an unwelcome interloper in the domains of British, French, and Italian statesmen, and a threat to their secret treaties. His British and French colleagues in Paris were determined that the Middle East question be delayed so that it would be addressed only after Wilson, with his curiously ingenuous anti-imperial fixation, had decamped. The failure to resolve the future of the peoples and lands of the Ottoman Empire during Wilson's six months in Paris left Great Britain and France free subsequently to divide the spoils between them. Disinclined ever to adopt Wilson's ideas, the British and French denied the peoples of the Ottoman Empire the self-determination and independence they thought within their grasp. This changed the face of the Middle East forever, with disastrous ramifications for the region and for world peace.

WILSON IN PARIS

When considering Wilson, most historians focus on the rejection of the League of Nations by the U.S. Congress. Doubtless, this had dramatic effects on international relations and even domestic politics, but it is not the only event of his career with persistent aftershocks. Wilson's complete disappearance from the negotiations surrounding the Ottoman Empire meant that the decisions taken at the Paris Peace Conference would be subject to the old diplomacy of the European powers, and despite the influence Wilson had on the leaders' thinking, the people of the Ottoman Empire would ultimately be denied the benefits of Wilson's innovative ideas.

Since both Theodore Roosevelt and Woodrow Wilson saw foreign policy primarily through the lens of foreign trade and economic development, the Middle East would not play an important role for America until the era of oil discovery beginning in the 1930s. However, the multiethnic mosaic of the Ottoman lands had already become of interest to American civil society in the nineteenth century, especially with regard to religious life and educational institutions. American religious and educational outreach fostered a strong identification with the Holy Land, especially Jerusalem and the surrounding territory, as the birthplace of Christianity and with the presence of numerous Christian minorities in many predominantly Muslim areas. Americans had also started their tradition of developing important local educational institutions in the Ottoman Empire, beginning with Robert College in Constantinople and the Protestant College of Beirut, which eventually became the American University of Beirut. Many of these institutions still play valuable roles in the education of young men and women in Turkey and in the Arab world, and have trained many key leaders of the region.

These Christian and institutional ties played an important role in President Wilson's decision to refrain from declaring war on the Ottoman Empire even after the United States had declared war on Germany and its other allies. In this, Wilson began the tradition of American Middle East foreign policy's being heavily influenced by American civil society's concerns and lobbies. As a result, the U.S. Navy was restricted to its peaceful role of transferring refugees from one part of the Ottoman Empire to another, including from Palestine to Egypt, and was involved in humanitarian efforts on behalf of the Christians of Armenia and, to a lesser extent, the Kurds on the border areas of Turkey, Syria, and Iraq. This focus on minorities had the be-clouding effect at that time of limiting popular perception in America of the plight of the majority Muslim populations, who suffered from poor government, economic underdevelopment, and foreign control and occupation.

During his six months in Paris, Wilson became increasingly aware of the various secret agreements and understandings that had been concluded among the Allied Powers during the war: the Sykes-Picot Agreement of 1916 between Britain and France, in which territories in Syria and Palestine were divided between them; the Balfour Declaration of 1917, in which the British government promised the Jewish people a national homeland in Palestine; and the McMahon-Hussein Correspondence, in which the British government gave the Hussein family reason to believe that the British intended to create an independent Arab state in Arabia under Hashemite rule in return for the Arabs rising in revolt against the Ottomans. While Wilson was clearly troubled by the colonialist intentions of Britain, France, and Italy[9] toward the lands of the former Ottoman Empire, he was more focused on the settlement with Germany and the formation of the League of Nations. He felt that if he could implement the League, it would be a barrier to the Allied Powers' plans to annex the former Ottoman lands. Wilson had complete faith in his own prediction that the League was the antidote to the old diplomacy of Europe. So while he abhorred the "land grab" that seemed foremost in the minds of the British and French, it was not where he was placing his primary attention.

Wilson was confident enough in the power of the newly created League of Nations that he left Paris in June of 1919 with few concerns as to the remains of the Ottoman Empire. It might be said that he was not committed enough to the issues of Ottoman succession to extend his stay long enough to attend the second phase of the conference, to be held in San Remo, which was to dispose of the Ottoman Empire. However, it is more likely that he believed that the main thrust of his work was done. He had developed, presented, and implemented the League of Nations, and now it was up to that institution to serve its purpose. (It is also important to note that since the United States had never declared war against the Ottoman Empire, many in Wilson's administration felt that it was inappropriate for the president to preside over the decisions being made with respect to that region.)

Despite his absence from San Remo, the imprint of Wilson's ideas remained on the deliberations of the European leaders and eventually reverberated, albeit not loudly, in the settlement. His influence was felt in the hesitancy of the other Great Powers to establish direct colonial rule in the Arab areas of the Ottoman Empire. Even if the principle of self-determination was to be denied, and independent states were not proposed, the compromise eventually reached was shaped in part by Wilsonian sensitivities against empire. During his time in Paris, Wilson had become an advocate of the idea of mandates as a form of transitional rule. A mandate offered less direct control by the foreign power than direct colonial rule and was supposed to become a training ground for local peoples to later independence. It was this idea of mandates that the leaders chose to implement at San Remo as a palatable compromise between the old structures of colonialism and the Wilsonian principle of self-determination.

FAILED MANDATES

It is unclear if Woodrow Wilson, when he sailed for Paris, understood the extent to which the Great Powers were still mired in the paradigm of the old diplomacy of Europe. Wilson sought to begin the conference with the creation of a League of Nations. He argued that "the war had its roots in Europe, not Africa or the Pacific, and that European settlements came before the disposition of colonies."[10] Britain and France entered into the conference with territorial agendas and wanted to decide the fate of German and Ottoman possessions before the League was discussed. Wilson quickly realized that his colleagues spoke publicly of a peace without victory, but at the negotiating table demanded reparations and territory from the German aggressors. He felt strongly that "if the process of annexation went on . . . the League of Nations would be discredited from the beginning. The world expected more of them. They must not go back to the old games, parceling out helpless peoples."[11]

But Wilson also began to doubt the feasibility of his ideas. First, he became increasingly convinced that there were peoples in Eastern Europe and the former German colonies who were not ready for complete independence, peoples who could not yet govern themselves. Second, as Wilson began to learn the extent of the secret agreements between and among the Allied powers, he feared that each nation with territorial claims flowing from these agreements would leave the conference, and the League would be destroyed. Based on these growing fears, and with the encouragement of the South African general Jan Smuts, the idea of mandates developed.[12]

Initially, Wilson wanted nonimperial states such as the Scandinavian countries to take trusteeship over the former German and Ottoman colonies.[13] However, this trusteeship idea faced implacable opposition from the other Great Powers. They argued that if there were to be mandates rather than colonies, they had the right to govern those mandates. Eventually Wilson compromised further and allowed that the Great Powers, through the League of Nations, could hold temporary mandates. He hoped that the process of granting mandates through the League would inhibit imperialistic opportunism, while at the same time allowing for the development of new states under the tutelage of Western nations. He became convinced enough by the idea of mandates that when offered a U.S. mandate over Armenia, he was willing to present it to the American people with his full backing.[14] The Great Powers accepted Wilson's idea of mandates, thinking that they could appease him for the moment and do as they wished with their territories once the mandates were granted.

The system of mandates seemed apt for Eastern Europe: it was enshrined in the Treaty of Versailles. What Wilson did not stay long enough to do was to ensure that the idea of the mandates was accepted and internalized both by the Great Powers holding the mandates and by the peoples in the former Ottoman Empire over which the mandates were to be held. William Westermann, Wilson's top adviser on the Ottoman Empire, explained in an essay, "What Really Happened at Paris," that

> The liberation of Armenia was the one outstanding result expected from the Near Eastern negotiations at the Peace Conference. The failure to meet this general expectation was indirectly a result of the struggle among the Allied Powers [Britain and France] for equality or priority of opportunity in the commercial exploitation of the old Turkish Empire . . . In the pursuit of these objects the independence and protection of Armenia became a thing men talked about, but did not work for.[15]

As a result, the mandate period following the war was not to be characterized by peaceful agreed transitions to training in self-rule and democratic self-government, but instead by a struggle, often an armed struggle, between the imperial powers and local national popular movements. Often, it was not democracy that was to emerge from these struggles, but autocracy, whether of monarchs or of military dictators. Herbert Hoover later wrote that he was

> convinced that the judgment and attitude of the President in these matters were due to his unfamiliarity with Old World diplomacy and too much confidence in General Smuts when that statesman's own imperial interests were at stake . . . It is my belief that the President, to put it bluntly, was just fooled. He was certainly under an illusion as to the ultimate effect of the mandates.[16]

DIVIDING THE UNIFIED ARAB STATE

The story of Syria and Palestine is the best example of the breakdown of the idea of mandates. This case makes it clear that mandates were not a means to a democratic and independent end, but an imposed solution that became indistinguishable from colonial rule once popular revolt was suppressed.

One of Wilson's Fourteen Points was that "the other nationalities which are now under Turkish rule should be assured an undoubted security of life and an absolutely unmolested opportunity of autonomous development."[17] This idea led him, during one of the rare conversations at the Paris Peace Conference that addressed the Ottoman Empire, to propose the creation of an Inter-Allied Commission of Inquiry that would consult with the local Arab leadership and the indigenous people and then report back on the desires of the people. However, the French and British feared that this plan would jeopardize the secret Sykes-Picot Agreement they had concluded during the war. And so, though they publicly agreed to the Commission of Inquiry in principle, they found ways to stall and avoid the actual mission. As we have said earlier, the Americans, on the other hand, appointed commissioners immediately and brought them to Paris to prepare for their expedition. One, Charles R. Crane, was a Democratic Party campaign contributor and fund-raiser, and the other, Henry Churchill King, was the president of Oberlin College.

After more than six weeks of waiting for the British and French to appoint their commissioners, Wilson passed along an ultimatum to his colleagues, saying that his two commissioners, King and Crane, would be leaving the following Monday with or without the commissioners from France and Britain.[18] In these last moments, the French announced that they were not willing to participate in the commission unless French troops had first replaced British troops in the occupation of Damascus. The British, for their part, were unwilling to send their commissioners without the French commissioners, but were also unwilling to change the troop deployment in Damascus. Faced with this stalemate, the Americans went alone, and thus what was meant to be an Inter-Allied Commission became simply an American enterprise known thereafter as the King-Crane Commission.

The people of the Ottoman region knew about Wilson's Fourteen Points and pinned their hopes on his ideas of self-determination. They enthusiastically welcomed King and Crane as ambassadors of Wilson's ideas. But despite the good intentions and strongly affirmative reception the American mission received, by the time King and

Crane returned to Paris the next fall to report on their findings, Wilson had already left for home. Their report became a dead letter and would form no part of American policy planning. And finally,

> in December 1919 the United States Government withdrew from active participation in the work of the Peace Conference. This removed the chief deterrent to the settlement of the Turkish problems, in the sense that no force opposed to the secret treaties was any longer represented in the meetings of the Supreme Council.[19]

The Allied Powers were left with a free hand to carve up the Ottoman lands between them, as they had originally intended.

King and Crane reached two main findings, both of which were completely ignored in the disposition of the territories. First, the people they spoke with wanted the area, Syria (including Lebanon) and Palestine, to be maintained as one undivided state. Second, if the people were to be under mandate and not become independent states, they wanted a mandate under the United States. They would have grudgingly accepted a British mandate, but they were especially hostile to a French mandate over Syria. And yet the decision reached by the French and British at San Remo was to make Syria and Lebanon separate from Palestine and to give the mandate for Syria to France. The decisions reached at San Remo began the tradition of differences between the United States and Europe over the Middle East and set a course for the disaster that has been the relationship between the West and the Arab world over nearly the last century.

In the United States, King-Crane garnered little attention and less support. By the time Wilson received their report, he had already suffered from the stroke that would essentially incapacitate him for the rest of his term, and the report never really proceeded beyond his sickbed. But even if the report had been passed along to the State Department or to Congress, given the rejection of Wilson's cherished idea of the League of Nations by the U.S. Senate and its Republican leadership, it is highly doubtful that the King-Crane ideas would have had any takers among the U.S. leadership. Moreover, American leaders demonstrated no interest in the idea of an American mandate for Christian Armenia, which had been offered as part of the Ottoman settlement.

There was one deep complication for American foreign policy evident in the King-Crane report, even though it was not the main thrust of its recommendations. Still, it is an issue of much longer staying power and significance: the British government's Balfour Declaration formally enunciating its sympathy with the concept of a Jewish homeland in Palestine. Wilson had expressed support for the Balfour Declaration in Paris, and earlier in America,[20] but the King-Crane report had found this idea anathema to their Syrian interlocutors. In June 1919, King and Crane sent a message to Wilson trying to explain how hostile the region was toward a Jewish homeland in Palestine. Their letter intimated that the only way the "Zionist program" could be initiated in the region was through military force.[21] But for Wilson the idea of a Jewish homeland in Palestine was compatible with two of his main concerns after the Great War: self-determination (and a Jewish state was a species of self-determination for the Jewish people) and the plight of the Jewish minority in Eastern Europe and Russia (and this was responsive to that concern, albeit not an immediate answer to their present suffering, their marginalized political and social status, and their severely circumscribed freedom of religion in Russia and the new Poland). Also for these reasons, the King-Crane recommendations therefore went unheeded.

The coup of getting the Balfour Declaration endorsed by Wilson is an important part of the story of the British cabinet decision to issue the declaration and paved the way for Wilson's decision to publicly support the idea of a Jewish homeland. This was the first example of the Jews of the United States beginning to support the Zionist idea at the diplomatic level. Ever since the presidency of Benjamin Harrison, American Jews had had access to American presidents to plead the case of oppressed Jews in Eastern Europe, but during World War I the idea of a Jewish homeland became supported by a large enough part of the Jewish community to overcome the anti-Zionism of the early Reform Movement and the fear of Zionism in the American Jewish Committee and among other successful German Jewish immigrants to the United States. An interesting aside is that Christian Zionists, led by William Blackstone, petitioned President Harrison to support the Jewish resettlement of Palestine some twenty-five years before Jewish Zionists first broached the issue with President Wilson.

American Middle East policy, ever since Wilson, has had to deal with the cross-pressure of intense lobbying from Arabists such as Henry Churchill Crane on the one hand and Jewish leaders such as Louis Brandeis and Felix Frankfurter on the other. Unfortunately, neither Wilson nor his successors were ever able to bring about a fully open and rational policy discussion with the American people about these issues, and they continue to be the source of internal conflict among American interest groups, with their contradictory demands on each successive American president.

It is hard to judge how much Wilson himself foresaw the emerging clash between Arabs and Jews or if he realized that the Zionists and Arabs of Palestine would come to see their respective claims for self-determination in the land of Palestine as fundamentally in contradiction. Did Wilson face up to the problems of the concept of self-determination in deciding who was a proper candidate for what, and when they were to be deemed ready for independence? Did Wilson see that the "self" in the concept of self-determination presupposed a solidary, unified nation, failing which self-determination could turn into a formula for the "self" being an autocratic ruler and not a democratic people, or that there could be struggles to define who was part of the nation and who was not?

CONCLUSION

When Wilson arrived in Paris in 1919, the old empires on the losing side of the war had already devolved into a congerie of new nations. Twenty-seven of them had already been approved to sit at the negotiating table, and seven more were at the conference as observers. It was clear that the ideas of nationalism and self-determination were powerful forces sweeping across the globe. In this respect, Wilson's intentions were honorable and timely. He sincerely longed for a new world order that would do away with the ideas of imperialism, but his decision to return home rather than participate in the creation of an Ottoman settlement contributed to a new world disorder and sowed the seeds for the troubles that the United States would face after World War II. This failure, especially in the realm of the Ottoman Empire, contributed to the inability of the Great Powers to establish political systems that could rest on the legitimacy of the assent of the governed. Because the mandate system was so contrary to what the people of the Ottoman Empire wanted, it required strong military power on the part of the French and British, and the installation of authoritarian rulers to keep control of the people. And when the Europeans finally had to concede their mandates because they could no longer afford to keep up the large armies needed to support the corrupt rulers, they left behind a legacy of military leaderships that were no more capable of facing up to the problems of modernization and the challenges of creating democratic societies than were the imperialist regimes that had preceded them.

To understand the history of America in the Middle East, we must pause to point out that the advocacy of Wilson, with its wide gap between his high principles and the emergent political situation on the ground, was the beginning of the perennially vexing problem of the Arab and Muslim perception of the United States. This problem is one of perceived hypocrisy and double standards, the belief that the United States advocates great values, but does not behave in conformity with those values and, when it comes to Arab states, often acts in direct contradiction to them. Wilson helped create the high expectations of America that many Arabs have maintained, alongside their disappointment in the gap between those expectations and the perceived lack of fulfillment. America's lack of participation in the implementation of an international system based on the principles it advocates helped to contribute to one of the persistent and devastating critiques of America in the Arab and Muslim world.

It is also crucial to point out that while America made the decision (correctly or incorrectly) not to become engaged with the European powers in haggling over the future of the Ottoman Empire, in the end it is America that has inherited the bitter legacy left by the European mandates and the imperial regimes that supported them.

Wilson left a confused legacy. Despite the deep antipathy he felt toward colonial and imperial regimes, the desire for American leadership resulted in the United States assuming a large measure of Great Power responsibility. At the same time, its absenting itself from a crucial stage of the postwar process regarding the Middle East evoked the anger and disappointment of the people in the region. This confused legacy continues to be at the heart of the problem between the United States and the Middle East.

A PERSONAL APOLOGIA

This American-educated academic finds in the emergence of Woodrow Wilson a striking point of identification with the saga of America's emergence on the world scene and its great impact on the societies and states of the Middle East that struggled to emerge after the fall of the Ottoman Empire. Wilson had been a university president at Princeton, and his moral, religious, and intellectual foundations would not allow him simply to fall into the imperialistic mold of his most recent presidential predecessors. His ambition for America in world affairs was to have the nation as a new actor in world leadership, not to join the eternal struggle among great powers for dominance, but instead to transform the very game by turning competition into cooperation. The combination of religious commitment and intellectual maturation led him to see America not as Teddy Roosevelt had envisaged her, an imperial power dominant in the Pacific and controlling the states of the Western Hemisphere. Wilson was the first, but not the last, American president who imagined creating a new world order by the force and originality of his vision and the power and wealth of the new American colossus.

Wilson, who had a progressive vision of economic and political reform within the United States, was going to propose ideas for a peaceful, cooperative world order with freedom of world commerce, with peoples casting off colonial rule for self-determination, and with the Great Powers turning away from antagonistic coalitions to a League of Nations that would provide multilaterally guaranteed security for all. This exaggeration of the power of ideas coming from an academic entering the realpolitik field of world affairs has been seductive to many intellectuals (including myself) seeking a way to bring resolution to the protracted conflicts in the Middle East that have destroyed so many lives and quashed so much hope for Arab and Jew alike.

CHAPTER 2

EGYPT

*Between the Arabs and the peoples of the West there existed
a chasm of incomprehension and suspicion.*[1]

Like much of the Middle East, Egypt underwent a long period as a colonial holding of the British Empire. Britain first occupied Egypt in 1882, and despite the existence there of small, private American commercial interests, the United States was content to regard Egypt as fully within the British sphere of influence. Egypt was seen by the British mostly through the lens of its commitment to the security of India, its jewel in the Crown, the cornerstone of the British Empire. Such began the dangerous tradition of looking at Egypt with an eye not to its development and identity, but rather to how it served external interests. If Egyptians have come to see the future of their country too much and too often as a result of the actions of others and the influence of foreign powers, they have come to this distorted perception with much encouragement, extending back to Napoleon's invasion and culminating in American military dominance, financial aid dependence, and several wars with Israel.

During World War II, Egypt became an essential military staging ground for the Allied powers, and the American-Egyptian relationship blossomed. President Roosevelt took the trouble to publicly acknowledge this relationship by stopping his yacht in the Suez Canal on his way back from his last wartime summit meeting at the Black Sea port of Yalta with Stalin and Churchill, to meet with Egypt's King Farouk. Later, in 1945, President Truman invited King Farouk to Washington, and in 1946, Egypt and the United States exchanged ambassadors for the first time. Unfortunately, this personal attention to Farouk was soon to be made irrelevant by the Free Officers Movement in Egypt, which ended Farouk's rule and brought about the rule of Colonel Gamal Abdel Nasser. Few Egyptians had felt any national pride in the dissipated monarch, but Nasser initiated a period of nationalistic identification with the state.

After World War II, Egyptians became increasingly disenchanted with the British presence in their country. Yet, though they wanted the British out, most understood the need for some other power to fill the financial gap that would be left. The United States was the obvious and desired candidate for the replacement, but America and Britain had been the closest of allies in World War II, and the United States did not want to harm British interests in Egypt. Still, the United States knew that reinforcing an American relationship with Egypt would advance important economic and strategic benefits. The British knew that the United States did not share its interest in maintaining its empire. What they did share now was the fear that the iron curtain might be extended beyond Europe, and they both wanted to prevent Communist influence from penetrating Egypt. Meanwhile, Egypt was being humiliated by the new state of Israel in the war of 1948–49. King Farouk tried to ignore public anger over the war and the U.S. support of Israel and saw his interest as building the U.S.-Egyptian relationship. Truman agreed, but underneath their intergovernmental agreement, Farouk's control of the country was becoming more and more shaky. Egyptian officers who had fought in the Palestine war resented greatly that Farouk had not properly prepared them for the war, and they already resented his failure to remove the British presence from their lives. Britain and the United States shared the desire to protect Farouk from Communist plotters, but they did not understand the growing power of Arab nationalism.

Through most of the Truman administration, the United States was satisfied to let Britain maintain control and stability in the Middle East. The American administration considered a Soviet invasion of the Middle East to be a real possibility, and that spurred it to take a more active role in Egypt. In order to save Egypt and thus the Middle East from the Soviets, the Americans felt they had to find a way to diminish the tensions growing between Egypt and Britain.

As the Americans worked between the Egyptians and the British, they began to realize that King Farouk was never going to be a useful partner in the battle for containment. This realization came in part from Farouk's unwillingness to implement land reform in Egypt. The Americans saw land reform as a way to begin to alleviate the problem of widespread Egyptian poverty, something they believed the Communists would exploit in their campaign to take over Egypt. Still, Farouk stubbornly continued to oppose land reform and other similar programs. This explains why the Americans chose not to intervene, even when they heard rumblings of an intended coup by the Free Officers.

These two failings of Farouk—his failure to push Britain out of control of Egypt and his unwillingness to engage in the kind of reforms, including land reform, necessary to overcome the fundamental problem of rural poverty in Egypt—were fatally augmented by the anger of the army, especially those who had been defeated in the Palestine war and blamed Farouk for failing to train them or to properly arm them. The humiliated young officers now had the motivation and the energy to try to overthrow Farouk and his regime. Thus, on July 23, 1952, the Young Officers Corps, including the dynamic Colonel Nasser, were able to carry out a bloodless coup against Farouk. The United States and Britain could not bring themselves to defend Farouk against the officers because they had themselves come to understand that Farouk could not be their partner in keeping communism out of Egypt and the Arab world. However, when the coup succeeded, neither the United States nor Britain had any idea how they could keep in the good graces of Nasser and his colleagues because neither America nor Britain had made any progress in solving the problem of Egyptian disillusionment with British control of

Egypt. Nor could they reverse the successes of the new Jewish state against Egypt, the Palestinian irregulars, and other Arab forces. Britain and America feared the porousness of Nasser's Egypt to Soviet penetration, but they had no formula for being on the right side of the new forces of Arab nationalism.

But support for this new government did not prove an entirely good idea for the British. In keeping with the nascent nationalist fervor, the new Egyptian government wanted the Suez Canal bases back from the British. Egyptians considered British control of the bases an illegal occupation. Though the British did not entirely need or want the canal bases any longer, they wanted to withdraw on their own timetable and with their dignity intact. They could not let it appear that they were being kicked out of Egypt.

As soon as the Eisenhower administration came to power in early 1953, the United States became the de facto mediator between Britain and Egypt over the Suez Canal bases issue. The United States promised Egypt economic and military aid in exchange for an acceptable agreement with Britain, and asked the British to be more conciliatory. One must note that the Suez bases and British control over them were perceived as a critical asset for NATO and therefore important in the fight against communism. So although the United States wanted to appease the Egyptians and get them "on their side," it also needed to keep NATO strong. The resolution of the issue of the bases was important for both these reasons.

Even though at this early stage it seemed as though Britain and the United States could agree on nonintervention against the Free Officers, they already had very divergent motives and interests. Britain had by this time ceded control of India to its own people, but it wanted—perhaps more desperately than ever—to maintain its imperial standing in key Arab countries. The United States was angling for the support of these indigenous nationalist movements and knew that British conflict with them would be a crisis for America in its joint control of Egypt and the canal area. It took a few years, but when it came, the clash rocked the world for all three.

American mediation, combined with domestic changes in Egypt

and Britain, allowed an accord to be reached in 1954. Britain was still suffering from serious economic problems resulting from World War II and had to make substantial changes. Reducing its involvement, and therefore its manpower, in the Middle East was an obvious place to start. In Egypt, Nasser took over as prime minister in March 1954. He needed a political success to solidify his control. An accord that would largely remove the British presence would be a huge boost for him, and so he pursued this cause forcefully.

In the end, an agreement was signed on July 27, 1954. The British agreed to leave some British civilian maintenance workers on one base and to withdraw their troops over the course of twenty months. The bases would be turned over to Egypt, but could be reactivated for British use if there were an attack on the Arab states or Turkey.

COMPETING INTERESTS: ANTICOMMUNISM AND NATIONALISM

Under the Eisenhower administration and the rule of Nasser, it appeared that the United States and Egypt had forged a strong alliance, but there was a critical problem, over which their friendship would eventually founder. The United States never fully accepted Egyptian aspirations to nationalism; it would not break with Britain at the stage that was critical for Nasser. By the time of the Suez Canal crisis in 1956, when the United States did break with Britain—a much more public and damaging blow to the British—it was too late for that act to cement an American-Egyptian partnership.

The Eisenhower administration was so completely focused on the threat of communism that it ignored Nasser's strong Pan-Arabist desires. As Ray Takeyh, a senior fellow at the Council on Foreign Relations, points out, the United States wanted to "mobilize the Middle East for the task of containment,"[2] and Egypt was crucial to the implementation of American plans. The United States knew it was taking over from the British, and yet in so many ways still seemed totally unprepared. It viewed the world predominantly through the narrow lens of anticommunism, a lens through which Nasser had little interest in peering. Eventually, America's unclear and myopic view of Egypt and the Middle East would frustrate its plans for the region.

The United States approached Egypt at the time with two main goals in mind. The first was the creation of a Middle East Defense Organization (MEDO). Eisenhower wanted to create a united front against the Soviet Union that would stretch across Europe and the Middle East. In 1953, just four months after the Eisenhower inauguration, Secretary of State John Foster Dulles went to Cairo to meet with Nasser. This demonstrated that for the Eisenhower administration the fear of Soviet advances in the third world, especially in the Middle East, had become a major cold war concern.

But the United States did not look solely to Egypt among Middle Eastern states to battle communism. It concluded an agreement with Iraq to supply it with arms in exchange for Iraqi support for MEDO. America also brokered an agreement between Turkey and Pakistan under which those countries would work together to contain communism. It is these secondary and tertiary agreements that exemplify America's misunderstanding of Egypt, of Arab nationalism, and of its own potential role in the Middle East. Nasser was very unhappy with these agreements because they precluded a regional Pan-Arab arrangement, his stated goal.

Egypt feared Iraq's joining the Turco-Pakistani alliance and forging an Arab unity agreement under the auspices of the United States rather than having Arab unity emerge under the auspices of Nasser and Egypt. Nasser therefore declared that any Arab state that joined MEDO would be part of a Western imperialist pact. America's goal to get Egypt, the strongest and most populous Arab state, to be a leader in MEDO therefore backfired and created a rift in the American-Egyptian relationship. The United States did not then, and has not since, penetrated deeply enough into inter-Arab relations to avoid running afoul of inter-Arab rivalry.

The second American goal in the Middle East was an end to the Arab-Israeli conflict. The 1954 Suez agreement between Britain and Egypt called for the United States to send arms to Egypt. Despite

American assurances of protection, Israel felt that it was being exposed to assault: not only would there no longer be a British buffer between Israel and Egypt, but now Egypt would be better armed. Unfortunately, the resolution to the problem of the Suez bases intensified the problem of the Arab-Israeli conflict. The United States could not seem to achieve its policy goals or to think ahead to the interconnected repercussions of all its decisions in the region.

Even though the resolution of the Suez base problem seemed only to aggravate problems between the Egyptians and Israelis, the United States still felt it had the clout and ability to solve the problems of the region, and it developed what it called the Alpha Plan, to try to end the Arab-Israeli conflict. The Alpha Plan called for the end of belligerency between Israel and Egypt. Israel would be asked to accept the return of seventy-five thousand Palestinian refugees. Compensation for the rest of the refugees would come through an international effort. Israel would also have to make territorial concessions in the Negev, and Jerusalem would be under an international mandate. In return, the Western powers would guarantee Israel's borders and try to persuade Arab regimes to lift their economic embargoes.

The Alpha Plan was not acceptable to any party involved. Israel would not give up the Negev, an important natural barrier between itself and its enemies. "Nasser and the Free Officers recognized that compromise with Israel would lead to the de-legitimization of their rule and subversion of the tenets of Arab nationalism."[3] Thus the fundamental goals of Egypt and Nasser were opposed to, and the fears of Israel were incompatible with, the main Alpha Plan goal of the United States.

As Takeyh explains:

The Anglo-American conception for a solution had almost no chance of being realized since it clashed with both Egyptian and Israeli ideas. This was one of the persistent weaknesses of Western policy toward the Middle East; the State Department and Foreign Office continually conceived plans and strategies which had limited applicability to the reality on the ground. The chasm between Western objectives and the disposition of regional states was most obvious in the Alpha Plan.[4]

Eisenhower would not push Israel hard enough to overcome its Negev retention stance. By the time he was willing to use the full force of an American ultimatum on Israel, it was after the 1956 Suez War, and by then he was forcing Israel out of the Sinai in return for only a soon-to-be-broken promise of free Israeli merchant marine passage through the Straits of Tiran. It was no longer a question of achieving a full-scale Israeli-Egyptian agreement, and the United States found itself after the 1956 war alienated from both Israel and Egypt and having seriously weakened the positions of the French and British in the Middle East and in international affairs generally. It is very hard for the United States to summon its energies to move on Middle East matters early enough in any presidential administration to produce a major result. Instead, it is easier for decision makers to wait for a crisis. However, alleviating the crisis is not the same as eradicating the roots of the problem, and those roots live on to again break through the surface to create still another crisis.

After Dulles's failure to find a point of rapprochement with Nasser, and after the Alpha Plan fell flat on its face, the Egyptian-Israeli relationship began quickly to deteriorate—through fedayeen raids from Egyptian-controlled Gaza; through Israeli retaliation—leading to a major Egyptian arms deal with the Soviet Union and Czechoslovakia, Eastern European client state of the Soviet Union.

By 1955, the Eisenhower administration had grown closer to the Nasser regime, but had not achieved either of its stated goals: Arab-Israeli peace or a solid Middle East defense against communism. Then things began to fall apart.

THE GAZA RAID (FEBRUARY 1955)

Despite ongoing attempts at brokering peace by the Eisenhower administration, the relationship between Egypt and Israel was not improving. In fact, in February of 1955 the possibility for a settlement was dealt a severe blow. In reaction to skirmishes on the Israel-Egypt border, the Israel Defense Forces staged a raid on Gaza (then under Egyptian control). The Egyptian forces were easily overwhelmed by the Israelis and suffered heavy losses. The raid was a public humiliation for Egypt. Until this point, Nasser had been concentrating his economic efforts on rebuilding the domestic economy and alleviating poverty. After the raid on Gaza, he realized that he could no longer afford to divert money from the military. If Egypt were ever to become a regional leader as he hoped, it could not continue to suffer such defeats. Most embarrassing for Nasser was that "throughout the preceding years, [he] had maintained that the Arabs could handle their defense obligations effectively through the Arab Collective Security Pact led by Egypt."[5] The utter trampling of the Egyptian army in the Gaza raid called this notion into question, and so Nasser not only began to build up his military but also initiated a program of propaganda that would bring the other Arab leaders back into the fold. He condemned them for collusion with the West and thus, by association, with Israel. To an extent, the tactics worked, and Nasser managed to persuade the Syrian, Lebanese, and Jordanian governments to form a new Pan-Arab alliance. This was Nasser's first tangible diplomatic victory.

BAGHDAD PACT (FEBRUARY 1955)

As discussed earlier, creating a Middle East alliance to combat communism was of utmost importance to the Eisenhower administration. John Foster Dulles saw the creation of such a bloc as the key to the encirclement of the Soviet Union. Bridging NATO and the South East Asia Treaty Organization (SEATO) through a select group of Middle Eastern states would inhibit the Soviet Union from spreading its ideology and influence. The problem with the plan was that the Americans, not wishing to involve Nasser, did not want to expand the alliance south of Iraq, beyond the so-called Northern Tier. This would, of course, eliminate Egypt from the alliance and consequently alienate Nasser. Despite the American desire for an Israeli-Egyptian treaty, the Eisenhower administration decided not to include Egypt in its planning. Turkey and Pakistan formed a pact of friendship coordinated by the Americans. Iraq and the United States worked out an arms arrangement, and it seemed that Iraq would be the next state to join the new alliance.

Britain had been trying for some time to reassert its dominance in the Middle East, and saw an alliance with Iraq as a means of doing just that. In February of 1955, the same month as the Gaza raid, Iraq, to the delight of the British, joined the Turco-Pakistani Alliance. Nasser was furious. He feared Iraqi regional dominance; he feared a polarization of the Arab world; he feared Western control in the Middle East; and, most of all, he was furious that Egypt was being excluded from a Middle East alliance. Nasser condemned the Iraqi decision, seeing it as an act of colonial subservience. Iraq saw it differently and viewed this as a chance for regional hegemony. Iraq and Britain both joined the alliance, which became known as the Baghdad Pact.

Nasser's deepest fears were being realized, and so he tried to retaliate by turning to the Soviets for aid and protection.

BANDUNG CONFERENCE/SOVIET ARMS DEAL (SPRING 1955)

As Nasser struggled against Western defense plans, including the American effort to build up Iraq as the linchpin of a new alliance against an anticipated Soviet assault, he chose to focus on the second part of his platform, namely third world neutralism. Nasser believed that the emerging nations of the world should not be coerced into alliances and defense pacts in order to serve the interests of the Great Powers. In April of 1955, he expressed this view at the Bandung Conference, in Indonesia, a pathbreaking gathering of many emerging countries to declare the solidarity of the third world and its refusal to be drawn into the Soviet/Warsaw Pact versus United States/NATO world conflict.

Nasser's participation in the conference helped him regain the international and domestic popularity and prestige that he had lost with the creation of the Baghdad Pact. His version of neutralism and Pan-Arabism had mass appeal and provided him with the practical benefit of Soviet arms and eventually Soviet financing of the Aswan High Dam project. It is not surprising, therefore, that Nasser's nonalignment seemed dangerously similar to anti-Americanism in the eyes of American cold warriors. He was placed in the company of Nehru and Sukarno as a major figure in this third world defiance. Given the high-flown rhetoric of anti-imperialism and anticolonialism, it cannot be a great surprise that American observers could not discern any sharp distinction between this defiance and any other form of anti-Americanism.

The Soviet Union seized on the British and American missteps with Egypt. Since the Gaza raid, it had become imperative for Nasser's grand image of himself that Egypt acquire new armaments. He had been trying to get the requisite matériel from the United States, but it had been continually denied. Nasser did not immediately turn to the Soviet Union for arms, but when the United States denied his request, even after there had been indications of a Russian offer, he felt it was time to look for support elsewhere. The Soviet Union's offer was a generous package of arms and the possibility of financing Nasser's pet project, the Aswan High Dam, in exchange for Egyptian cotton. In September of 1955, Egypt agreed to the deal. In an attempt to allay American fears, the Soviets and the Egyptians made their transfers through Czechoslovakia, but it was well known that the deal was in fact a Soviet creation.

As a result of this arms deal, Nasser's prestige in Egypt skyrocketed. He had defied the United States and gotten what he wanted without compromising. His triumph was unsettling to the region, to the Americans, and most of all to the Israelis. Their enemy was gaining political and military power right under their noses, and the United States did not seem capable of controlling Egypt.

ANDERSON MISSION (1955–56)/ASWAN HIGH DAM

The United States was shocked and disturbed by the Soviet-Egyptian arms deal. But interestingly, it is here that the story of Egypt and the West takes a turn very different from that of Iran and the West (see chapter 3 on Iran). Whereas in Iran the decision was made to subversively overthrow a problematic ruler, Nasser and Egypt were too important to the cold war effort for the West to follow this path. So, in order to compete with and, it was hoped, supersede the Soviet influence, the United States and Britain decided to entice Nasser back into the fold. The two governments offered to finance the Aswan High Dam, a project that would regulate the flow of the Nile and create a desperately needed reservoir of fresh water. In exchange, they required Egyptian support and assistance on the Alpha Plan. The dam project was the crown jewel of Nasser's plan for Egyptian regional dominance, and even though the Anglo-American offer came packaged with demands for Arab-Israeli peacemaking, Nasser could not turn it down. He seized the opportunity. What better policy for him than to accept arms from the Soviet Union and money from the Americans and British? This was the way to turn the cold war from a threat into an opportunity to gouge both sides.

The process for gaining American government approval for the dam funds was set in motion, as were attempts to act on the Alpha Plan. In early 1956, Robert Anderson, a former undersecretary of defense, was sent to the region to try to mediate between Egypt and Israel. He immediately hit a wall. Both sides were willing to talk with him, but neither was willing to make any concession to the other. Though both Israel and Egypt declined Anderson's offer to mediate, the Eisenhower administration found the most fault with Nasser, and therefore placed the blame for failure on Egypt. The United States chose to implement punitive measures. It developed the Omega Plan, designed to marginalize Egypt's influence in the region. What was remarkable about Omega was that it demanded from Nasser not only the abandonment of the tenets of Arab nationalism but also his taking the lead in the transformation of the Middle East into a bulwark of anticommunism. In sum, the United States, after having been turned down in its offers that made modest demands on Egypt, proceeded to make offers that made major demands on Egypt.

In May of 1956, Nasser was once again concerned about being denied arms. It appeared that all the Great Powers were going to discontinue arms sales to the Middle East, and so Nasser began a search for a new supplier. He quickly hit upon China, shocking and angering the West when he recognized the Chinese Communist government at the height of America's attempt to isolate that regime.

After Nasser's recognition of China, it became quite clear to the Eisenhower administration that the Omega Plan was not working and that Nasser seemed to be drawing nearer to the Soviets. In July of 1956, the United States and Britain cut off funding for the Aswan High Dam. "Western policy had gradually shifted from accommodation to hostility."[6]

Dulles, who had initiated the American relationship with Nasser by his early visit to Cairo and who had enticed Nasser by the offer of Aswan High Dam funding, found a way to add insult to injury by broadly hinting that the loan would not be forthcoming because Egypt was no longer creditworthy. Thus, Dulles was not willing to accept responsibility for canceling the deal because he no longer thought that Nasser could be dissuaded from his hostile attitude toward American interests.

Nasser's riposte was to declare on July 26, 1956, his intention to nationalize the Suez Canal in order to fund the construction of the Aswan High Dam with canal revenues.

THE SUEZ CRISIS

The United States viewed Omega as a plan of gradualism that would serve eventually to reorient Egyptian policy. The British, discerning in Nasser's tactics a disturbing similarity to those of Hitler vis-à-vis

Czechoslovakia, could no longer believe in gradualism. It seemed to them to be nothing more than appeasement redux. Britain and France planned an ignominious end for Nasser.

The British cabinet wanted to take joint military action with the French and Americans. However, the Americans wanted to exhaust all diplomatic options first. They proposed a tripartite statement. A conference to craft the statement would be held in London.

The Americans also tried to create groups that would work to ensure that the Suez Canal stayed open for trade, such as SCUA, the Suez Canal Users Association. They also tried to persuade Britain and France to bring their complaints to the UN Security Council. Britain and France felt there would be no chance of successful resolution there. The discussions at the United Nations did take place, but were not very effective. (The irony is that the principles elaborated in those United Nations discussions would be the basis for a resolution in 1957 that demanded the withdrawal of Britain, France, and Israel from Egyptian territory.)

France had been secretly supplying arms to Israel since 1950, and was considering asking Israel to join the venture to get rid of Nasser. The French proposed the idea, and the British prime minister, Anthony Eden, jumped at it.

The British-French discussions moved quickly, and in highly secret conversations France, Britain, and Israel agreed upon the "Sèvres strategy" (the Sinai Campaign). The CIA had some indication that there was going to be an attack on Egypt, but did not know the details. As the first Israeli parachute troops landed on October 29, 1956, Eisenhower telegraphed Eden to find out what was going on.

The British and French had devised a plan whereby Israel would take the canal and, on the pretense of separating the two sides and securing the safety of the canal, the French and British would intervene. When the Israelis attacked on October 29, Britain and France called for the Egyptian combatants to fall back ten miles from the canal. Egypt refused, and the British and French invaded.

Eden sent Eisenhower a telegram describing the steps Britain would take to "intervene." The telegram was delayed, and so the U.S. administration learned of the ultimata that were put to Nasser from the press instead of from Eden. American officials were furious. Eisenhower issued a serious rebuke of Eden in the press and put before the United Nations Security Council a resolution on Middle East aggression, calling for the suspension of all aid to Israel until it complied with UN-U.S. demands to withdraw from the Sinai completely. This created a huge rift between the United States and the United Kingdom.

In a unique protest against its allies Britain and France, the United States called an emergency session of the Security Council, which soon after morphed into a General Assembly special meeting. The option of sending UN peacekeeping forces was put forward. Not expecting that the United Nations could react quickly, Eden said that he welcomed peacekeepers. However, when he saw the speed with which they were deployed, he soon regretted his statement. He accelerated his own military actions in order to seize the canal before the UN troops arrived.

In the first days of November, Britain was isolated from the international community and there was discussion in the General Assembly of sanctions being placed on the British and French unless they agreed to an immediate cease-fire.

The hypocrisy inherent in the British invasion was telling in the eyes of the Americans. The Western powers had condemned the Soviet invasion of Hungary when the Soviets observed the growth of nationalist sentiment there. Now the British attack on Egyptian nationalism pulled the rug out from under American claims to being the leader of the defenders of the national pride of smaller and weaker states.

The British cabinet began to talk about a cease-fire on November 5. Although they had not taken the entire canal back and had not deposed Nasser, they were not sure they could afford to continue the campaign (either financially or in the currency of international and domestic public opinion).

On November 6 the British and French declared a cease-fire, and Eden turned his attention immediately to repairing relations with the United States.

America made it clear that unless Britain withdrew there would be no oil supplies forthcoming. In early December, British and French troops were withdrawn from Egypt unconditionally, and the United States immediately resumed aid to Britain. A few days later, Eden resigned, and while the sun may not have set on the British Empire with his resignation, it had dipped a long way toward the horizon.

Eden had turned decisively against Nasser because he felt that Egypt was undermining the Jordanian relationship with Britain. In particular, King Hussein had dismissed Glubb Pasha, the longtime British commander of the Jordanian Hashemite Arab Legion. In Eden's view, Nasser had intimidated Hussein into dismissing Glubb Pasha with his propaganda campaign on the radio. Eden had seen Nasser as a dangerous enemy to the waning British Empire. With Nasser surviving and Eden resigning, Egypt's Arab nationalism had won the battle over British control in the Arab Middle East, and soon afterward the British-implanted Hashemite rule in Iraq collapsed as well.

For the United States, Nasser's unforgivable act was to recognize the Communist regime in China at a time when Dulles was still fighting to maintain Formosa (later Taiwan) as the legitimate government of China. Once again, the British were focused on the decline of their empire, while the Americans were single-mindedly absorbed with cold war rivalry. Thus, as the battle over Arab nationalism extended to Syria and Lebanon, the United States was more hostile to Syria than was Britain, and it was the United States that considered seriously the overthrow of the Syrian regime in 1957 and 1958.

Nasser's ploy of threatening to nationalize the Suez Canal had proved a stunning success, and it had had even greater effects than he could have imagined as it created major tension between Britain and the United States. In the end, the invasion of the Suez Canal was a disaster for Britain and France. Not only did it not achieve its goals—

it blocked the canal for six months—but it also gave Nasser a great and unexpected victory that reinforced his dominance in the Arab world.

THE CONSEQUENCES OF SUEZ

Eisenhower did not sanction or support the invasion of Nasser's Egypt by Israel with the support of the British and French, and he showed that even during an election campaign he was able to pursue his Middle East policy without regard to domestic pressures from pro-Israel Jewish groups. He faced down Israel's prime minister, Ben-Gurion, and forced a historic Israeli withdrawal from the Sinai.

Despite the fact that Eisenhower had so strongly opposed the British-French-Israeli tripartite plan for the invasion of Egypt, and that John Foster Dulles, the grand anti-Communist, was now suffering from cancer and was out of the picture, Eisenhower's relationship with Nasser continued to deteriorate through the last years of his presidency. Eisenhower had now come to see Nasser as the poison-tipped spearhead for an avowedly nonaligned but in fact anti-American coalition within the Arab world that would undermine the standing of America in the Middle East. He saw Nasser's handiwork in the developing troubles of the Chamoun government in Lebanon and in the eventual fall of the Iraqi monarchy to Arab nationalist army officers in Baghdad, thus putting an end to the pro-Western regimes as a powerful Arab bloc.

The question remains why Eisenhower, with all his animosity toward Nasser, never gave the order to treat the Egyptian leader to another American-organized coup à la Mossadegh. Fortunately, by refraining from doing so, he left open the possibility of a rapprochement between America and Egypt after the death of Nasser. However, Eisenhower was much maligned by his successor, President Kennedy, for a policy that left the United States with strained relations with both Israel and Egypt.

Kennedy tried to warm up both, but succeeded only in creating a warmer Israeli relationship for the United States while Egypt-U.S. relations remained strained. An attempt at rapprochement in the early sixties by Kennedy fell victim to Nasser's intervention in Yemen against Saudi Arabian interests in favor of a fledgling Arab nationalist leftist regime. Kennedy's attempts to improve America's standing with both Egypt and Israel were not taken much notice of at the time, but they set the stage for the polarization of the cold war to link with the Arab-Israeli conflict in the period leading up to, during, and following the momentous Six-Day War of 1967. President Lyndon Johnson slipped comfortably into the pro-Israel defender role when the Soviets condemned Israel as the aggressor in that war. Later, when the Soviets and their Arab partners tried to fashion a pro-Arab resolution on Middle East issues to sum up the 1967 War, Johnson outflanked them by American diplomacy that helped produce UN Security Council Resolution 242. Resolution 242 bowed to the inadmissibility of the acquisition of territory by force, but in its operative paragraphs insisted on every state in the region having the right to secure defensible boundaries, a phrase that became the watchword for decades of Israeli diplomacy seeking to prevent a return to the 1967 borders.

It is important to note that the United States never did adjust its thinking about the Alpha Plan and Arab nationalism, but simply changed its strategy for getting what it wanted. The idea that what America wanted was unattainable or incorrect simply never arose in official circles.

After he succeeded Eisenhower, President Kennedy thought he could reach out to Israel and Egypt and improve the United States' standing with both of them. He was able to put the American-Israeli relationship back on track, but, sadly, it was on the basis of the first American arms sale to Israel, the Hawk air defense missile system, in 1962. This arms sale was followed in the time of President Johnson by the United States replacing France as the main arms supplier to Israel, and eventually led to the sale of the Phantom jets that solidly reinforced Israeli air superiority. The United States would not take a decisive step to try to prevent the 1967 War by upholding Israel's freedom of passage through the Straits of Tiran that had been assured after the Suez War. Instead, the Johnson administration became much more active after the war in an attempt to create the possibility of an Egyptian-Israeli agreement that would stave off a next war; however, having waited until after the 1967 War, America's leverage on both the winner and the loser was much more limited, and the next war did come.

President Nixon, like Johnson, preoccupied with Vietnam, did not intervene vigorously in the Middle East conflict until after the 1973 War and the renewed threat of Soviet-American confrontation brought about by the confrontation between Egypt and Israel and between Syria and Israel. This time Henry Kissinger, Nixon's right-hand man for national security, began intensive diplomacy to separate Israeli forces from those of Syria and Egypt, but the breakthrough came only when there was a historic initiative by Nasser's successor, President Anwar Sadat, to himself travel to the Israeli Knesset in Jerusalem in November of 1977. Fortunately, at the right moment, President Jimmy Carter played a highly active, even sometimes aggressive, role in bringing Sadat and the Israeli prime minister, Begin, to an agreement and did not leave it either to them or to chance to determine if they would successfully complete these very tough negotiations.

After the 1979 Egypt-Israel Peace Treaty, the United States moved sharply to reinforce its relationship with both Egypt and Israel, and made them the two largest recipients of American foreign aid for the next two decades.

CONCLUSION

Mirroring the situation in Iran, the United States ended up inheriting from the British an Egypt that felt great animosity and hostility toward the British for their imperialistic control and their imperious attitude. Instead of cultivating a better relationship, the United States demanded from the new Egypt under Nasser that it cooperate with and serve the purposes of the United States in the cold war before the United States would consider offering to help Nasser move to solve the problems of British control of the Suez Canal and of the continued presence of British forces on Egyptian soil. Nasser's Free Officers Movement coincided with the installation of the Eisenhower administration and the arrival of John Foster Dulles as secretary of state. The new administration was astute enough to understand the centrality of Egypt and Nasser in Arab politics of the time, but did not grasp, or perhaps chose not to deal with, the major obstacles to Nasser's joining the American cold war effort.

In the Suez period, the United States tended to view all events through the lens of cold war competition and confrontation, and could not measure Arab nationalism and inter-Arab rivalry on its own terms. It could never seem to grasp that this was not the lens through which the Arabs saw the world. The Arabs were seen by America as too fractious and simply would not be made to fit on the Procrustean bed of American cold war foreign policy.

As a result, not only was the United States unable to recruit Nasser to its goals. It also inadvertently helped to create the conditions for his leadership in the nonaligned movement and Egypt's policy of purchasing Soviet arms. A combination of neutralism as developed by Nasser in Bandung and his decision to have the Soviet Union arm Egypt were strong evidence that the U.S. policy had backfired. What happened was that the Soviet Union had become much more deeply involved in Arab politics and was now a major Arab supporter in the Arab-Israeli conflict. The United States, having invested in developing a relationship with Egypt through World War II, and building that relationship further by personal diplomacy with King Farouk, had squandered any new opportunities arising from the transition from a corrupt monarch unwilling to adopt land reform policies that would make the poor less vulnerable to Soviet advances, to a nationalist hero who was to become the major symbol of Arab nationalism for the next decades in the Arab world.

In much the same way, the United States now sees the world through the lens of the War on Terror, and it is very hard for it to assess the processes of struggle over religious identity, economic development, and government corruption and inefficiency as the engines of Arab politics on the ground in their own right and not as reflections of a single-minded Al Qaeda–related force attacking America. Only this time it is America that launched an invasion under George W. Bush to remove Saddam Hussein, a pale copy of the original charismatic Nasser model for Arab nationalism.

For the United States to extricate itself from the Iraq civil war without leaving the problem even worse than it found it will require a much more acute and nuanced American analysis of the differences among various Arab states and Islamic movements in their politics, their warfare, and even their propaganda against America. It is not possible now any more than in the fifties to have a one-size-fits-all policy and expect to be able to manage the complexities of the Arab street and the imperative to make progress on the heretofore intractable Israeli-Palestinian conflict.

Egyptian society was the most cohesive of the Arab societies that came into conflict with Israel and the United States. This solidarity and the long experience of Egypt with a variety of colonial powers could have made the country the best instance of a Wilsonian outcome. It could have been a nation-state with strong enough social resources to have become an effective and well-governed political and social system. Such an Egypt could have been a model for legitimate, effective government in the Middle East. However, Britain's persistent effort at controlling it for its own imperial purposes, followed by the mobilization of America through the cold war conflict to shape Arab politics as a bulwark against the Soviet Union, delayed Egyptian self-determination for decades. This cost Egypt precious opportunities for economic development at a time when nationalist enthusiasm was high and the nation's energies were well focused. Among the worst results were Nasser's suppression of freedom of speech and freedom of association and his driving out of many productive foreign elements from Egyptian society. This deprived Egypt of the benefits of diversity and artistic and intellectual creativity. Egypt still has not been able to integrate fully its secular nationalist aspirations as a modern state with its strong Islamic traditions. The United States, with its own tradition of independence and formation of a national identity, with strong components of religious belief and nationalist solidarity, should be able to encourage these strains in another nation rather than respond with fear and attempts at suppression.

CHAPTER 3

IRAN

The British and the Russians maintained a high degree of control over Iran in the years before World War I. Each of them saw Iran as a linchpin in their ability to extend power deep into the Middle East. They also competed to shape the Iranian economy to their own trade purposes. This rivalry between Britain and Russia was temporarily resolved by British victory over the Ottoman Empire and by the Russian Revolution, but the competition took on a more dramatic significance after World War II, when the cold war threatened to extend itself into the third world. Iran made a historic arrangement with Britain in the creation of the Anglo-Persian (later Anglo-Iranian) Oil Company (APOC), but Britain successfully helped persuade Iran to deny any concession to the Russians.

In much of the Middle East, the United States is treated today as the Great Satan, but many of the issues that soured Iran on modern Western ideas and policies are heirlooms of the British era and perhaps even remnants of the rivalry between Britain and Russia in the nineteenth century.

The first layer of the problem is economic policy and practice. The traditional imperialist policy of imposing capitulation was applied in Iran. This meant that foreign businessmen from the north, especially Russians, and from the south, predominantly British coming to Iran through the raj of India, were able to control the economic direction of Iran well into the twentieth century. Agriculture, Iran's biggest source of employment, was redirected so that basic foodstuffs, staple crops, were increasingly replaced by cash crops, especially opium. This led to such severe food shortages in the World War I period that cereals had to be imported, even though Iran was traditionally a net exporter of barley and wheat.

Local guild structures, which maintained an important economic tradition of fine handicrafts and handmade goods, were overwhelmed and undermined by cheap imported textiles from Britain and other imports. Little capital was invested and no manufacturing was developed, so underemployment and unemployment grew. Employment opportunities could not keep pace with population growth. This was the start of the massive youth unemployment that has led to a huge problem in the contemporary Middle East. Trade policy that created a structural preference for imports from Britain and Russia over any other trade relations also determined that Iran could not go in the direction of import substitution at an early stage of industrialization. Thus imperial policy completely forestalled any kind of industrialization when it might have taken root prior to the development of the oil industry. When oil was eventually discovered, the revenues were used to support income rather than to serve as an engine of economic development.

In 1907, Britain and Russia forged an agreement to combat the rapidly growing German influence in Asia, dividing Iran into Russian and British spheres of influence. Iran reacted to this decision with indignation, and was especially disappointed in Britain, from which it had expected better, including protection from the embrace of the Russian bear. And so, when World War I began, Iran, though technically neutral, was pro-German at heart.

The relationship between Britain and Iran soon became dominated by the politics and economics of oil. In 1901, William Knox D'Arcy had obtained a concession from Iran that provided the British with exclusive control over oil extraction in the region. In 1908, the Anglo-

Persian Oil Company was formed, and the British government closed its fist around the oil industry in Persia.

For almost a decade, the financial arrangements agreed upon in the original concession were left uncontested, but in the early 1920s disputes over royalties erupted between APOC and Persian leaders. An American financial adviser to the Persian government, Sydney Armitage-Smith, was appointed by the Persian government to oversee the resolution of the dispute. In the end, the questions of royalties and ownership that were plaguing the concession relationship were resolved, at least for the nonce, by the 1920 Armitage-Smith Agreement.[1] The British saw this new agreement as an end to the dissatisfaction in Persia, while the Persians viewed it as merely a stopgap until a more advantageous agreement could be reached. The separate and very different understandings of the impact of the Armitage-Smith Agreement led to further conflicts between the parties.

In 1925, Reza Shah Pahlavi, the newly installed leader of Persia, insisted on renegotiating the Armitage-Smith Agreement. The renegotiation process was a tedious endeavor, taking years to conclude. At some point in the discussion the Persian government threatened to cancel the concession entirely. The British said they could not afford to increase the royalties they paid on Persian oil, but the shah would not allow the status quo to stand. The problem of the concession became so intractable that in 1933 the British brought it before the League of Nations. In the midst of oral presentations to the Council of the League, the Persian government and APOC decided to go back to the negotiating table. By May of 1933, after almost three months of talks, APOC and the Persian government agreed to a new concession. Persia's need for higher royalty payments was met; in return, the duration of the concession was extended. The conflict—between the nationalist Persians, with their insistence on having a greater share of the revenues of their own oil, and the British, with their sense that as the discoverers of the oil, and its extractors, processors, and marketers, they fully deserved the share they had previously negotiated—was resolved temporarily in these negotiations, but the fundamental conflict of perspectives was destined to return, the next time with a vengeance.

An interesting feature of the Persian oil dispute was the absence of U.S. involvement, despite increasing American interest in foreign oil. The U.S. government did not have a military or financial interest in Persia, and so left the other Great Powers to act as they wished. In fact, in the 1920s the Persian government offered oil concessions to American companies in order to counterbalance the influence of Russia and Britain. The Americans never acted upon those proffered concessions, and it was not until World War II that the United States took an active interest in the problems and the natural resources of Iran.[2]

Once World War II broke out, Iran's location and its oil resources made it a valuable strategic asset. The United States formed policies based on the concept of Iran as an important factor in the war effort. Moreover, Iran was a buffer against potential Soviet invasion of the Persian Gulf. In order to protect its interests and block the feared advance of communism toward the south, the United States supplied Iran with military advisers and matériel throughout the war and beyond. But though the United States seemed to take a new interest in Iran, it still did not attribute any great inherent worth to it. America did not perceive Iran as a crucial ally or as a state in which it needed to invest much.

The most notable display of this type of thinking was in America's refusal to provide the economic aid Iranian officials repeatedly requested after World War II. In 1945, Iran, which had developed serious postwar economic problems, appealed for aid to President Truman, but the Americans had not been very involved with the Middle East before the war and did not see it as their role to become more involved now. American officials remarked that the British were to a far greater degree responsible for the defense of Iran, and consequently America was already doing more than its part. After World War II, despite wartime focus on oil supplies, the United States continued to think of the Middle East as a region outside its sphere of interest. The American government believed that oil abundance was the means to a prosperous Iran. If Iran and Britain could find a way to produce and sell oil effectively, both nations would benefit. The United States thus reasoned that it did not need to provide loans or grants to the Iranian government.

THE NATIONALIZATION MOVEMENT

A new national self-understanding began to emerge in Iran during the interwar period. Reza Shah had plans of "modernizing and secularizing his new Iran along the lines of a nationalist state."[3] Since the beginning of the twentieth century and the discovery of oil, foreign powers, especially Britain, had moved into Iran and gained control of the country through oil ownership, turning it into a puppet-like state. To reassert national pride required first of all the Iranians' reclaiming their oil. Nationalists wanted to stop Western interference in Iranian domestic issues, and many felt this would happen only if Iran took full control of its oil industry. Control of oil resources was thus paramount in Iran's struggle for national independence.

The disputes of the 1920s and 1930s between Iran and what was now called the Anglo-Iranian Oil Company (AIOC) gave birth to a new movement of middle-class Iranian nationalists. During World War II, the shah, because of his admiration for and connections with Germany, was forced into exile by the British and Russians.[4] His son, Mohammad Reza Pahlavi, succeeded him and signed the Tripartite Agreement with Great Britain and Russia. In exchange for Iran's alliance and cooperation, the Allies promised military protection and aid.

The rule of Mohammad Reza saw significant changes in Iranian politics. The middle class began to have a stronger voice in the government. They embodied growing feelings of nationalism, dislike of foreign power and influence in Iran, and a desire to make changes to benefit themselves. They wanted better education, a more responsible government, and a higher standard of living.[5] Ironically, American advisers such as Dr. Arthur C. Millspaugh were invited to Iran to promote these goals and were asked to help Iran devise ways to escape from its economic predicament.

The new nationalists quickly found places in the Majlis, the Middle East equivalent of a consultative council, which was to develop in Iran into a legislative body. They tried to enact legislation that would put Iran's oil solely under the control of Iranians. Their first definitive move came in 1940, when the Majlis voted to suspend all new concessions until after the end of the war. This meant that the existing British concession could remain in effect, but the concession that the Russians had recently applied for in the northern provinces was postponed.

In the years immediately following World War II, the Russians tried again to be awarded an oil concession in Iran. In exchange, they agreed to remove all Russian troops that had been stationed in Iran during the war. At first it seemed that the concession would be granted, because it had the support of the shah, but in 1947 the nationalist elements prevailed and the Majlis enacted a law stipulating that no new concessions could be granted to foreign parties. The law thus foreclosed the option of a Russian concession. This was pleasing to the United States, until it realized that the nationalists also wanted to gain control over the British concession. Iran was quickly becoming a policy battlefield in the nascent cold war.

Though the AIOC concession pre-dated the new law, a provision of the law affected this concession as well. In an attempt to initiate the removal of foreign parties from the Iranian oil industry, the new law stipulated that the AIOC agreement of 1933 had to be renegotiated. The AIOC considered this new directive to be a breach of contract. Renegotiation of the concession was not acceptable under the provisions of the 1933 agreement. Still, the British government considered nationalism better than communism and therefore felt that the "accommodation of moderate nationalism to prevent political extremism" was worthwhile. The British were willing to do almost anything to avoid Communist infiltration. They tried to encourage economic and political modernization as a way of avoiding political revolution in Iran. The problem was that by 1947, when the new concession laws were created, Britain, drained by the war, was itself in too difficult an economic situation to give up much of the concession or offer higher payments for the right to maintain it. The idea of having to renegotiate the concession and possibly forgo large income streams was thus intolerable for the AIOC and the British government. Furthermore, Britain had experienced a severe energy shortage in 1947 that had shut down much of its industry and further weakened the British economy.

Meanwhile, the United States was facing similar problems in countries where it had oil concessions of its own. In order to assuage nationalist sentiments, it created fifty-fifty profit-sharing arrangements in Saudi Arabia and Venezuela. Aware of these agreements, Iran was demanding similar arrangements from Britain. What the AIOC failed to fully grasp was that it was more control, and not just more money, that motivated Iran.

The AIOC did understand that some changes to the 1933 concession would have to be made because of the altered political and economic state of the postwar world, and so it presented new options to the Iranian government. The result was the Gass-Golshayan Agreement, more commonly known as the Supplemental Oil Agreement, which ensured the Iranian government increased royalty payments, consistent annual payments, and various new rights with regard to the oil industry. In 1949, after almost two years of delay, the Supplemental Oil Agreement was presented to the Majlis. Though the shah supported the agreement, his voice was not as strong as it once had been. Because of the tense political climate in Iran, the Majlis was dissolved before the agreement could be voted on and a new Majlis was convened. In 1950, when the new Majlis took up the issue of the agreement, it decided to refer it to a newly created oil committee, headed by Dr. Mohammad Mossadegh, a fervent nationalist leader.

Mossadegh was the leader of the National Front, the major nationalist party in Iran, whose main objectives were the end of autocratic rule by the shah and of British control over Iranian oil. In December 1950, the oil committee rejected the Supplemental Oil Agreement, holding that it was not in the interests of Iran. Mossadegh then proposed nationalization of the Iranian oil industry. The committee accepted the idea and asked the current prime minister, Ali Razmara, to consider nationalization. Razmara convened a group of advisers to look into the question. He and his advisers concluded that nationalization was impracticable for the time being, and he presented this finding to the Majlis. Four days later, on March 7, 1951, Prime Minister Razmara was assassinated by the Fedayeen e-Islam, a nationalistic militant group. By April, Mossadegh had been appointed the new prime minister and the Majlis had approved the nationalization bill and enacted the legislative machinery that enabled the implementation of the process.

Thus began the epic battle over nationalization.

THE AMERICAN ROLE IN THE NATIONALIZATION CRISIS

Few international relationships have had a more positive beginning than that which characterized Iranian-American contacts for more than a century.[6]

From the beginning of the contact between Iran and the United States, with the dispute over the Supplemental Oil Agreement, the United States approached the issue from the vantage point of mediator and tried to promote compromise and flexibility between the AIOC and Iran.

American officials understood this to be the only way to solve the problem in an acceptable manner—one that maintained British interests, but also assuaged Iranian aggrievement. Washington was caught between competing interests, and so hoped to maintain neutrality publicly, but privately, American officials chastised Britain for its rigidity. The Truman administration was beginning to question Iran's ability to defend itself from a Soviet invasion and saw the conflict with AIOC as a source of further weakness.

The United States understood and was sympathetic to the emergence of nationalism, but that sympathy was trumped by the cold war fear that nationalists would turn out to be susceptible to Russian influence. The United States may have upset Britain by not acknowledging the full legitimacy of British demands in the negotiations with Iran, but America could not accept the emergence of an Iran that would not be aligned primarily with the Western camp.

Because the United States feared the spread of communism and focused its policies around that fear, "the U.S. pressed Britain to sacrifice its economic interests in Iran for the greater good of containment" and pushed the British to find a quick solution to the dispute.[7] The United States hoped that the British government would persuade the AIOC to follow the fifty-fifty profit-sharing model pioneered in Saudi Arabia and allow for more Iranian control of the oil industry. Instead of allowing for the distant neutrality the United States hoped for, however, this approach embroiled the AIOC further in the dispute.

After World War II, the economic troubles of Iran became increasingly worse, and the shah turned to the United States for help. Iran had developed a seven-year economic plan and, to fund it, wanted the same type of financial aid being granted to rebuild Western Europe under the Marshall Plan. The United States initially rejected the request, saying that Iranian oil revenues, if used wisely, could easily pay for Iran's seven-year plan. But as the economic situation in the country became more obviously dire, the United States' fear of Iranian economic collapse and infiltration by Iran's Soviet neighbor grew. The deputy director of the Office of Greek, Turkish, and Iranian Affairs was dispatched to Iran. He reported back that the economic situation was grim, and confirmed rumors of the Iranians' turning to Russia for help. The State Department posted one of its most respected ambassadors, Henry Grady, to Iran. Grady had been a key member of the commission that had developed the co-partition plan for Palestine (the Morrison-Grady Plan) and had most recently been in Greece, helping in the reconstruction efforts after the war.

The Iranians perceived the arrival of Ambassador Grady as a sign that assistance and attention would be forthcoming. Regardless of whether those were in fact America's intentions, this optimism did not last long. The Korean War largely diverted the U.S. focus away from Iran and its economic problems. The United States was now engaged in another war, but still feared a Communist takeover of Iran. Even though most resources were directed toward Korea, American concern spurred it to continue to participate in seeking a resolution to the dispute between the AIOC and Iran. The United States feared that problems in Iran would hurt the war supply effort by impeding oil flows. This led it to characterize the AIOC as inflexible and the British government as obstructionist, and to blame them both for their handling of the Iran issue. Tension increased between the United States and its most important ally. The Americans pressed the British to agree to Iranian demands so that the Supplemental Oil Agreement could be put into effect. The British government had tried to stay out of the dispute between the AIOC and the Iranian government, but in 1951, after the nationalization decision in Iran, Britain had started to work with the AIOC in an effort to find a resolution.

As the problems between the AIOC and Iran grew worse and the economy of Iran continued to crumble, America's position became more and more determined by cold war fears about the collapse of Iran or its falling into the Soviet camp, and less sympathetic to British economic demands. In order to try to shore up stability in Iran, America moved to help strengthen the shah. As the shah's status and strength grew with American assistance, he became more able to influence elections. The position of prime minister was highly sought after, but the shah forced the election of the candidate he wanted. In 1950, General Ali Razmara was elected prime minister. There was general agreement among American officials that Razmara "offered a chance of strong leadership that might undertake essential domestic reforms and guide the Supplemental Agreement through the Majlis."[8]

In January, Prime Minister Razmara tried to form a new oil commission to study the question of nationalization. The National Front, the party headed by Mohammad Mossadegh, had stirred up enough anger within the Majlis that it voted against the creation of a new commission and went as far as to place Mossadegh and his original commission in control of oil policy formulation in Iran. This new move caused panic among the British and Americans. To counteract this development, the AIOC and the British government put pressure on Razmara to publicly oppose nationalization and to present the Majlis with a British proposal that discussed why Iran could not control its own oil. Razmara asked the British for more concessions to the Majlis before he would go forward. While not unreceptive to the request, the AIOC did not grant him enough time. His assassination soon followed.

With little choice left but to follow the will of the Majlis, the shah signed the nationalization resolution into law on May 1, 1951. The resolution officially nationalized all AIOC holdings, created plans for Iran to assume control over all oil operations, and offered compensation to the AIOC only if counterclaims were settled.

In order to stop nationalization, the British government stepped in on behalf of the AIOC and brought the dispute before the International Court of Justice. The Iranians rejected the competence of the court to hear the case because the British government had no standing in the dispute. They argued that the dispute was between the Iranian government and the AIOC, and that the involvement of the British government was unlawful interference in the sovereignty of the Iranian state. In 1952, more than a year after the case came before the International Court of Justice, the court agreed with Iran's claims: even though the British government had large holdings in the AIOC, the dispute was not between two states, but between a state and a corporation, and so could not be heard by the court.

The year's delay during deliberation and, finally, the elimination of the International Court of Justice as a venue for deciding the dispute ushered in a more proactive role for the United States. President Truman wrote personal letters to the heads of the British and Iranian governments, making his own proposals for possible solutions. In 1951, he sent his personal representative, Averell Harriman, to Iran to mediate the dispute. Harriman was one of the first to use "shuttle diplomacy," flying from London to Tehran and back to try to find a way to break the impasse. Harriman helped bring the two sides close to an agreement. He even managed to persuade the British to accept nationalization in principle. (This was the first step in British-American policy coming closer together.[9]) But when the British representative Lord Stokes presented this proposal to the Majlis, it was quickly rejected as too similar to that of the oil company itself. Not long afterward, Harriman returned to the United States.

NEW LEADERS IN THE UNITED STATES AND BRITAIN

The nationalization crisis critically strained the special relationship between Britain and the United States. In 1951, Winston Churchill was reelected prime minister, and with the election of his World War II colleague Dwight David Eisenhower as the new American president, Churchill hoped to be able to repair their relationship and better coordinate their policies toward Iran. In January 1952, a joint British-American conference was convened in Washington, but it was unable to reach agreement on the main substantive issues. Eisenhower decided to change American policy from diplomacy and conciliation to intervention and confrontation. The rise of Joseph McCarthy and the continued difficulties in Korea had raised the fear of Communist spread to a new level of intensity. Like his new secretary of state, John Foster Dulles, Eisenhower could not tolerate the perceived dangers of Mossadegh's close connection to the Communist Tudeh Party in Iran.

Eisenhower decided to use the newly created Central Intelligence Agency to try to remove Mossadegh from power.

During the summer of 1953, the British and American administrations organized Operation Ajax, a countercoup designed to overthrow Mossadegh. Using swarms of paid Iranians, the Americans and British orchestrated vast protests against Mossadegh. He was forced to flee on August 19 and was quickly arrested. Three days later, the shah, supported by the Western powers, returned to Iran and regained control.

In the years that followed the overthrow of Mossadegh, two main changes in Iran further fomented anti-American sentiment. The first was the creation of the Iranian intelligence services, or SAVAK. Formed with American assistance in order to help maintain the rule of the shah, SAVAK became one of the most notorious and violent internal security organizations in the world. For decades, SAVAK and the shah's own grandiosity ensured that there would be no further liberalization and no legitimization of opposition, until the Islamic radicals forced the shah out of power, bringing the Khomeini revolution that sealed off legitimate opposition even more hermetically.

At a meeting of the National Security Council to discuss the idea of the coup in Iran, Eisenhower asked a question that has been repeated in the United States more aggressively since 9/11: "Why is it not possible to get some of the people in these downtrodden countries to like us instead of hating us?" The CIA-executed coup denying Iran its chance for a secular nationalist popular leader contributed mightily to that hatred.

The second change was in the control over Iranian oil. Between August and October of 1953, British and American government officials met to figure out how to revive the oil industry in Iran, and decided that a consortium would be best. After almost a year of negotiating with Tehran, an agreement was reached. The Iranian Consortium consisted of British Petroleum (the former AIOC), which had a 40 percent share; the United States oil majors, which had a combined 40 percent share; Royal Dutch Shell, which had a 14 percent share; and Compagnie Française des Pétroles, the French oil company, which had a 6 percent share. The agreement recognized that Iran fully owned its oil reserves, but the consortium would be responsible for the operation of the industry. The agreement may have been acceptable to the shah and his coterie, but it rankled the Iranian populace. They saw it as leaving the oil industry under foreign management. Nevertheless, their nationalist protests subsided when they saw the Majlis ratify the agreement, and the shah's agents made sure the protests did not rematerialize.

Though Operation Ajax and the political machinations of its aftermath were successful in the short term, in the end they were a failure that poisoned American-Iranian relations. The crucial issue to understand is that Iranians felt that America, once an ally and friend, had betrayed its Wilsonian legacy and taken up arms against them, and perceived what America had done as equal to or even worse than the historic imperialist actions of Great Britain.

The people involved with Operation Ajax exploited many of the scholars and missionaries who had taken up residence in Iran over the previous decades. Intelligence agents used these contacts to gain entry into Iranian society. As James Bill, the author of *The Eagle and the Lion: The Tragedy of American-Iranian Relations*, points out in his discussion of Operation Ajax, the subversion practiced by the CIA

> demonstrates well a symbolic crossover point between the time when American missionaries, scholars, and knowledgeable diplomats who had been central to Iran-American relations since the 1930s were replaced by the Dulles school of thought in Washington and intelligence and military operatives in the field.[10]

The tragedy was not that Mossadegh maintained all his popularity until he was overthrown: he did not. He had made some serious errors and had lost much of his support. Rather, the tragedy is that the modality of his removal sapped the strength of the forces of secular nationalism and paved the way for the revolution against the shah by Islamic radicals. The nationalist, secular, and liberal forces could no longer revive themselves after the years of the Mossadegh overthrow, the shah's rule, and the Khomeini takeover.

The shah's rule after the overthrow of Mossadegh did not become more open to nationalist sentiment. Instead, the shah tried to replace popular nationalism by a glorification of his rule of Iran and a push toward modernization that left behind the mass support for traditional Islam. In this context his mounting corruption, including his enormously self-indulgent world celebration of the creation of Iran, aroused more and more anger among the people, and instead of meeting the demands, the shah used his SAVAK to oppress opposition, often brutally. By now the only place where effective opposition could emerge was in the mosque. No liberal nationalism could resurface after the Mossadegh coup. Opposition to the shah grew more radical as Iranians found shelter in Paris and even in Iraq. The Khomeini revolution became even more focused on anti-American agitation when Henry Kissinger insisted that the U.S. government owed it to the shah to rescue him and give him American refuge and health treatment. The price of Eisenhower's coup and Kissinger's caring for the shah was one to be paid by Jimmy Carter, one that cost him his presidency. In 1979, young militants rose up, many of them pretending to be students, and attacked the U.S. embassy in Tehran, breaking through its security and taking all of the American personnel as hostages. The hostage crisis was the cause célèbre that dominated the news every night the hostages were held. Carter could not find a way to free them and finally tried to rescue them by an ill-planned secret raid that became a military humiliation when a plane and a helicopter involved in the raid crashed in the Iranian desert and a political disaster ensued when Secretary of State Cyrus Vance resigned in protest against the military action. Until the day of the inauguration of his successor, Ronald Reagan, Carter could not get a moment's peace away from the crisis, and the Reagan team made sure that the hostages' release came only as soon as Reagan was inaugurated.

THE IRAN-IRAQ WAR AND THE TANKER WAR

Perhaps the greatest trauma of the new Iranian regime of the ayatollahs was the invasion by Iraq only a few years after the Revolution. Saddam Hussein seems to have believed that this war against the Shiite Islamic regime—the regime that had aroused so much anger in the United States through the hostage-taking of American embassy staff and officials, and had awakened so much concern in the Arab states of the Gulf region—was a perfect opportunity for him to assert his ambition for leadership of the Arab world. At first the attack looked like it was succeeding militarily, but the mullahs of Iran found Iranian nationalism to be a strong unifying force they could marshal to mobilize a counterattack.

A day or two after the invasion began, I had a conversation with Boutros Boutros-Ghali, who was then the acting foreign minister of Egypt. He told me it was not going to end well for either Saddam or Iran. Saddam did not realize that the offensive would eventually bog down, Boutros-Ghali said, because the Iraqi leader would be unable to manage the complicated logistics of such a complex war, and the conflict would grind to a halt with great anguish for everyone.

> This is the third world [Boutros-Ghali emphasized] and this war is a war in the third world and will have all the inefficiencies and logistical problems of two third world countries. You have to learn what a war in the third world becomes and how it does not progress like a war in the West but becomes a bloody confusion and a disaster for the masses. Saddam will see in a few months that this is the great mistake which will bring him down in the long run.[11]

Boutros-Ghali was right that this was the beginning of the reckless warmongering that led to the destruction of Saddam's regime and its conquest by the United States. Boutros-Ghali needed to teach this lesson about wars of third world countries not only to me but to the government of the United States. Far from trying to stop the war, the United States was happy to see the Iranians battered and the regime there threatened. It did not understand that the long bloodletting would introduce into the region powerful additional elements of rage, resentment, vengefulness, and brutality, as well as the militarization of both regimes and their search for weapons of mass destruction.

The United States started soon afterward to supply the Saddam regime with information on Iran's military positioning, intelligence gathered from satellites, and other sources unavailable to Iraq. As the war continued, Israeli and American officials would often express the unofficial view that they were happy to see the war continue and both sides lose, and in this they showed their lack of understanding about how a long war between these two Gulf forces would poison the atmosphere of Gulf security for decades and lead to the outbreak of war and terrorism that has plagued the participants and their neighbors, and even the United States, ever since. The Iran-Iraq War became the strongest argument for Iran to seek nuclear weapons and to seize the small islands of the Gulf (Greater and Lesser Tunb and Abu Musa) from the United Arab Emirates, a move that has kept tensions high among the Arab countries of the Gulf Cooperation Council and Iran ever since. The war built the military capability of Iraq and strengthened the national solidarity of Iran at a time when the regime there was very unpopular and not fully consolidated.

The involvement of the United States when the Iraqis and Iranians started to attack each other's shipping in the Gulf went beyond fishing in troubled waters. Both nations were highly dependent on oil exports to maintain their economic equilibrium in a very costly war in which so much counter-city warfare was taking place and so much wanton destruction was being inflicted. The war strengthened the dictatorial control of both regimes and saw the first large-scale use of chemical weapons since World War I. Both sides attacked each other's tankers in the Gulf—with the intelligence information provided by the United States greatly increasing the accuracy of Iraqi attacks and the efficacy of Iraqi defenses.

The American aid to Iraq in the Tanker War belied the official U.S. claim of neutrality. The aid also misled Iraq about how tolerant the United States would be of any aggression by Saddam Hussein.

As often happens when war penetrates deeply into civilian society and life, a shocking civilian air disaster occurred in 1988 when the United States inadvertently shot down an Iranian passenger plane over the Gulf, killing more than two hundred passengers. This was yet another reason for the fury of Iranians against the United States, and it continues to represent a further human grievance for which Iran expects compensation if relations between the countries are to change. Iran has a legitimate need for new civilian airplanes, which the United States has embargoed in its sanctions against the country. This is one Iranian wound that continues to fester. If the United States moved to heal this toxic memory, it could be a well-received signal of an American desire to initiate a thaw in the relations of the two countries and their peoples.

Neither the United States nor the riparian powers of the Gulf have been able to work out an effective agreed-upon regime of Gulf security since the Iran-Iraq War. Certainly, the likelihood of further major acts of aggression in this area will be heightened as the demand for oil continues to intensify and as the conflict among Saudi Arabia, Iraq, and Iran continues its slow boil.

Iran was happy to see the defeat of the Saddam regime first by a United States–led coalition in the first Gulf War and then by the United States in its invasion of Iraq in 2003. However, Iran does not wish the United States to use its presence in Iraq to implant a long-term military presence in the Gulf that could at some point be turned against Iran itself. Iran also has to figure out its optimal policy for relating to an Iraq for the first time led by the Shiites and in which the centers of Najaf and Karbala will be seeking to reassume theological primacy in Iranian Shiite Islam. Finally, Iran is going to have to search for an alternative guarantee for its long-term security rather than violating the Nuclear Non-Proliferation Treaty and becoming a small nuclear power, and thus too tempting a target for larger nuclear powers.

The United States' uncertainty and discomfort about Iran and its foreign policy go beyond Iran's present nuclear potential. Iran and its Revolutionary Guard have played a pivotal role in the growth of Hizbollah in Lebanon as a way of leading the Shiites to a much greater share of political power in that country. The Shiites of Lebanon and of Iran have close religious and family ties, so the Iranian relationship with Hizbollah is deeply rooted in more than Hizbollah's enmity for Israel. Iran may see some benefit in Palestinian guerrilla warfare and even suicide bombings against Israel, as means to ensure that Israel and the Arabs do not solve their problems with each other before Iran has worked out an effective long-term relationship with the Arabs and has ceased to be a primary potential target of Israeli attack. However, Iran's relationship with Hizbollah is more organic than its relationship with either Hamas or Islamic Jihad, though Islamic Jihad has endeared itself to Iran by becoming the first Sunni Palestinian organization to treat the Khomeini revolution as a decisive historical event not only for Shiites but for Sunnis as well. Hizbollah, it should not be forgotten, perpetrated a major terrorist attack against Americans in Lebanon during the Reagan years. Neither Hamas nor Islamic Jihad has targeted America yet.

In the years of Iran's president Khatami (1997–2005), who was elected on a moderate platform largely by the female and youth vote, there was a great deal of whispered disappointment in the United States that Khatami had not emerged as a powerful enough force in Iran to counter either the Supreme Leader, Khamenei, or other sources of power inimical to Khatami's reformist policies. During his tenure, Iran remained radical and maintained a high level of hostility toward the United States. Even when the American secretary of state, Madeleine Albright, made a major overture to Iran, the Iranian government was unable to respond.

Khatami did open channels of communication with a number of European countries and introduced a new concept into international discourse that provided hope for a major change in Iran's relationship with the West. His concept of a "Dialogue Among Civilizations" even seemed to contain a kernel of hope for dialogue between Islam and Judaism that might eventually reduce the dangerous tension between Iran and Israel. However, Khatami's decline within Iran opened the way for the surprising electoral victory of the former Tehran mayor Mahmoud Ahmadinejad. Ahmadinejad, who had volunteered as a Revolutionary Guard in the early stages of the Revolution, turned sharply away from the rhetoric of Dialogue Among Civilizations in his harsh speeches, denying the Holocaust and insisting that Israel had no right to exist. Also, he became a major advocate of Iran's nuclear program, rejecting proposals for solutions coming from Europe and even Russia. This new face of leadership heightened the Western perception that Iran was trying to reconstruct its revolutionary fervor and export it to Arab countries. Although Ahmadinejad did not launch any campaign, either by word or deed, against the Arab Gulf countries, his foreign policy became more aggressive. Not only did he insist on continuing his nuclear program, but he strongly supported Hizbollah in Lebanon and Islamic Jihad in

Palestine, and he brought together leaders of Hamas from outside Palestine to encourage them to reject Israeli, American, and European pressures to accept Israel. He also offered financial aid to counteract the cuts in aid from the international community following Hamas's election as the legislative majority in the government of the Palestinian Authority.

With the rise of Ahmadinejad, Iran was once again on the path of confrontation with American national security interests on several fronts. The feeling that the Iranian relationship with the United States was headed for big trouble reached its tipping point with the 2006 war between Hizbollah and Israel, which was widely interpreted—although without convincing evidence—as an Iranian stratagem.

The relationship between Iran and Syria, so much strengthened by Syria's willingness to support Iran against its fellow Arab Ba'athist state in the 1980s, continued to be a source of anxiety and suspicion in Israel and the United States, though the direction of influence and the extent to which the two countries shared a truly close relationship remains very unclear. However, Iran puts much emphasis on maintaining its relationship with Syria, to keep itself from becoming estranged from the Sunni Arab world, and Israel and the United States are often tempted to engage deeply with Syria as a way of loosening if not breaking the Syria-Iran alliance.

In any case, Iran's influence in Iraq, based to a large degree on the two countries' shared Shiite Islam, remains a source of strong anxiety to the United States in its highly troubled attempt to forge an effective Iraqi government over the whole country. That worry is heightened by the role of Muqtada al-Sadr, head of the Shi'a militia in Iraq, called the Mahdi Army, and a claimant to religious authority, who is more openly hostile to the American presence in Iraq and the elected Iraqi government than the more moderate Ayatollah Ali al-Sistani, the main religious leader of the Iraqi Shiites, who has tried to be more cooperative with the new regime in Iraq and consequently less hostile to the United States. Iran therefore, both directly and through its channels of influence, has become a major force in the region, strongly opposed to the American assertion of dominance in the Middle East, insisting that Iran be acknowledged in any new security system in the Gulf, and becoming a potential dominant regional power in the years ahead. (This is particularly so given Egypt's moderate role and the Egyptian and Saudi focus on cleaning their own houses before trying to assert themselves too dramatically on the regional political and economic systems.) This allowed Iran to seize the role of being the prime hater of Israel.

The question of whether the sum of these sources of influence will lead to Shi'a dominance over the Sunni power bloc has become a very important uncertainty for America's future in the Middle East.

CONCLUSION

The U.S. relationship with Iran has always been a product of primary American relationships with others, whether Britain or the Soviet Union, or now Iraq on the one hand and Israel on the other. Iran has given the United States a veiled hint of what it needs to begin to reduce the enmity between itself and the United States by developing the phrase "Dialogue Among Civilizations." They are suggesting that it is time for the United States to deal with Iran directly as a society in itself, and not as part of a subgame to other strategic relationships.

Iran is an important intellectual and theological center of Islam. The United States, through its own clergy, should try to build a structure of communication with Iranian mullahs, imams, and influential religious teachers and theologians to provide American policy makers with a deeper understanding of what moves post-Khomeini minds in the Iranian Shiite leadership. The United States needs to engage in a serious encounter with this fundamental dimension of Iranian life. To begin to make the relationship between Americans and Iranians less weighed down by historical resentment, it would also be useful to open channels of communication that do not immediately lead to zones of mutual hostility.

In addition, the United States needs to have a dialogue between its

civil society and Iranian civil society to understand what Iranian nationalism means today and which aspects of it Americans can affirm
and which they will feel the need to challenge and debate. The notion
that the United States and Iran can somehow overcome this long
period of alienation in one step and move directly to a strategic agreement at best is fanciful and at worst would exacerbate an already dangerous situation by increasing the intensity of mutual hostility to the
flashpoint.

CHAPTER 4

SAUDI ARABIA

bn Saud, the founder of modern Saudi Arabia, was quite remarkable for his ability to master the several critical elements necessary
to unite a highly divided nomadic society and to maintain its cohesion over years of shocking developments. He was able to conquer
the various parts of Saudi Arabia by bringing together cadres of nomadic tribesmen who became adherents to the traditional Saudi Wahabi version of Islam, and he came to see their loyalty to Islam as
including fealty to the line of succession established by him. They became his fierce and devoted army, ready to meet all challenges, even
from other important families in the Arabian Peninsula. Ibn Saud
maintained wise judgment about sustaining the religious culture of his
people and of himself, even when he found that he mastered untold
riches, beyond anything he could have imagined while growing up in
his native country. Moreover, despite his reliance at certain critical
moments on help and sustenance, military and economic, he never
gave up his close commitment to and partnership with Wahabi Islam,
which provided the backbone of national solidarity and mass faithful-
ness to his rule. The deep strategic alliance Ibn Saud formed with
President Franklin Roosevelt was strong enough to continue through
the crisis generated by the Iraqi invasion of Kuwait to the courageous
decision of Ibn Saud's descendants to invite American military power

to crush that invasion from the launching point of Saudi soil. Ibn Saud had confidence in himself, something he transmitted to his successors, who were confident enough to know both that even the massive presence of American troops on the kingdom's territory would not undermine their kingdom and sovereignty and that George Herbert Walker Bush, whom they saw as a true successor to Franklin Roosevelt, would never violate the trust relationship between the two allies. To explain this confidence requires a brief excursion for the twenty-first-century reader into the history of this unusual and intensely significant Islamic kingdom.

The involvement of so many young Saudi men in the attacks on the World Trade Center and the Pentagon on September 11, 2001, created an image of Saudi Arabia as a haven for enemies of the West, and particularly of the United States. The stories we hear today in the news depict a fanatic form of Islam propagated throughout Saudi Arabia and by Saudis throughout the world, the human rights atrocities perpetrated in the country, and the hatred emanating from there toward the United States. It would be shocking, then, for many to discover that since early in World War II, the Saudis have been one of the closest and staunchest allies of the United States in the Middle East. A reliable and steadily flowing supply of Saudi oil has been one of the pillars supporting American prosperity and military effectiveness. The Saudis joined the Allied side just prior to the end of World War II, and directly helped American cold war efforts in the Middle East and Central America. What has changed to create the present atmosphere of distrust? What has changed in Saudi Arabian and American society that has so degraded the relationship? What conditions are necessary to restore the alliance that once prevailed? Will the two societies work to meet those conditions?

The Arabian Peninsula, with its vast deserts and scorching summer heat, has never been a heavily populated area. Its fame rests on the hydrocarbons that lie beneath its ground and on the religion that developed there. It was in Arabia that Muhammad founded Islam. Arabia is home to the towns that were the original sites of his prophecy, Mecca and Medina, and that became the most sacred places of worship for hundreds of millions of believers in Islam. Integrating this vast territory with its small, dispersed tribal populations into states and nations required much shrewdness, political skill, and, when needed, military force. Despite the efforts of the Western imperialist forces that seized the edges and coasts of the Arabian Peninsula in order to take control of ports and shipping routes, by the 1930s a unified greater Saudi Arabia had emerged as a major power in the Middle East.

The story of Saudi Arabia and its creation therefore stretches back before the era of European imperialism and long before the entry of America on the scene, in the 1930s. It is a tale with elements of cultural and religious drama and a strategic logic that pre-dates the powerful commercial oil logic of the past seventy years. But the energy story is so important to Western economic growth and American wealth that its glare pervades the landscape, and earlier history is not much understood or appreciated by either the actors of the oil generations or the fighters against terrorism of this last decade.

The development of Arabia into the nation-state of Saudi Arabia and other, smaller states began at about the turn of the twentieth century. Three main factors were material to Saudi Arabia's successful incubation.

The first is religion: its strict adherence and rigorous practice. Throughout the peninsula there were multitudes of fiercely independent tribes that had no tradition of solidarity with one another. The idea of a unified state having sovereignty was foreign to them, and could not take root without the inculcation of powerful reasons. The question of cohesion found its first answer in a shared and authoritative religion: the religious ideology of Islam was and remains a core element of the state's national identity. This centrality was reinforced by its local, highly rigorous (or at least highly orthodox and rigorous) variant, the Wahabi sect. Thus Saudi Arabia was not only the founding place of Islam and the homeland of its originator, but was also the locus of the most intensely devout, orthodox, and unreconstructed version of its religious practice. Saudi Islam did not tolerate any elements of folk religion, such as reverence of local saints. Moreover, Wahabi Islam was not softened by the tolerance that emerges from living in the direct presence of people of other faiths, as was true for Morocco and, to a certain extent, Egypt. Third, Wahabi Islam did not rest on a profound intellectual discourse on and study of the Koran and the Hadith. In Saudi Islam, traditional practice stood alone. In distinction, at Al-Azhar University, the oldest and most influential Sunni Islam seminary, intellectually rigorous immersion in the Koran and Sharia law bestowed a status of high honor, and through teaching and the training of so many imams throughout the Sunni world, Islam could not become so completely hidebound that no new religious and theological thinking could enter.

A second factor in the emergence of the Arabian nation-state was the declining influence of the Ottoman Empire. Although formally still part of the empire, the tribal hinterlands of Arabia were not under the effective control of Constantinople, especially at the beginning of the twentieth century. Ottoman rule did not penetrate very deeply into the society, and its military power was much less forbidding than it had been at the empire's height. Moreover, the caliphate, based in Turkey, did not have the same importance to Muslims in Arabia as it might have for others in the Ottoman territories. The local religious sites of Mecca and Medina provided close-to-home religious authority of the highest order, obviating the need for a strong connection to the distant caliphate.

The third factor was the emergence of a strong and charismatic leader, Abd al-Aziz Ibn Abd al-Rahman Ibn Faysal Ibn Turki Abd Allah Ibn Muhammad al-Saud, known as Ibn Saud, head of the Saud family as World War I broke out and as Ottoman suzerainty over Arabia approached its end. Ibn Saud was a remarkable father of his nation. He united the disparate tribes into a single sovereign state under his leadership. He developed an effective alliance both with the religious leadership of Arabia and with nomadic tribes, including those with strong military traditions, and was effective in negotiating the relationship between his nation, with its precious resource underground, and foreign interests and powers without undermining the religious and cultural traditions of his people and himself.

The Saud family of Arabia had allied itself with the Wahabi religious movement in the eighteenth century. That alliance was integral to the Sauds' gaining control of Arabia, notwithstanding repeated challenges by a powerful rival tribal family, the Rashids. In one of those ebbs and flows of fortune, the Sauds were expelled from Arabia in the 1890s, but at the turn of the century, Prince Ibn Saud drew upon the loyalty to Wahabi Islam to recruit the men who would become his military force in seizing control of Arabia. These men, known as the Ikhwan, were mostly Bedouin tribesmen, and under the tutelage of Ibn Saud they became strong adherents of Wahabi Islam. Once firm in their faith, they developed into the political base and source of military strength for Ibn Saud. For them, loyalty to Islam demanded loyalty to the royal line represented by Ibn Saud. This primordial alliance between the Saud family and Wahabi Islam is not something that could or would be eroded, not even by the flood of oil or landslides of petrodollars or the intense pressure of superpower threats.

As Ibn Saud began to consolidate his power over Arabia through military conquest and his alliance with the Ikhwan, he found that he needed financial support to maintain his rule. His refusal to accept full Ottoman suzerainty created the context for him to turn for assistance to the emerging power in the region, Britain. The British, as the preeminent naval power of the world, had established a network of ports from the Mediterranean to India, and had already made the Middle East an important strategic area for shipping, both commercial and naval. They were powerful, interested, and conveniently present.

The British were at first careful not to do anything to undermine Turkey's hold on its empire, and consequently resisted involving themselves with the Saud family. They did not want to contribute to the disintegration of the Ottoman Empire, at least not before Britain was positioned to take it over. But once war broke out and the Ottomans had thrown their lot in on the side of the Central Powers, the British no longer had any reason to support the Ottoman Empire—

quite the contrary. They decided to aid Ibn Saud directly. However, at the same time, ever careful to hedge their bets, the British began to make alliances with other Arab leaders, in particular the Hashemite family, long a rival of the Sauds. Eventually, this stratagem of distributed support led to the unraveling of Britain's relationship with the Sauds only a few years before the great Arabian oil field discoveries. By that time, the Sauds had discovered the Americans and cared little about Britain's choice.

The British preferred the Hashemites, the dominant family of Mecca and Medina, in the Hejaz. They were recognized to have direct descent from Muhammad and were at the time in control of both the holy cities. Moreover, the Hashemites were aware enough of what was happening internationally and astute enough to approach the British shortly after World War I broke out. They put forward an offer: they would help bring about an Arab revolt to assist in the overthrow of the Turkish Empire in Arabia if the British supported Arab unity and the Hashemite family's claims to leadership of that unity. A deal was struck, one that led, after the 1919 Paris Peace Conference, to the installation of members of the Hashemite family as rulers in Iraq and Transjordan, the immediate neighbors of the Arabian Peninsula.

Britain wanted secure sea routes, prospective oil reserves, safe passage to the holy cities for the many Muslim pilgrims from within its empire, and the imposition of order on the disorder resulting from the sudden disintegration and dismemberment of the four-hundred-year-old Ottoman Empire. It saw in the Hashemites a family who could deliver those results and, what is more, who could provide rulers to mediate the rising tide of Arab nationalism and the exigencies of British imperial needs and aspirations. Finally, it is especially important to note that no aspect of postwar policy was more personally determined.

Winston Churchill, who served for two years as head of the Colonial Office after the war, and T. E. Lawrence, who was a real British expert on the Middle East, fashioned between them the Sharifian Policy of placing the crown on the heads of Sharif Hussein and his sons. This policy was designed, among other things, in the hope that each Hashemite ruler would feel sufficiently responsible toward the other members of his family to behave in ways consistent with British interests so that each family member succeeded in his own particular area of responsibility. The British were more confident in Faisal I as ruler in Iraq than in Abdullah I as ruler in Transjordan, but they went ahead with all three (Sharif Hussein was supported as ruler in the Hejaz) as their best-guess solution at a time when Britain's primary goal was to install friendly (and tractable) rulers as a way to maintain and even broaden its influence and still reduce British expenses and manpower in the Middle East.

British support for Sharif Hussein in the Hejaz would go only so far. It definitely did not include military backing, and as a result, by 1924, Hussein had abdicated and left the Arabian Peninsula for exile in Cyprus, where he died in 1931. The polite illusion that Sharif Hussein and his Arab revolt had played a major role in the defeat of the Ottoman Empire could not be sustained for very long. General Allenby's campaign to conquer the Middle East had been a sideshow to the great battles on the Western Front; Sharif's Arab revolt had been a minor attraction in that sideshow.

This preference for the Hashemites, who ultimately would lose out in the struggle for hegemony over the Arabian Peninsula, had many problematic consequences for the British, but it left open an unobstructed path for the eventual American domination of the Saudi oil business, once petroleum was discovered in commercial quantities in the 1930s, and for the strategic Saudi-American relationship, once the exigencies of World War II led America to build up Saudi defense capabilities.

The British, meanwhile, continued to focus on Iran for oil through World War I and its aftermath, and then concentrated on the resources of Iraq, its new mandatory territory.

IBN SAUD RECLAIMS ARABIA WITH (AND WITHOUT) BRITISH AID

As a young man in the 1890s, Ibn Saud found himself in exile. He and his family had been deposed by the Rashidi family in another round of the intertribal rivalry that had gone on for decades. In 1893 they were welcomed into Kuwait, and Ibn Saud spent his formative years in a close friendship with one of Kuwait's leaders, Sheik Mubarak. While in Kuwait, Ibn Saud watched Mubarak interact with representatives of the Western powers in the process of negotiating, first the basic definition of Kuwait's independence from Iraq and its dependence on Britain for foreign affairs and, later, the terms under which Kuwait became a protectorate of Britain. That experience gave Ibn Saud deep insights into the ways of dealing with the British and other imperial powers. He learned early on that their interest in his family was subordinate to many other priorities of British imperial politics. Primarily, the British did not then want to alienate the Turks and, accordingly, wanted the Sauds and other Arabian families to remain patiently loyal to the Ottoman Empire and to recognize its authority. Internal tribal wars did not concern the British unless that unrest in some way served to destabilize the Ottoman Empire.

This zigzagging about Ibn Saud and his family by the British exemplified the British view that Arab regional politics should be handled only as a subsidiary to the primary British interest in the region: keeping India within the British sphere of influence. At that time the British saw the Middle East principally as the gateway to India, and were willing to support any number of Arab leaders if doing so secured that gateway. To the British, India had become not only the jewel in the Crown, but also an important source of the matériel and manpower that sustained British power.

Which foreign nations, if any, have achieved such a status in the American view of the world by becoming primary interests rather than subordinate ones? For many years, it seemed that Saudi Arabia, Israel, and perhaps Egypt had, but since 9/11, heavy questions have been raised about both Saudi Arabia and Egypt. Saudi Arabia, as a pillar of American global economic interests, and Egypt, as the pillar of the American strategic position in the Arab world, are well over-due for a major infusion of new ideas for government and civil society relations, so that these interests are not overwhelmed by fears of Islamic terrorism emerging from the huge and disaffected younger generation growing up in these and related societies.

As for the U.S.-Israel relationship, it is based on the most solid footing of American citizens committed to Israel's welfare and to her relationship with the United States. However, it would be foolhardy to ignore the fact that the continued failure to solve the problem of Israel's integration into the region and the delays in creating a Palestinian state both threaten major American interests. They enhance hostility to the United States and also create antagonism for Israel itself. They threaten to erode Israel's relationship with the United States. They pose a basic contradiction between America's ethnic and democratic solidarity with Israel and the possibility of America maintaining positive relations with the Arab and wider Muslim world as its own Arab and Muslim population increases. This problem cannot be allowed to fester any longer.

Seeing the Arabs as subordinate to other primary interests would become the approach pursued by the United States as well, at least until the era of the Bush-named "War on Terror." However, in the early days around 1930, the United States approached Saudi Arabia as the only Arab object of its attention, and thus at this early phase the Saudis got from the United States the clear sense of priority that they could not get from the British.

Tired of living in Kuwait, and chafing to reclaim his ancestral land, Ibn Saud began his attempts to regain control of Arabia as the twentieth century dawned. He reentered Arabia, gathering Bedouin troops and other loyalists to him as he advanced. His progress was swift, and with the aid of the Ikhwan, whom, with their newly inculcated religious fervor, he had carefully prepared for the battle to come, he took Riyadh from the Rashids. As happened repeatedly in his career, he was able to combine his military adventurousness with his grasp of the importance of religious motivation in the formation of his state-to-be. It is no surprise that the United States, with all of its military superiority, has not yet been able to find a key to unlocking that motivation for its agenda of Saudi moderation, modernization, and democratization. Ibn Saud used the fire of religious fervor to forge a sword. America will have to learn to respect and understand Islamic fervor and duty before that sword can ever be beaten into a plowshare.

But Ibn Saud's victory at Riyadh was far from any form of solidified control over Arabia. Other tribal chieftains constantly challenged him. He deployed the Ikhwan militarily to consolidate control, but he also sent out Wahabi preachers to, and provided economic support for, the desert tribes. He wanted to consolidate their settlements into small societies fully loyal to the Saud family. The combination of religion, armed force, and financial inducement was a highly effective triad for Ibn Saud and his successors. However, it also established a pattern of Saudi rule that became much more problematic as the Saudi indigenous population grew dramatically into the present century.

Ibn Saud, having achieved a strong foundation of support by his recruitment of the Ikhwan and his capture of Riyadh, moved on to conquer other parts of Arabia, including the Hejaz. The major problem he now faced was how to continue his subsidies to the Ikhwan. Although the British had made it clear that their support would not be military, he had hoped they would continue to provide financial support. He quickly found that British interest lay with the perpetuation of the Ottoman Empire. He thus turned to the Turks to find a means of supporting the Ikhwan.

But Britain's loyalties in this period were fickle, and varied according to British interests and priorities in the region rather than on the basis of a close assessment of the Saud family relative to other contending Arab tribal families on the peninsula. This was important for Ibn Saud, because as soon as World War I broke out, with the Turks entering on the wrong side, Britain changed its view of him. Once the Ottomans allied themselves with Germany and Austria in the war against the British, French, and Russians, Britain no longer felt constrained to take pains not to offend Ottoman sensitivities. Quite to the contrary, it was now eager to find an Arab partner who would move to overthrow Ottoman rule, or at least legitimize British seizure of Ottoman lands. It found such a partner (albeit not the only one) in Ibn Saud, and quickly supported his rule in word and deed by supplying him with promised protection and a monthly subsidy. Ibn Saud received one thousand rifles and £20,000 upon signing the understanding and £5,000 a month thereafter, as well as regular shipments of matériel and ordnance. This subsidy continued until 1924.

For his part, Ibn Saud agreed not to be "antagonistic to the British Government in any war" and to "refrain from entering into any correspondence, agreement, or treaty with any (other) foreign nation or power." In addition, in recognition of Britain's special interest in the coastal emirates of the peninsula, Ibn Saud agreed not to interfere in the British protectorates of Kuwait and Bahrain, or in the territories of Qatar and the Omani Coast,[1] thus beginning the formal division of the Arabian Peninsula that survived the British withdrawal from the Emirates and their assumption of independence and joining together with the Saudis in the Gulf Cooperation Council in May 1981.

The British indeed needed Ibn Saud's military help, but they had other motives. Oil had been found in Persia in 1908, and the British thought there might be prospects of oil in Arabia, too. The agreement they reached was designed to ensure that no other power could interfere if oil were discovered there.

It took two years during World War I for the agreement between Ibn Saud and the British to be finalized, and then, just after the end of the war, the carefully conceived agreement began to break down as the British preference for the Hashemites played itself out.

THE END OF WORLD WAR I AND THE PARIS PEACE CONFERENCE

During World War I, the British needed stronger support in their struggle to defeat the Ottoman Empire than Ibn Saud alone could provide, so they turned to other tribal leaders in the Arab world. In fact, throughout the war, Britain subsidized many Arab leaders, not fully understanding that they had cobbled together a "coalition" of sworn enemies. To this end, the British found strong support among the Hashemite leaders in the Hejaz region of Arabia—the historic enemies of the Saud family. This would prove hugely problematic for Britain after the end of the war.

The story of Britain's relationship with the Hashemites is in itself an important one of trust and deception, and of the planting of Hashemite influence in Iraq and Transjordan and, temporarily, even in Syria. These plantings yielded fruits both bitter and sweet for Western relations in the region—bitter in Iraq and Syria, and a long-term, still deep, and mutually productive relationship with Transjordan, later the Hashemite Kingdom of Jordan. These tribal rivalries and the Saud-Hashemite competition have continued in various forms and with varying intensity into our days.

When the carnage ended in 1918, Germany had been defeated, America had entered the European power arena, the Ottoman Empire had fallen, and there was economic and social turmoil from Russia to the Atlantic and down through Africa. To create a peace agreement and perhaps even a new world order, the Great Powers (minus Germany and postrevolutionary Russia) gathered in Paris in 1919. The leaders of Britain, France, and the United States came to the conference with vastly different priorities. President Woodrow Wilson brought with him grand ideas of self-determination, the League of Nations, and putting an end to war. The French prime minister, Georges Clemençeau, feared a resurgence of Germany and sought to do everything to prevent it. The British prime minister, Lloyd George, wanted to find a feasible way to perpetuate Britain's imperial status.

The leaders brought with them hundreds of advisers and spent six months working on a settlement, but despite the far-reaching effects of the war, they talked mainly about the rebuilding of Europe and the redistribution of German colonies. They barely touched upon what was to happen to the remains of the Ottoman Empire. In 1920, six months after the signing of the Treaty of Versailles, long after Woodrow Wilson had returned to America, the British and French met in the Italian Riviera resort town of San Remo to decide the fate of the Middle East. In doing so, they were motivated only to a very small extent by the high principles Wilson had enunciated; they for the most part reverted simply to implementing the secret agreements they had contrived in the context of the war.

Though they had exploited the idea of Arab nationalism to their advantage during the war in order to destabilize Ottoman rule, Britain and France now wanted to ignore nationalism in order to legitimize their own rule. These contradictory positions engendered what would become a long history of Arab mistrust of the West and resentment over what Arabs have imputed to be deceptions and false promises. For the United States, this created a huge gap between the expectations generated by Wilsonian idealism and the continued denial of Arab independence. The so-called compromise of mandate was intended by the British and French not as a halfway house to Arab independence and unity, but rather as a fortress to consolidate and perpetuate imperial control. The division of Arab land into newly designed and exogenously determined entities that would be more amenable to management from London or Paris contributed greatly to the breaking of the spirit of excitement over nationalism, which would help engender the Arab government leitmotif of blaming the West and not tending to its own garden.

The greatest problem the British and French faced in trying to decide how to design a governance structure for the Arab lands now under their tutelage was that after fostering and exploiting the idea of Arab nationalism to their advantage during the war, they now wanted to suppress and ignore it. Britain and France had supported leaders such as Ibn Saud and Sharif Hussein who were willing to take up arms against the Turks because they were trying to consolidate and unite either their own people or the whole of the Arab people in an independent state. The British and French had also made deals and promises to each other and to Arab leaders in exchange for cooperation. Many of these promises were mutually incompatible. (See the Sykes-Picot Agreement, the McMahon-Hussein Correspondence, and the Balfour Declaration in the index.) Also, by the end of the Paris Peace Conference there had been so much discussion of national self-determination and Woodrow Wilson's ideas of autonomous development that the Arabs thirsted after their independence more than ever.

But Britain and France were not prepared to give up control of such potentially oil-rich and strategically well-positioned territories. The decision they made was to hold mandates over certain areas; the British were determined to give some position of power to the Hashemites, but one outside the Arabian Peninsula.

Saudi Arabia was never even addressed—"presumably because no one thought all those miles of sand worth worrying about."[2] Ibn Saud was left with a precarious hold on power and a weakening agreement with the British carried over from wartime. He also had seen the Hashemites installed in Iraq and Transjordan, on the borders of the Arabian Peninsula.

DIVIDING THE REMAINS

By the middle of 1920 the remains of the Ottoman Empire had been divided by agreement between Britain and France, and the League of Nations had accepted the division, even though many of the peoples there had already started to resist. A Syrian National Congress had been held, the Iraqis had started to rebel, and the pattern of peasant revolt in Palestine had already been set. The new mandates would eventually prove extremely detrimental to the regional relations of both France and Britain, and were the backdrop against which political movements of violent hostility against the West would develop. And the door would be opened for America to enter.

In compliance with some of their wartime undertakings, the British and French installed friendly rulers throughout the newly created mandates. Some who were given territories next to one another were age-old enemies; some were unfamiliar with the areas and the people they were to govern. The British decision to install the various leaders around Ibn Saud was badly founded and based on underestimations of the Saudis' determination and military and political skill. By losing the trust of Ibn Saud in such a way, the British opened the door to competitors for Saudi oil. In return for political and security support, Britain typically wanted a right of first refusal for any oil discoveries, if not a flat promise of exclusivity. But such exclusivity would not be won from the Saudis, since the British were installing Hashemites, Ibn Saud's rivals, as rulers of areas neighboring the Arabian Peninsula. The British did not foresee or take fully into account the centrality Saudi Arabia would come to have in the world's oil economy and its eventual importance in regional political and economic developments.

So, in 1922, when Sir Percy Cox, the British high commissioner in Mesopotamia, came seeking an oil concession for the Anglo-Persian Oil Company, Ibn Saud was not ready to offer it. In fact, Ibn Saud and his advisers felt compelled to offer the concession to Frank Holmes, a New Zealander working for a private syndicate looking for concessions to exploit and then sell. Holmes had begun his oil campaign on the small island of Bahrain, where he had been attracted by reports of oil seepage. He also won an option for an oil concession in Al-Hasa, in the eastern part of what was to become the kingdom, and the next year in the neutral zone between Saudi Arabia and Kuwait. It is probable that the attraction of Holmes was not only his charm but also the absence of any close association with an imperial power or even a major oil company.

Angered at the competition for the concession, Cox threatened to terminate the subsidy Ibn Saud was receiving from the British government. Ibn Saud, still embroiled in tribal fighting, could not afford to lose the cash flow, but Frank Holmes's offer for the concession was enough to satisfy Ibn Saud's immediate needs. Ibn Saud also gloried in the fact that he could deny the British something they wanted. He was eager to prove to them and to his own people that he was not a colonial puppet. By granting the concession to Holmes, Ibn Saud made his point resoundingly.

THE NEW AMERICAN ROLE IN SAUDI ARABIA

Unfortunately for Holmes, and notwithstanding his efforts throughout the 1920s, he somehow, against all odds, managed to avoid finding oil and could not sell his concession to an oil company before American competitors arrived. Eventually, he let it lapse.

By the beginning of the 1930s, Ibn Saud, having had amicable dealings with Holmes and feeling a pressing need for money, wanted to grant another concession to someone who could pay him enough to bridge the gap that had opened between his revenues and his expenditures. Both a British company (the Iraq Petroleum Company, run as an adjunct of the British government) and an American company (SoCal, Standard Oil of California, in the American style fully independent from government control) bid on the concession.

The major oil companies were preoccupied after World War I with the reorganization of the Turkish Petroleum Company (TPC), which required first that they reassign the original German shares in TPC to France and, second, that they negotiate to accept the United States' Open Door Principle, and through it the inclusion of the American oil companies. Moreover, the partners in TPC had agreed that all consortium participants would have to act together as a group in the search for oil in the Middle East. Therefore, a concession in Saudi Arabia would either have to be shared among a wide number of partners or be taken up by a company not part of the TPC consortium. SoCal fit the bill by being one of the biggest producers in the United States that did not join in TPC.

Ibn Saud granted the concession to the Americans. While it is true that the American bid was significantly higher than the British, it is possible, and some would say likely, that Ibn Saud was motivated to grant the concession to the Americans because they were at that time interested solely in an economic interaction and, unlike the British, had no aspirations to exert political influence in the region, and certainly not to interfere in Arab politics.[3]

SoCal received a sixty-year concession covering an area of 360,000 square miles in the eastern part of the kingdom and preferential rights covering an adjoining region to the west. The Saudis were happy to deal with a company not officially associated with or owned by a government but that still had access to the most up-to-date exploration and extraction technology, as well as the required marketing capability. It was only after SoCal had signed the oil concession in 1933 that, later that year, the United States reached an agreement on diplomatic and consular representation with Saudi Arabia. However, there remained no collateral U.S. activity in the kingdom until 1940. In February of that year, the U.S. Department of State accredited its minister to Cairo to Jedda as well, it being the Saudi diplomatic capital. Saudi Arabia was rapidly becoming a major strategic asset to the United States. The American mission was upgraded to a legation in 1943.

SoCal (later called Chevron) was not going to interfere in Saudi internal affairs. It was not burdened with any holdover imperial complications, as were Shell and European oil companies. Eventually, the manifold interests of the United States in the region did prompt America to try to interfere in Saudi domestic affairs, but by then the problematic role of religious extremism was far too entrenched to be reversed, even by American pressure. However, Aramco (the Arab American Oil Company that in 1944 grew out of the concession to SoCal) first exerted pressure not on the Saudi government but on Washington, successfully lobbying for the Roosevelt administration's inclusion of Saudi Arabia as a beneficiary of America's Lend-Lease Fund. This allowed the Saudis to continue their construction, despite the wartime reduction in the flow of religious pilgrims (the hajj) and the flow of cash they represented. Oil exploration was carried on apace and the training of the first cadres of Saudi technical managers in the oil industry continued, so that by the end of the war oil revenues had surpassed foreign aid and grants to become the primary source of government revenue in the kingdom.

By 1940, SoCal had invested more than $30 million in infrastructure and development of the concession. But with the onset of World War II, Ibn Saud was again in need of money. SoCal could not see putting even more money into Arabia, but it also feared an increase in the British subsidy to the Saudis of £1 million a year, and, with it, increased British influence in the region. In order to protect their concession, the executives at SoCal turned to the American government for help. Franklin Roosevelt considered the request "too far afield"[4] for the United States to get involved. America remained uninterested in involving itself in the domestic affairs of other nations. In short, the reason Ibn Saud was interested in working with the United States was the same reason the United States would not enter into that partnership.

Gradually, as war issues loomed larger, Roosevelt's hesitation to get involved with SoCal was overcome, and the question of an American role in Saudi oil was reopened with a different perspective. There were growing oil shortages due to the war effort, and "concern for future petroleum resources was woven all through the discussions of America's strategic position during the war years."[5] Secretary of the Interior Harold Ickes convinced President Roosevelt and other government officials that locating foreign sources of oil had become a vital part of the military requirements to pursue the war successfully. At first the United States tried to gain controlling interest in SoCal, but there was a backlash against the idea of government in business, even though the relationship with Saudi Arabia and Aramco had been made possible only by the U.S. government working carefully with American oil companies.

But oil is not the whole story: Saudi Arabia is also important because of its strategic location. Lend-Lease was extended to the nation in 1943 in exchange for permission to build and utilize an air force base in Dhahran. The location of this base later made it a useful tool for the Americans during the cold war. Once they realized the strategic importance of Saudi Arabia, both economically and militarily, the political lives of both countries were linked—for better or for worse.

The official relationship was launched at the highest level in the most dramatic of circumstances: at President Franklin Roosevelt's post-Yalta meeting with Ibn Saud. The distance between the two in world understanding and perspective was obvious and huge, but the strategic partnership they established was nonetheless deep and lasting.

FDR spoke of Palestine and pleaded for Saudi support for Jewish refugees to be allowed into Palestine. Ibn Saud spoke of Saudi independence and proposed that the Jewish state be established on conquered German territory, since the United States was the victor in the war and could therefore simply impose its will. This exchange of wildly different notions of how the world worked was repeated a number of times in their long talk, but neither allowed it to get in the way of the main bilateral issue: Saudi oil supply and American security guarantees for the kingdom. On Palestine, FDR promised to consult the Saudi king before any decisions were made, but that was not a very deeply internalized presidential commitment, nor was it a binding legacy for Truman.

American support for Israel quickly became a point of contention between the Saudis and the Americans, but they never worked hard enough to resolve it. When their relationship was at its best it was because the issue was not central to their leadership. This proved to Ibn Saud that the Americans were in one basic way no different from the British: they would take from Saudi Arabia what they needed under the agreed premise of cooperation, but U.S. priorities would always outweigh Saudi interests in the implementation of policy.

Still, they both wanted to believe their meeting had gone well. Each side needed to keep the relationship positive, so despite the wide divergences in politics and culture, both left the Suez Canal with the sense that they had conducted a successful meeting that had consolidated their state-to-state relationship based on oil for security.

The United States and Saudi Arabia developed a good working relationship because they related to each other on only one subject: oil. It was a straightforward and mutually beneficial exchange of interests that did not entail interference in each other's internal affairs. Later, when Western culture started to infiltrate Saudi Arabia, the relationship changed. The emergence of a struggle within the royal family in the late 1940s and early 1950s was accompanied by a race for luxurious living in royal circles. At this point foreign NGOs began to talk about the corruption in the kingdom and its violations of human rights. The United States still had its predominant interest in oil, which led it to avoid attention to these internal problems lest they complicate the basic agreement. American civil society was again playing a role that could direct changes in U.S. foreign policy. This permitted those who seek change in Saudi Arabia toward more equality and a greater respect for human rights to form an antipathy against the United States for what they see as its blanket and indiscriminate support of the Saudi royal regime. On the other hand, some conservative elements in Saudi Arabia began to resent America's influence on the culture of their country. Religious zealots came to think that the United States had become too involved in domestic Saudi issues.

All of these factors have intensified as Saudi Arabia has become wealthier and much more of a factor in regional and world affairs. The short oil embargo after the 1973 War (the Yom Kippur War) rocketed Saudi Arabia into prominence as the fulfillment of Arab hopes for finally being able to find a weapon powerful enough to overcome the pro-Israel influence in American society. Then Saudi Arabia was propelled into a central role in world finance as the price of oil increased substantially and Saudi money (petrodollars) became a major financial investment factor in the United States, Europe, and Japan.

Once Saddam Hussein invaded Kuwait, the Saudi regime was called upon to make the historic decision of inviting the United States to mount a major military campaign to protect Saudi Arabia and save Kuwait for the royal family of Kuwait, who had been for so long a friend of the Sauds. Having large numbers of American personnel in Saudi society for those months, and an American presence maintained in Saudi Arabia for more than a decade, produced new kinds and levels of tension. There was a palpable clash between American cultural norms as practiced by American men and women in uniform and the very different norms of Saudi society, especially regarding the role of women. Saudis had to deal with Christian religious observances in the American enclaves within their land and even with the visits of some Jews.

On another front, the United States had begun to involve Saudi Arabia in assuming certain responsibilities in the American cold war rivalry with the Soviet Union. The most important and enduring impact was made by Saudi involvement in anti-Soviet guerrilla warfare in Afghanistan. As the Soviets were being defeated, a new political force was emerging in Afghanistan. The Taliban, who had taken upon themselves many of the rigors of Wahabi Islam, created a highly restrictive society that denied literacy to women and banned any artistic expression not deemed sufficiently Islamic, music included. The Taliban made of Afghanistan the perfect training ground for a new organization of Islamic extremism that had declared war on the United States and had been trained in war through the battle against the Soviets.

This Al Qaeda movement began to turn on American targets abroad and eventually within the United States. It recruited terrorists from a number of Arab countries and among Muslims who had moved to Europe and North America. The U.S. government and people not only were determined to destroy the Taliban and Al Qaeda wherever they operated, but insisted that Saudi Arabia itself extirpate the Al Qaeda movement within its borders. The Saudis for their part did not wish to see Islamic extremism either in their own country or as their export to the world; however, they were reluctant to go to war against too big a part of the religious sector and Wahabi life in their own country and elsewhere.

Thus, as America became fully focused in its foreign policy on what it called the War on Terror and included in that the war on Iraq and potential confrontations with Iran or Syria, or both, the hostile energy of their mutual anger and recriminations threatened to make the relationship explosive. American civil society and the private sector of the American oil industry will now have to make a major new effort to create positive civil society links, or else stand by and watch this important and mutually beneficial relationship fall casualty to government conflict and popular distrust despite the fact that both peoples and both governments do not want to have their common enterprise blow up in their faces.

A STABLE EXCHANGE

While Saudi Arabia was never directly a colony, it was often encircled by enemies—especially enemies installed by imperial governments—

and thus made to feel insecure and ambivalent about its relationships with outside powers. It also depended a great deal on the subsidies the Western countries offered in its early years, and therefore shared some of the discomforts of dependence that were shared by colonized peoples. It was clear to Ibn Saud that British support of Arab nationalism was as transitory, contingent, and expedient as its support of the Ottoman Empire had been. It was not for the British in itself a primary interest, but rather a derivative of primary interests, such as the protection of their shipping and naval routes to India and oil supply from Iran, Iraq, Saudi Arabia, and other Gulf countries. By not sufficiently taking account of the relationships among Arab rulers and by treating the Arab world as only a tool sometimes useful to the British Empire, Britain eventually lost the loyalty and, as a consequence, the resources of one of the most important Arab rulers of the period.

The American presence on the Saudi scene began in 1932 after the consolidation of Saudi control over the Arabian Peninsula. By this time, Ibn Saud had conquered the Hejaz, the pilgrimage areas of the Islamic holy sites, and had extended his rule to the borders of Bahrain, Kuwait, Qatar, and Oman. Saudi Arabia was now its name and it was already an unusual state diplomatically in that its treaties were basically agreements between an individual monarch and the British Empire.

By 1914, Ibn Saud had already negotiated his way through a period in which he had contradictory exclusive agreements with the Ottoman Empire and with Britain, and had worked those agreements to his favor to expand his territorial control and deepen his rule. He had already formed the effective alliance with religious authorities (mutawa'a) who saw themselves as the guardians of Islam and enforcers of obedience to Ibn Saud.

The American independent oilmen and their backers in the major oil companies did not need to concern themselves with the ideological underpinnings of the state. They focused only on the state's stability and its ability to meet its commercial obligations and to provide a conflict-free atmosphere for exploration, extraction, and export of oil. For their part, the oilmen concentrated on paying for and providing the services necessary to develop the industry on a sound, profitable, and stable basis. The source of that stability, and the means by which it was achieved, were not at that time a concern to the American oil-men or their government.

It was thus easy for the two sides to reach an exchange agreement that was unchanging and solid for many years after World War II, un-til the disruptions of the Gulf wars. The Americans had gained eco-nomic growth and a major reinforcement of American leadership in the economy of the world. The Saudis gained a steady market and the income that ensured the American security umbrella. The nature of the Saudi state and its implicit Islamic social contract had always de-pended on Ibn Saud's being able to provide funding for the mainte-nance of core groups who supported the regime. Once oil was discovered and was being produced in commercial quantities, it be-came the key to regime stability and to the centralized control that the royal family was able to maintain over its own growing numbers and over the various factions and tribes that it had to keep loyal and sub-servient. This American-Saudi exchange worked well as long as nei-ther side had to "look under the hood" of what maintained the stability and what kind of society was being developed and sustained based on that exchange.

THE BREAKDOWN

The United States had inherited a wary ruler in Ibn Saud, and it did nothing to mitigate that wariness. By World War II, the U.S. govern-ment was also interested in what it could get from Saudi Arabia with regard to concessions, control over oil, and the strategic barrier against communism. And so an old relationship with new actors was restaged: one in which the priorities of neither the regional leaders nor their people were considered, and the priorities of the superpow-ers were paramount. The Americans picked up where the British left off, though without the active search for empire and with more focus on the economic aspects of the relationship.

The strange and intense meeting between Ibn Saud and Franklin Roosevelt in the waning days of World War II was an indication of how far the two worlds diverged in their basic concerns and understanding. It is a chasm that has yet to be bridged effectively by policy adjustment of either party or by the education of their respective publics and elites. That Ibn Saud could have proposed at that moment that FDR create a Jewish state in occupied Germany or that FDR could have proposed that Ibn Saud sponsor a major influx of Jewish refugees into Palestine was a clear sign that the two leaders were coming from different planets and that each knew nothing of the other's real political environment. Neither had any idea how to modify his view to make a proposal to the other that had a chance of being taken seriously. The clash between maintaining the stable monarchy (and therefore also the religious conservatism) of Saudi Arabia and satisfying the potential American interest in the creation of Israel was a major consideration and concern of many leading American foreign affairs specialists and is a continual source of tension between Saudi Arabia and the United States.

During the cold-war period the United States was content to see Saudi influence and ambition spread to other Arab and Muslim countries as a bulwark against Arab socialism and supposed Communist infiltration and tendencies. The 1962 conflict between the Saudis and Egypt's Nasser over Yemen is a good example of a temporary convergence of interest against Nasserism and perceived Soviet penetration of the region. But as Ibn Saud and his successors became more engaged in regional politics in South Asia and the Middle East, they brought their ideas with their money to the playing field. This new involvement in foreign affairs would lead to difficulties in the Saudi-American alliance.

These gaps grew as the United States became the singular power of the West in the Middle East. The withdrawal of Britain first from Suez and then from the Persian Gulf and Aden left the United States and Saudi Arabia in a wholly different relationship than either had bargained for. The Saudis now found the United States to be only secondarily its partner in energy exchange and, primarily, the main military and strategic power in the Gulf Area. This new role meant that for the first time the United States was really affected by what went on within the borders of Saudi Arabia and what the political and eventually ideological exports of the region would be.

The issue of Israel and the Palestinians created differences of opinion and sharp words, but the security of the Gulf and the growing impact of the strategic partnership between the United States and Saudi Arabia on the support and legitimacy of the Saudi regime was not something that either could allow to be ignored any longer. For a while, both sides tried to keep it the subject of gentlemanly disagreement, but as security issues became more intense with the growth of threats from Iraq and Iran and the dawning of awareness of religious-state tensions, they could no longer simply agree to disagree. Everybody needed answers.

Other events in the region widened the growing gap and strained the Saudi-American alliance even further. This intensity of mutual engagement was heightened dramatically by the Khomeini revolution in Iran, as well as by the ambitions of Saddam Hussein. In his challenge to Iran's sovereignty and his search for a financial backer for further adventures, Saddam Hussein created serious difficulties for the Saudis and the Americans. Their evaluations of the political situation in the Gulf and the Arab world in general became more divergent and more consequential.

Gradually, after the conclusion of the Gulf War, the full implications of the Saudi decision to invite Americans onto sovereign Saudi soil to fight against another Muslim country and to stay for years in the kingdom with its soldiers—men and women—began to sink in for both sides and to penetrate especially the content of anti-royal-family-opposition rhetoric and incitement. This coincided with the intensification of anti-American animosity in religious opposition groups.

The tensions between the American military presence and Saudi society led to a proclivity on both sides toward lowering the visibility and presence of American forces on Saudi land even before the ultimate decision was taken after 9/11. It was 9/11 that was the signal for

Saudi-bashing to become a common form of talk in American political circles. What was more striking was the failure of the old associates of the Saudi-American relationship to come to its public defense. The alliance has become too radioactive for their overt public advocacy.

The Saudis emphasized the animus of their old rivals for influence in America, such as the pro-Israel lobbies, but the new critical fact is the disappearance of the pro-Saudi consensus from the American corporate community and from the wide circle of the foreign policy elite of America. They, too, were stung by the events of 9/11, the failure of the Saudis to take a forthright role in fighting the Al Qaeda phenomenon, the tendency of many Saudis to repeat if not to promote conspiracy theories of Jewish or Israeli responsibility for 9/11, and the ostensible unwillingness of the Saudi government to address the problem with sufficient energy and forthrightness.

This moment of crisis has enhanced the willingness and indeed enthusiasm in America for insisting on Saudi internal reform and even on moves to democracy, despite the explicit clash it entails with the royal family and its traditional forms of succession and rule by nepotism. For the first time, the nature of the religious life of the two countries and their value systems began to be as important in the discussion as oil prices and production levels. It was only a sharp rise in oil prices close to election season that brought Americans back to their traditional concerns about Saudi Arabia, but even then it was with more than a tinge of anger and a desire to reduce the importance of Saudi Arabia in American economic life.

Some Americans have become very facile and superficial in their willingness to jettison the relationship with Saudi Arabia as a pillar of American national policy in the region and in the energy market. One can only hope that Saudis and Americans will both have a second wind of rationality about the mutual importance of their relationship, which has grown far beyond the bounds of its origins. The consequences of their alliance are of much greater importance now that the United States is such a central player in Middle East policy and life and that Saudi Arabia has achieved such a place of primacy in the politics, religion, and economic future of the Gulf and of the Arab and Muslim worlds.

Indeed, America would be in a much better place in its relations with the Middle East and the world community if it was clear to itself and its elites that its relationships with Israel, Saudi Arabia, and Egypt are not temporary anomalies, but of bedrock importance to the American people and their conception of U.S. national interest. We must move to a place where Americans no longer play fast and loose with partisan and secretarian ideas that one or another of these relationships is to be reduced to irrelevance in America's future. For this to happen, the three parties will also have to come not only to relate to America at the government level and at the level of the special interest that brought each of them to the party, but to develop a relationship with much wider and deeper elements of American society and political culture.

It was fortunate for Saudi Arabia in many ways that oil was not discovered until Ibn Saud had succeeded in uniting the Arabian Peninsula into one country, and that the elements of its identity pre-existed the West's starting to treat it as a huge gas station. Americans are going to have to face up to the fact that Saudi identity will be the bedrock of Saudi Arabia and will not be forfeited either for oil wealth or for relationships with other powers. Indeed, the Saudis will have to recognize how important religion is also in American society, that it is at the core of American identity. Therefore the dialogue they have never had about intimate internal issues of identity is going to have to take the place of priority that has always been accorded the discussion of oil reserves and oil prices and the strategic defense of the Saudi state by American power.

For many years, it seemed as though the oil under the feet of Ibn Saud would suffice to maintain the cohesiveness and solidity of the kingdom. Ibn Saud had what seemed like an impregnable triad: military force, religious intensity, and financial inducement. Each of the pillars of the triad has had its moment of shakiness. The military force of Saudi Arabia could not match the power accumulated by Saddam Hussein, which led not only to the invasion of Kuwait but to the eventual need to rely more heavily on the protective power of the United States. The economic pillar became stronger as oil prices rose, but was also subject to the whims of change that brought oil prices sharply down and led to declines in demand because the world's economy was in recession. Most important, however, was the emergence of unexpected consequences of religious fervor. The growing population of young men and women in the kingdom, who maintained the ferocity of their religious allegiance but were no longer content to receive government handouts while they remained unemployed, required a very different kind of Saudi governance and education. Most of all, as the younger generation gave evidence of a growing gap between their religious conviction and their unhappiness with their lack of meaningful work as adults and the scarcity of world respect for their culture and religion, some Saudi young people turned to extremism. A significant number of Arabs, including Saudis and Yemenis, had been recruited to join the jihad against the Soviet Union in Afghanistan. In addition to military training, they were exposed to the reactionary notions of Islamic rule preached by the Taliban and the radical hatred of the United States spread by Al Qaeda. Indeed, the religious fervor of the young now threatens to overwhelm the Saudi leadership, and its consequences threaten to visit upon Saudi Arabia the wrath of its longtime strategic partner, the United States.

When the United States first engaged with Ibn Saud, the exchange relationship was very clear and well delimited. The Saudis would sell oil to the United States through Aramco and the American oil companies, and the U.S. government would reciprocate by providing the kingdom with a strategic umbrella against any foreign intervention or invasion. Neither had any desire to understand the internal structure and culture of the other, and neither considered any possible attempt to change each other's internal life. This gentleman's agreement could not survive the shocks of the Iraqi invasion of Kuwait, the Al Qaeda terrorist attacks on the Twin Towers and the Pentagon, and the realization by both of them that the greatest threats to Saudi Arabian stability were now internal or from the great reemergence of Shiite power that resulted from the American invasion of Iraq and the power ambitions of Iran. These new realities coming to the fore at the beginning of the twenty-first century made Americans and Saudis much more conscious of and concerned about the other's political life and national values.

If they do not engage in a respectful dialogue about their identities, they may lose the great benefits they have both enjoyed: the Roosevelt–Ibn Saud exchange of a military umbrella for a reliable oil market relationship must now be augmented by the coming together of the leadership of the two countries about the future of Middle East regional politics and the role that each of them will play.

 **CHAPTER 5**

SYRIA

How did Syria come to be such a militant opponent of Western interests in the Middle East?

Syrian relations with the United States are in one sense the counterexample to America's inheriting leftover Middle East woes from the residua of the British Empire, in that Syria had a French mandate. On the other hand, Syria is also the exception that proves the rule, because the residua of the French mandate had much the same composition as that of the British. Syrian nationalism had emerged even before World War I, and it was intensified by local antagonism to a French mandate.

The French did little to provide the basis for economic modernization. They underinvested in health and education, and directed most of their spending to their own military presence.

The French mandate not only failed to prepare Syria for democratic self-rule but actually exacerbated the internal ethnic conflicts that have continued to impede effective governance and national development to this day.

The tendency to play on ethnic and religious rivalries was a preferred tactic not only of the French in Syria but also of the British in Iraq. The resultant ethnic-conflict-laced politics created an openness in both countries to the ideas of Ba'athism, which combined a strong

unitary Arab nationalism, a nonreligious political culture, and autocratic control in the style of European authoritarian movements of
the thirties and forties. This reaction to ethnic divisiveness through
authoritarian nationalism was highly appealing for a short time.
Notwithstanding the rhetoric of national unity, a specific minority
ethnic/religious group came to be dominant over all others, partly by
identifying itself with the development of new military capability. In
Iraq, the Sunni minority, concentrated in a geographical triangle
around Baghdad, became the base of the ruling group, and its dominance became much reinforced as the Hashemite monarchy, itself
Sunni, was replaced by the authoritarian leader Saddam Hussein, who
did not hesitate to use brutal torture and summary execution to
strengthen his rule.

In Syria, the minorities nurtured by the French were first the
Maronite Christians located around Mount Lebanon and mostly
northeast of Beirut and the Alawite quasi-Shi'a focused in the Latakia
and northeast areas of Syria extending to the Mediterranean coast.
Alawi control was greatly reinforced by the long rule of the strongman Hafez Al-Assad, who came to leadership in the 1970 crisis over
the struggle for power between King Hussein of Jordan and the
Palestinian guerrilla force that unsuccessfully challenged his regime;
in Iraq it was Saddam Hussein who eventually came to power some
years after the overthrow of the sister Hashemite regime in 1958.

The United States began to deal with Syria as a significant factor
in foreign policy not as a British colonial legacy but through the single
lens of the cold war. Eisenhower and Dulles saw Syria as the Arab
country most under Soviet influence, and because they saw it as the
Arab socialist and nationalist regime most inimical to American interests, they developed a hostile attitude toward it. Syria's Communist
Party had not only been permitted to operate, but had actually been
part of the government coalition under the Ba'ath Party. Syria was
engaged in arms deals with the Soviet Union, though at first unpub-
licized, and was objecting to any kind of Egyptian participation
in Western defense plans. The relationship grew especially tense
through the Syrian-American crisis of 1957, part of the aftermath of

the 1956 Suez Crisis. Even when Nasser finally accepted a compromise with Britain that specified a date of British military withdrawal from Suez, Syria objected to the compromise. It denounced Egypt's acceptance of the British condition for withdrawal, which would have allowed Britain's return to Suez as a military base if any of a number of specified countries were attacked.

Syria's transition from imperial rule to independence was not a smooth one. First of all, its urban notables and landowners were pioneers in the support of the ideas underpinning first Arab nationalism vis-à-vis the Ottoman Empire and then both Arab nationalism and Greater Syrian nationalism.

From the beginning, Syria was strongly opposed to the disposition planned for it in the Paris Peace Conference of 1919. Syrian interlocutors had made it clear both directly in Paris and through Woodrow Wilson's King-Crane Commission that Syria was strongly averse to its division from Palestine, had already been deeply affected by both the idea of Arab national unity and the idea of Greater Syrian unity, and did not want any mandate foisted upon it. It especially did not want a French mandate, with a proclivity to separating Lebanon from the rest of Syria and favoring the Christians over all other groups in the multiethnic and multireligious Syrian society.

The Syrian National Congress of 1920 went so far as to agree with the British idea of crowning Faisal I, a son of Sharif Hussein of Hejaz, as the Hashemite ruler of Syria, but the French would have nothing to do with that plan. They were planning to rule in their own way and not through a pro-British Hashemite protégé. These early expressions of Syrian nationalism were brushed away by the French, who proceeded to create a structure of four substates in the already divided Syria.

One state was Lebanon. A second was created for the Druze population centered on Jebel el-Druz (Druz Mountain). In keeping with their special attention to the heterodox Muslim sects, they also created an Alawi state bordering on the Mediterranean, in the northwest, which later came to be called Latakia. The fourth state was the Syrian heartland, and included the two dominant classes, mentioned earlier, as well as the majority population, which was Sunni. They were largely small merchants and the urban and rural poor. As a result, even the emerging Syrian nationalists did not find an inclusive way of organizing all the major subgroups of the society into a unified movement.

Syria's neighbors, Palestine, Transjordan, and Iraq, were under separate British mandates. In Iraq, the British were also unable to find a point of integration among the key subgroups of the state created by their mandate, and in Palestine the British chose the Mufti of Jerusalem to hold power in Palestinian Arab society, giving the back of their hand to other key families, some of them more moderate and more oriented toward cooperation with the mandatory authority.

The United States, although not happy with the British-French division of Syria into mandates, did recognize the mandatory authority in 1924. Serious nationalist and popular resistance to the mandate began soon afterward, and the interwar years were marked by a predictable series of revolts against the mandatory regime. Meanwhile, the new Turkey had revived her claim to Alexandretta, in northern Syria, and in 1939 the French mandate ceded it to the Turks, thus arousing more tension between Turkey and Syria, tension the United States and others have exploited from time to time.

The French mandate was largely a failure in preparing Syria to become a modern state. Virtually no progress was made toward the establishment of an independent government. Only halfhearted attempts were made to establish representative institutions. The French did not go far in the necessary land reform. Almost no progress was made on improvement in agriculture, the sector that was the main employer in the region. Some progress was made in helping foreign trade by extending the harbor in Beirut and accessory facilities, and a state system of schools was initiated, but it did not approach the level of the private schools.

In the fifties, Syrian coups d'état became a way of life, with governments coming and going and no stability established. Arab nationalism was able to produce its strong leader in Syria only after the Ba'ath Party revolution in 1963 that brought to the fore a political structure that was quite doctrinaire in its socialism. That party interpreted democracy in ways that did not encourage consent of the governed, democratic elections, or private enterprise, but did encourage close support of the Soviet Union, even though Soviet leadership perceived Syria's own doctrinaire leftism as somewhat reckless. Syria's stability emerged with Hafez Al-Assad, who, paradoxically, objected to the doctrinaire socialism of his predecessor, Jadid Al-Salah, but understood well what he needed to do to create a more businesslike relationship with the Soviets so that they would provide the arms and training that would permit Assad to go to war with Israel, as he did in 1973.

Assad expanded the party base to include many middle- and lower-class Sunnis, but he focused his attention on gaining control of the military, which had been heavily Alawi and which, much more than the party, became the pillar of his rule. So the United States found itself with a less doctrinaire leftist regime in Syria, but one with much greater determination to build its military capability on the basis of Soviet arms and try to recapture the territory lost in the 1967 War. Moreover, Syria was led by a man who was willing to look beyond his great distrust of Egypt and Sadat in order to create a coalition that could challenge Israel in a two-front war.

Assad, who saw himself as the only possible successor to Nasser as a Pan-Arab leader, not only proved himself effective in dealing with Brezhnev, but was also able to persuade Henry Kissinger and a series of American presidents from Richard Nixon through Bill Clinton that he was the Arab leader most worthy of direct U.S. presidential attention and most interesting as a negotiating partner (though Henry Kissinger was the only American official actually able to reach a substantive agreement with him). Secretary of State James Baker, under George H. W. Bush, was able to convince Assad first to join the American military coalition that expelled Saddam Hussein from Kuwait and then to send Syrian high-level representation to join the American-organized Madrid Peace Conference of 1991, but he did not manage to achieve a substantive agreement between Syria and Israel.

After independence in 1944, Syria suffered almost two decades of recurrent coups d'état and continuous political instability. Having been under Ottoman control and then French mandate, a free and independent Syria could have been a close ally for the United States, but the Truman administration foreclosed that initial opportunity. By taking such a strong stand on the formation of the state of Israel, the United States became in the Syrian mind intrinsically identified with the ideas of Zionism, colonialism, and imperialism, the triple anathema of the Arab nationalist world. Syria in particular was a sworn enemy of the formation of a Jewish state on land it considered its own, and this hostility was intensified through the 1948 War and the tidal wave of the ensuing refugee problem that brought many thousands of Palestinians streaming into Lebanon and Syria, among other states.

The Arab-Israeli War in 1948 was a turning point for Syria. When the Israelis easily defeated the Syrian army, Syrians began to believe that their leaders had been criminally negligent. Similar to the experience in Egypt, the young officers began to see themselves as responsible for the defense of Syria from external threats and internal incompetence. An intense feeling of nationalism grew within the country. The United States, focused only on its own immediate interests, did not quite grasp the heated transition to nationalist anger occurring in Syria. In order to achieve its goals there, it is believed that the CIA, under the auspices of the Truman administration, supported a 1949 coup by Colonel Husni al-Za'im.

In the five months that Za'im held power, he made it clear that he was a friend of the Truman administration. He concluded an armistice with Israel regarding the War of 1948; approved Tapline, an oil pipeline construction between Saudi Arabia and the Mediterranean; outlawed communism; said he would consider taking in Palestinian refugees; and renounced any claim to Alexandretta, the disputed area ceded to Turkey by the French mandate against Syrian nationalist sentiment. Za'im had apparently adopted all of the American initiatives in the Middle East. Unfortunately for the Truman administration, he was soon overthrown, and the favorable United States–Syria relationship was over before it ever really got started. Za'im was assassinated by Colonel Sami al-Hinnawi, who immediately reversed many of Za'im's decisions.

In late 1949, Colonel Adib al-Shishakli staged the third coup of the year. The United States thought it could restore a working relationship with Syria through Shishakli and offered him economic and technical aid under Truman's Point Four Program, but Syria, still stinging from its defeat in the 1948 War, was interested only in direct military aid. The United States therefore created a policy by which it would supply military aid to an Arab country only if that country signed on to the 1950 Tripartite Agreement among the United States, France, and Britain, which stipulated that military aid would be used for defensive purposes only and not for an attack on Israel. Syria refused to sign the agreement and was consequently denied military aid.

It is clear that successive American administrations did not grasp how much of an enemy Syria was becoming. When the Syrian minister of national economy Dawalibi said that he would "become a Soviet republic rather than become prey to world Jewry," the United States interpreted this to mean that Syria was falling into Communist hands. The Truman administration did not regard the statement as an exaggeration of Syria's real attitude. They did not understand that it was more an expression of hatred toward Israel than a warming-up to communism, and saw it as representing a real threat of potential Soviet penetration in the Middle East and a breach of Truman's containment policy. There was no sense in Washington that Syria's attitude could be reversed by the simple expedients of allaying Syrian fears of Israeli expansion and addressing the problem of Palestinian refugees.

The Syrians hoped (and to a certain extent believed) that the Eisenhower administration would understand their needs and fears better than Truman's had. They, and most of the Arab world, were to be sorely disappointed.

PRE-EISENHOWER DOCTRINE (1953–57)

A month before Eisenhower took office there was yet another coup attempt in Syria. The Syrian leader Shishakli survived the coup, but his hold on power was weakened, and widespread animosity toward

America made it difficult for Shishakli to work with the United States. He was not able to reconstruct a stable government, and so any concession to the West would have meant his overthrow. In fact, his hold on power was so tenuous that not only could he not reach agreements with the United States, but he was now also forced to "strong-arm" the West. When he spoke of any possible U.S.-Syrian agreement, he made clear that any such agreement would have to be in Syria's favor and based on equality. To show his independence from the West, he reversed the Tapline negotiations and demanded 49 percent of all savings the pipeline would yield. He wanted to ensure that Arab nationalist aspirations were met and that Syria not become a plaything of the West.

The main concern of the Eisenhower administration was the spread of communism. Its foremost policy goal was to surround the Soviet Union with non-Communist states, in order to dam up communism within Soviet borders. For this to happen, the countries of the Middle East would have to play a vital role. Given the new situation in Syria and the problems throughout the Middle East, Eisenhower felt that an entirely new approach was in order if the United States was to achieve its aims. Thus one of the major policy purposes of the administration, which was to solve the Arab-Israeli conflict, became known as the Alpha Plan. Eisenhower understood that if he could find a solution to this problem he would have the support of the Arab leaders. To begin his efforts in the region, Eisenhower sent his secretary of state, John Foster Dulles, to the Middle East three months after inauguration. Dulles met with many Arab leaders; they all told him they disliked the favoritism the United States displayed toward Israel and complained about continued British imperialism in the region.

Shishakli told Dulles that if the United States took a completely impartial stance on the Arab-Israeli conflict, persuaded Israel to abide by UN resolutions, and supplied Syria with military aid, then Syria would consider a defense pact with the United States. He emphasized that he wanted not to destroy Israel, but rather for Israel to abide by the UN resolutions. He also gave the impression that any military aid would be used not against Israel, but to defend Syria against communism. It was everything Dulles wanted to hear, but what he imparted to the National Security Council when he returned home was that Syria was considering joining a defense pact. It is unclear why Dulles gave such a warped interpretation of his conversation with Shishakli, but perhaps he did so because he knew it would be almost impossible to meet the Syrian leader's requests without seeming to abandon Israel, sure to be a very unpopular move in the United States. Dulles's misrepresentation was the first step in a long series of missteps that would estrange the United States further from the Arab world.

For Shishakli's part, his meeting with Dulles garnered him great opposition in Syria. In order to try to quell the suspicion that he was in the pocket of the West, he signed a treaty of friendship with Iran, a state then at bitter odds with the United States.

In early 1954, due in large part to the problems the United States was then dealing with in Egypt, the Eisenhower administration decided it had to create a defense plan against the Soviet Union that was not linked to the Arab-Israeli conflict or other Arab issues. This evolved into the so-called Northern Tier concept. The administration felt that it could isolate the Soviet Union by joining Pakistan and Turkey in a defense pact, called the Baghdad Pact, when it came to center on Iraq as the link in the Northern Tier between Asian Pakistan and Turkey, which bridged Europe and Asia. Shishakli had conflicting feelings about the pact. He did not want it to exist because that would lead to strong American involvement in the region. However, if it was inevitable, he wanted to ensure that Syria was not left out of it.

Prime Minister Shishakli did not have much time to ponder his dilemma because in February of 1954 he was overthrown by a coup led by Colonel Adnan al-Maliki. This coup set off another string of short-lived regimes. As a result of the Maliki coup, Sabri al-Asali became prime minister. The Asali government quickly self-destructed and was replaced by that of Said al-Ghazzi. Syria's chronic instability made the United States fear that Communist influences could easily infiltrate it. In the mid-fifties there was a growing Syrian Communist Party, and even though it was not strong, the United States was deeply concerned by any intimation of penetration by the Soviet Union. The growth of an indigenous Communist Party was the strongest and clearest signal of that danger.

THE NORTHERN TIER

Contrary to the Northern Tier concept, many in the United States started to see value in including Iraq in the mix (even though this would destroy the idea of "de-linking" Arab issues from the Northern Tier defense). In April of 1955, the Eisenhower administration believed that the best course of action was to bring Iraq into the Turco-Pakistani pact, thus making it the Baghdad Pact. It was ironic that the United States would implement this new alliance just then, at the same time that the Syrians were expelling all pro-Iraqi elements from their government.

The new move to include Iraq created huge problems for the U.S.-Syrian relationship. The Syrian-Iraqi relationship—involving two states linked by their Ba'athist parties and ideologies, and sharing the problems of deep internal fissures based on religion, ethnicity, and historical rivalry—has been little understood by the United States from the fifties through the Iraqi-U.S. military confrontation that began in 2003. The United States cannot hope to successfully influence the direction of policy decisions by the leadership of these countries without a much firmer grasp of the intricacies of the relationship between Iraq and Syria and the consequences of their unresolved internal divisions. Syria's revolving-door government required far deeper social and political analysis if the United States wanted to find a foundation for a stable and nonhostile relationship with this fractionated society. Syria was one of the post-Ottoman lands that became a state before its nation had coalesced. This is true of Iraq as well and, to a certain extent, of Palestinian Arab society. The chronic instability of these countries reflected the troubled relations among ethnic groups, religious groups, and tribes that had yet to be worked through to create a solid basis for national solidarity and identity.

The newly created Baghdad Pact and the debate over the Syrian reaction to it created rifts within the Syrian government that eventually led to its resignation. A growing group of leftists in Syria, helped by a propaganda upsurge provided by Nasser of Egypt, was able to take power. Under this new Syrian leadership, Egypt, Syria, and Saudi Arabia created a joint Arab defense and economic cooperation pact as an autochthonous Arab alternative to the Baghdad Pact.

The growing tension in the region was exacerbated in 1955 by Israeli raids into Gaza and into Syrian territory near Lake Tiberias. The Israeli raids and the Egyptian-Syrian weakness in responding to them forced Egypt to look to the Soviet Union for arms. Military aid was granted, but the arms were supplied through Czechoslovakia, in order to lower the profile of the arrangement. The Lake Tiberias raid made Syria, too, more intent on gaining arms and rebuilding its military capabilities.

The United States could not decide whether to bring Iraq closer, when that surely would entail greater alienation of Nasser, but could also mean temporarily perpetuating the vestiges of British influence over its former mandate in the Fertile Crescent (at least until the United States was itself firmly enough engaged in Arab politics to assume the responsibilities Britain had shouldered since General Allenby's conquest of the Ottoman Arab lands). The United States also needed to decide if it had a real chance of winning over Syrian support, because a closer relationship with Iraq would further complicate its chances with Syria. Eventually, in 1958, the United States made a last-ditch effort to structure a strong anti-Nasserist alliance based on Iraq, Jordan, and Lebanon, but by then the Hashemite regime of Iraq had been overthrown and the country had moved into the Nasserist camp. Camille Chamoun, the Christian leader of Lebanon, and the teenage King Hussein of Jordan, still unable to work with the Saudis because of the historic rivalry between the Hashemis and the Sauds, were too feeble a combination to compete against the dynamic force that was Nasser and his now strongest supporter, Syria.

In 1956 a further blow was dealt to those who still hoped to create an alliance between moderate Syrians and the United States. Adnan al-Maliki, an important Syrian military official and strong Ba'ath supporter, and the colonel responsible for overthrowing Shishakli, was assassinated by a member of the Syrian People's Party (PPS), at the right wing of Syria's political spectrum. The United States and specifically the CIA had had connections to the PPS, and many in Syria thought the assassination was coordinated by the United States. Though there are no documents to support this theory and almost no evidence to this effect, the dissemination of propaganda about "the plot" was enough to energize anti-West sentiments in Syria. The Ba'athists in the army used the assassination as justification to purge the military of PPS members and to round up pro-Iraqi supporters. After the assassination, the Ba'ath Party was well on its way to consolidating its stranglehold on power in Syria, a process it completed in a 1963 coup.

In 1956 the United States had considered aiding a PPS coup in order to install a friendly pro-Western government. However, Dulles decided that helping the PPS was simply too risky, as there was a chance of its leading to a leftist decision in Syria to overtly ally itself with the Soviet Union. Despite the American hesitation, the British developed Operation Straggle, a plan to establish a Western-friendly government in Syria. Although Dulles publicly denounced any covert actions there, it seems he recommended that the CIA cooperate in Operation Straggle. The CIA agent Wilbur Eveland was dispatched to Syria to scout out possible internal allies, and a coup was planned for October 29—which turned out to be the day the Israelis attacked the Suez Canal. The coup was postponed, and it appears that the Americans withdrew their support from Operation Straggle.

The Eisenhower plan to "de-link" the issues of the Arab-Israeli conflict and the fight against communism had failed. The administration was caught between the competing interests of creating good bilateral U.S.-Syrian relations and taking steps toward solving the Israeli-Palestinian conflict. American commitments at the regional and international levels were made, inter alia, at the expense of a potential improvement in the U.S. relationship with Syria.

The State Department knew that what Syria wanted was an arms deal, but its officials thought that if Syria had a stronger military it would not feel the pressure to negotiate peace with Israel. Dulles also thought the Israelis would be less likely to negotiate from a weakened position. But the biggest fear was that Russia would swoop in as it had in Egypt and fill the vacant role of arms provider in Syria. The Americans were caught in an untenable position, but the choice was soon made for them. When Syria discovered the covert intentions of the United States to change its government by force, any thoughts of an improved relationship were obliterated.

THE EISENHOWER DOCTRINE

In January 1957, the Eisenhower administration announced the Eisenhower Doctrine, its new Middle East foreign policy, which pledged that the United States would come to the aid of any country that had fallen prey to international communism. By the time this new policy was created, Syria had already declared its neutralist attitude (with an implied hostility toward the United States). Syrians felt that the Eisenhower Doctrine furthered only American interests (i.e., stopping the spread of international communism) and did not address Arab concerns (i.e., Israel and the Baghdad Pact). They also saw the doctrine as anti-Nasser and therefore incompatible with their interests and their new decision for union with Egypt and the creation of a United Arab Republic.

As Bonnie Saunders, the author of *The United States and Arab Nationalism: The Syrian Case, 1953–1960*, explains:

Arab governments, however, hesitated to endorse the Eisenhower Doctrine because it provided no assistance against the persistent twin threats of Zionism and imperialism, manifested most recently by the invasion of Egypt by Israel, Britain and France. Instead, the Doctrine offered help against Soviet or Soviet-inspired aggression, which most Arab leaders found irrelevant since the Soviet Union had never invaded an Arab country. The United States now was asking Arab leaders to ignore what they saw as the critical realities of regional politics.[1]

As a corollary to the Eisenhower Doctrine, the United States tried to court King Saud of Saudi Arabia to become the conservative, pro-Western alternative to Nasser and his radicalism. This was a foolish idea. The personalities were too different. Nasser's charisma was not going to be outshone by an obscenely rich, self-indulgent, socially reclusive potentate with more wives than Nasser had generals.

Still, emboldened by his American support and confident of the new power it gave him, King Saud held himself out to the Arab world as having the ability to persuade the United States to pressure Israel to withdraw from the Sinai and to find a solution to the question of Suez Canal sovereignty, a resolution of the Gulf of Aqaba dispute, and an answer to the Palestinian refugee problem. In order to build up King Saud's prestige and not embarrass him, President Eisenhower exerted pressure on Israel to withdraw from Sinai. The irony of the story was that although the United States had launched much of its policy to contain Nasser, by this time it was seeking Nasser's help to push the Communists out of the National Front coalition government in Syria, as Nasser had started to express his own misgivings about communism. Indeed, important elements in Syria maintained that the United States was fully supporting Syria's union with Egypt in order to eliminate leftist political elements from Syrian politics and to permit settlement of the Palestine question.

In 1957, King Saud helped King Hussein assert control over leftist and pro-Nasser elements in Jordan. To further consolidate the pro-West sentiment, the United States brokered a rapprochement between the longtime enemies King Faisal of Iraq and King Saud of Saudi Arabia. The left-wing political figures in Syria immediately launched a propaganda (and media) campaign against Saudi Arabia. In response, Saudi Arabia froze all Syrian assets in its banks and recalled its ambassador from Damascus. The Syrian government quickly decided that it did not want to be estranged from Saudi Arabia, and the two countries began to reconcile.

In order to reconstruct relations with Saudi Arabia and simultaneously undermine the U.S.-Saudi relationship, the Syrians expressed support for an issue of major importance for the Saudis: the question of the Gulf of Aqaba; the Arab world wanted to keep Israeli ships from passing through those waters. Saudi Arabia assumed "ownership" of the dispute over the Gulf. Syria continued to question the United States as to why it had not taken action on this issue. Syria and Egypt's agreement to let the Saudis take the lead on the Gulf of Aqaba issue, and a shared frustration over America's inaction, opened the door to reconciliation among Saudi Arabia, Syria, and Egypt.

In 1957, a new leader emerged in Iraq, Ali Jawdat, who wanted to improve the long-troubled relations between Syria and Iraq. Meanwhile, the United States and Britain were very unhappy with the new relationship being constructed between Egypt and Syria.

EISENHOWER'S LAST STAND

In 1957 U.S. concern about the Soviet infiltration of Syria became intense. In order to stem the tide, America turned to its friends in the Middle East, but no one wanted to take military action. On August 24, 1957, Eisenhower had sent Deputy Undersecretary of State Loy Henderson to the region. Henderson had been intimately involved in the overthrow of Iran's Mossadegh and in the creation of the Truman Doctrine, presented by President Truman to a joint session of Congress in 1947. The Truman Doctrine proposed that the United States take responsibility for protecting Greece and Turkey both economically and militarily in order to prevent those two countries from falling under Soviet control. Henderson's presence, therefore, immediately caused a stir, as many feared that he was up to his old tricks and would try to replicate in Syria what had happened in Iran. Henderson had hoped to form an Arab coalition that would invade Syria and drive out the Communists. But the Arab states had many reservations and could not reach consensus. So the United States had to change its tack and look to Turkey to do the work. Through not-so-subtle diplomatic exchanges, the United States gave Turkey the green light to intervene in Syria.

Henderson's diplomatic tour caused apprehension in Moscow, too. On September 3, 1957, the Soviets sent a letter to the other Great Powers calling for a four-power declaration renouncing the use of force in the Middle East. At the same time, Moscow condemned the United States as an imperial aggressor in the region. Khrushchev had invested a lot in intervention in the third world, and though he was not confident in any partner state that did not have a dominant Communist Party, he did cleverly find a way to position Soviet interests as if they supported local nationalism and the struggle for full independence for the Arab states. This positioning proved to be highly successful, especially in the perceptions of the United States, which construed neutralism as little more than a thinly veiled subterfuge for anti-Americanism, and often fought the national movements just at the height of their enthusiasm and energy, thus opening a path for Soviet arms, advisers, and ideology. Fortunately, the Soviets and Americans agreed on one red line of their engagement: they would not allow these local conflicts to degenerate into superpower confrontations. They both knew the big difference between deterrent threat and "mad" (mutual assured destruction). However, it was very difficult for them to adjust the rules of their competition from the European theater, which they knew very well, to third world venues, and especially the Middle East, which was developing rules of engagement only as the cold war deepened.

The Eisenhower administration had convinced itself that Syria was completely under Soviet control and was becoming a Communist satellite. On August 13, 1957, the Syrians uncovered Operation Wappen, an American plot to overthrow the current government. The Eisenhower administration denied the accusations, but there is a great deal of evidence that points to the truth of these claims. The alleged plot pushed Syria further toward the Soviet Union.

Eisenhower and Dulles believed it was time for more drastic action against the "Communist infiltration," and let the leaders of Turkey, Iraq, and Jordan know that if any of them felt inclined to take action against aggression from the Syrians, the United States would see to it that they were well armed and supplied.

And so the president sent Loy Henderson to the Middle East to discuss military action against Syria. None of the Arab countries was enthusiastically receptive. The Americans also consulted with and tried to enlist Saudi Arabia to help solve the problem of Syria. King Saud tried to mediate, and urged the United States to refrain from intervention in Syria for fear it would spark a conflagration that would grow into World War III.

Turkey was the state most receptive to armed intervention in Syria, as it has been more than once since then, and it began to mass troops on its Syrian border. The Soviet Union made it clear that it would defend Syria if Turkey attacked. In October, Egypt moved troops into Syria to forestall Turkish aggression.

At the 708th Plenary Session of the United Nations General Assembly, the Syrians brought a complaint against the Turks. After some discussion, Syria and Turkey agreed to allow Secretary-General Dag Hammarskjöld to go to the region to mediate the dispute.

When Moscow realized that Turkey was going to do the bidding of the United States, the Soviet Union submitted a not-so-veiled threat that regional conflicts could quickly become international ones. Not only was Dulles unwilling to accept an international perception that the Soviet Union was more committed to peace than the United States, he was also furious at the Soviet Union for its rhetoric of escalation from the regional conflict involving Turkey and Syria into a Soviet conflict with the United States. The goal of avoiding superpower confrontation was imperiled. This Syria crisis was the gravest threat of Soviet-U.S. confrontation until the nuclear alert of the United States in response to Soviet threats during the 1973 Yom Kippur War.

Such moments of spillover from Middle East conflict to the threat of world conflict pushed the superpowers to realize that they could not play the game of allowing client states to draw them across the line and into direct confrontation.

At this point the United States realized how close it had come to war with the Soviet Union and backed away, ending its encouragement of Turkey to continue harassing Syria. This interposition of Turkey between the Americans and the Soviets came back into focus a few years later as part of the solution to the Cuban missile crisis in 1962, when, in implicit return for Soviet withdrawal of missiles from Cuba, the United States withdrew bases from Turkey.

As the Syrian crisis intensified in October of 1957, the United States realized that the problem had become very complex, requiring management of the Arabs, Turks, Israelis, and Soviets. So the Americans relied a great deal on British advice and support (as they again did in the case of the George W. Bush crisis with Iraq). The British preference for trying to subvert the Syrian regime from within required more patience than the American approach of using superior force, but the former approach had the advantage of creating an internal basis for new policy from within Syria itself. This traditional imperial form of regime change, which requires a great deal of intimate knowledge of the internal dynamics of a country, was used to bolster Jordan and Lebanon so that Syria could not counter Western moves by generating trouble in one of those countries, if not both. By the end of 1957, the United States was already planning its interventions in Jordan and Lebanon, which were to take place in July of 1958, and was once again working closely with the British as if the Suez Crisis had come and gone and left no deep wounds. After the 1957 Loy Henderson trip, or perhaps because of it, the Arab countries continued to hold together to keep the United States out of Syria. Saudi Arabia turned 180 degrees and became Syria's strongest defender. Iraq got on board, too. Egypt agreed in principle, but Nasser was upset that King Saud was stealing the spotlight. By 1957, the leftist Syrian regime had been able to turn the tables on the Eisenhower administration by effectively playing on the Arab nationalist themes that forced the Jordanian, Iraqi, and Saudi regimes to distance themselves from American policy.

In many ways, America drove its Arab allies away. The perceived coup attempt in August 1957, followed by decidedly mixed signals over a response to the anticipated supposed Communist invasion of Syria, made America seem to be an unreliable ally. The United States was particularly inept in the use of soft power—exerting influence without deploying military power—in these crises in the Arab world. It did not devote enough of its efforts to the formulation of the message conveyed by its intended actions, so that, in the language of Arab nationalism, its actions could be convincing and it would not be outmaneuvered by Soviet self-promotion as the true supporter of Arab independence and nationalism. The United States must realize that in these Middle East crises the meaning is in the message, and the meaning of actions cannot be left to analysis by the Arabs alone. The United States must carefully place its message, expressed in the correct idiom, in the proper envelope and delivered by the proper messenger. Without that, the tenor of the American message becomes overwhelmed by the sheer forcefulness of U.S. actions: the message becomes only an insistence on witnessing American power, and no conceptual content is conveyed. Indeed, the demonstration of dominant power is so overwhelming that any content is drowned out.

SYRIA AND KENNEDY

By 1961, when John F. Kennedy assumed office, the situation in the Middle East had cooled somewhat and the region was not as high a priority as it had been during the Eisenhower administration. President Kennedy took office two years after the upheaval of 1958, and he had developed a new perspective from which to deal with the Middle East.

During his years in the Senate, Kennedy began to recognize the need to deal with the Middle East outside the East-West context of the cold war. "Essentially, [he] argued that the United States over-estimated its own strength and underestimated the forces of national-ism . . . Kennedy concluded that the United States must talk with Egypt in terms going beyond the vocabulary of the Cold War."[2] Based on these assumptions, Kennedy began his term by reaching out to both the Arabs and the Israelis.

Upon his inauguration, Kennedy attempted a rapprochement with Nasser. He appointed John Badeau, former president of the American University in Cairo, as ambassador to Egypt. Kennedy also felt that he had to form personal relationships with the leaders of third world nations. In order to build such a relationship with President Nasser, he instituted an ongoing correspondence with him. As one of his first attempts toward friendship, Kennedy sent a letter (that also went to Saudi Arabia, Jordan, Iraq, and Lebanon) calling for the repatriation or compensation of the Palestinian refugees. Kennedy said the United States would use its influence on the UN Conciliation Commission for Palestine to make this happen.

Kennedy also dramatically increased aid to Egypt. Between 1960 and 1962 the administration gave Nasser over $500 million in aid. (From 1946 to 1960 the total aid to Egypt had been $254 million.) Kennedy also sent leading economists and high-level members of the administration to help Nasser develop an economic plan for Egypt.

The other Arab countries, particularly Jordan, were bothered by the relationship that was growing between the United States and Egypt. Kennedy had to juggle these concerns while continuing to work with Egypt.

In September 1962, just after a coup in Yemen, Nasser recognized the new government of Yemen and sent troops to support it. The speed with which he acted reinforced suspicions that he had helped plan the coup. The coup was problematic for Kennedy and the United States because it put Saudi Arabia, a strong American ally, in a precar-ious position. Kennedy wanted to reassure Saudi Arabia that, if neces-sary, the United States would help defend it, but at the same time he did not want to strongly condemn the actions Nasser was taking in supporting the coup. The situation was particularly sensitive for

Kennedy because in the same week that Nasser sent his troops into Yemen, the United States advanced another loan to Egypt.

The fears of Jordan, Saudi Arabia, and even the British over the new regime in Yemen conflicted with Egypt's support for it and therefore made it hard for the United States to make a decision regarding recognition of the nascent regime. The United States did not want to scuttle its new relationship with Nasser at the first moment of trouble, but it was clear that the Egyptian leader gave higher priority to the Arab cold war in which he was competing with the Saudis than to the possibility of a rapprochement with the United States.

The Kennedy administration decided to try to appease both sides by trading the recognition of the new Yemeni regime for a phased Egyptian withdrawal from Yemen. The United States officially recognized the new government in Yemen on December 19, 1962, but the fighting between Yemeni royalists (supported by the Saudis) and the new regime (supported by the Egyptians) intensified. The United States felt forced to dispatch two destroyers toward Saudi Arabia in case American military aid was necessary. Eventually, a disengagement agreement was reached, in which the United Nations was to monitor the border between Yemen and Saudi Arabia. But in October 1963, Egypt had still not started its withdrawal, even though Saudi Arabia had fulfilled almost all its obligations under the terms of the agreement. In 1967, Egypt was caught at a disadvantage during the Six-Day War because fully a third of its military force was still stationed in Yemen.

Throughout the Kennedy administration, Israel and Syria were caught up in a cycle of attacks and reprisals across the Golan Heights and the Sea of Galilee. The most active the Kennedy administration was about this issue was in April of 1962, when the UN Security Council (including the United States) censured Israel over its reprisal raids. The Kennedy administration was focused considerably more on gaining the friendship of Egypt than on the Syrian-Israeli clashes. As others before it, the Kennedy administration saw Egypt as the key that would open up the Middle East.

DIMONA

Arguably one of the most crucial events in the history of U.S.–Middle East relations occurred during the Kennedy presidency. With the assistance of France, and unbeknownst to the Americans, Israel became a nuclear power.

All of Israel's neighbors and in fact most Arab countries were concerned about Israel's building its Dimona nuclear power plant. The Kennedy administration feared that Egypt or Syria, or both, would be tempted to hazard an assault on Dimona. Israel's fear of just that possibility was a significant factor in its decision making after Egypt amassed troops in the Sinai in the lead-up to the Six-Day War in 1967. Kennedy had tried to get the full story of Dimona from Prime Minister David Ben-Gurion and had even sent an American scientific team to examine Dimona, but under Ben-Gurion's instructions, Israel had successfully deceived the American team and, of course, Kennedy himself. It was only during the prewar crisis that Israel reportedly officially informed President Johnson of Dimona and Israel's nuclear program.

A more typical series of conflicts between Syria and Israel led up to the crisis of the 1967 War and, eventually, paradoxically served to consolidate the leadership of Assad as lifetime ruler of Syria. The series of events began with Nasser's attempt to institutionalize the Palestine issue in Arab politics by creating a new organization of the Palestinian people that would ostensibly be under the control of Egypt and the Arab League. However, Nasser's intention—to prevent the Palestinian issue and, at that time, prevent Israel's diversion of the headwaters of the Jordan River for its national water pipeline to the Negev from forcing the Arabs into a war with Israel for which they were not prepared—was overwhelmed by the emerging militancy of a new generation of Palestinian leaders. This group of young Palestinian militants—raised and educated in exile from Palestine and led by Yasser Arafat, a young engineer trained in Kuwait and a leader of the General Union of Palestine Students—was unwilling to accept what they saw as the shelving of the Palestine question and created a new organization called Fatah, which was to revive the Palestinian tradition of armed struggle.

On New Year's Day of 1965, Fatah launched a small and essentially ineffective military attack on Israel from Syria's Golan Heights. As inefficacious as it was, it resounded mightily, reverberating in a spate of violent exchanges between Syria and Israel and between Israel and the Palestinians in Jordan. This emergent guerrilla warfare, combined with attention around Israel's water-diversion plan, eventually escalated to Israel's shooting down six Syrian planes. This embarrassment of Assad, who had become defense minster and the head of the Syrian air force, was the proximate cause of Soviet and Egyptian accusations that Israel was about to launch a major attack on Syria. Israel tried to show the Soviet ambassador that this was not true, but its denials did not matter. In fact, rumor trumped reality when Israel attacked Egypt in early June of 1967. Once it had destroyed Egypt's military capability, it turned its attention to launching an overpowering assault on Syria.

THE END OF THE KENNEDY ADMINISTRATION

With Egyptian troops still in Yemen and the Israelis hiding their nuclear plans, the 1963 assassination of President Kennedy was met in the Middle East as a tragedy.

> To be sure, some of the response came from sheer shock, but some of it paid tribute to the innovations that Kennedy brought to his Middle East diplomacy and to the widespread regional perception of JFK as a progressive with no grudge against Arab nationalism.[3]

Two decades later, when I was in a meeting in Beirut with a Palestinian banker who was a leader in collecting funds for the Palestinian movement, he repeated to me, in a tone of intense and long-suppressed anger, a long-held conspiracy theory prevalent in Palestinian elite circles: that Kennedy had been assassinated by the Jews to prevent his winning a second term. A second-term president was not subject to the same pressures of the Jewish lobby of America, he said, and Kennedy would have turned away from the American tradition of one-sided support for Israel and given freer vent to his personal sympathy for Arab nationalism. Of course, the tragic irony is that Robert Kennedy fell victim to a Palestinian assassin, Sirhan Sirhan, who attributed his motivation to the younger Kennedy's support of Israel. But we cannot ask conspiracy theory to be rational when its very purpose is to provide emotional relief where reality is too painful.

SYRIA AND 1967 (JOHNSON)

Under the Johnson administration, American relations with Syria worsened. Syria severed diplomatic ties after Israel had conquered the Golan Heights, and the United States insisted that Israeli withdrawal be linked to Arab recognition of Israel, a condition completely unacceptable to Syria. The Syrians might not have believed the famous Nasser-Hussein canard that the destruction of the Egyptian air force had been carried out by American air power, but they certainly were sure that the United States was preserving Israel's conquest of Arab land and providing Israel with the military capability to continue this aggression against Arabs. Johnson also ended the American tradition of maintaining an arms balance in the Middle East and began to arm Israel heavily.

The 1967 War had its origin in the troubled relationship between Syria and Israel. For many years the two nations had exchanged gunfire across the Sea of Galilee over unresolved claims of who had the right to engage in agriculture in those borderland areas. The fighting became far more serious when Israel started to penetrate Syrian air space and demonstrated its air superiority over the Syrian air force. The United States under President Johnson was far too preoccupied elsewhere to devote the necessary energy to stop this escalation before it was too late. Instead, it followed its frequent pattern of intervening in a given Middle East problem not in a timely fashion but only after the problem had erupted in crisis.

Tensions between the United States and Syria escalated again when the United States rejected the Arab view of the UN Security Council resolution that would formally end the 1967 conflict. The United States insisted that it would not accept any one-sided condemnation of Israel and would link any demand for Israeli withdrawal from the territories occupied in the 1967 War, which of course included the Golan Heights, to Arab acceptance of the right of every state in the area "to live in peace within secure and recognized boundaries." Despite this phrase, which Israel used every time the issue of Resolution 242 was discussed, Syria persisted in claiming that 242 was a demand for Israel to withdraw from all of the occupied territories. This Syrian interpretation of 242 halted any substantive Syrian-Israeli negotiation until the Israeli prime minister Rabin communicated through the United States a secret commitment that Israel, with the proper security arrangements, would accept the June 1967 border as the permanent one between Israel and Syria. Even so, the Syrians continued to insist on hearing this commitment from each successive Israeli negotiator or interlocutor. Johnson's success in crafting and then negotiating the language of 242 turned out to be a legal victory, but it could not change the fundamental political relationship between Syria and Israel.

SYRIA AND KISSINGER

Syria broke off all diplomatic relations with Washington after the Six-Day War.

It was not until the Nixon administration began its second term, in 1973, that a new formula was devised for dealing with the Middle East. Nixon and Kissinger decided they needed to change the perception of America in the Middle East (very similar to the George W. Bush "public diplomacy" work). The Arab world officially believed that the United States had supported Israel in the 1967 War, so in order to establish a relationship, Nixon had to demonstrate a more "even-handed" interest in the Arab states and Israel.

Since Eisenhower's Alpha Plan, there had not been a strong American attempt to bring peace to the region. The Kennedy and Johnson administrations had tried to promote stability in the Middle East, but never had grand plans for peacemaking. However, the Nixon administration focused on finding a solution to the Arab-Israeli conflict and not simply inculcating a measure of general stability.

Nixon decided that the best way to begin a balanced diplomacy would be to support peace negotiations based on UN Resolutions 242 and 338, which called for negotiations to follow a cease-fire in the 1973 War. Nixon also believed that there had to be multiple partners: he wanted to work with the Soviet Union through bilateral talks in order to create a framework for peace in the Middle East; he wanted to have four-power talks—Britain, France, the Soviet Union, and the United States—at the United Nations; and he wanted to dispatch Kissinger, whom he had just strengthened by appointing him secretary of state in addition to national security adviser, to hold direct talks with the region's leaders. The first opportunity to try their hand at Middle East diplomacy came with the end of the 1973 War.

In December of 1973, Kissinger went to see President Assad for the first time, the first American secretary of state to visit Syria since John Foster Dulles twenty years earlier. It was clear to Kissinger that previous Syrian leaders had been torn regarding U.S. intervention, but he found himself dealing with a new kind of Syrian leader. Assad had confidence in himself and a strong hand in the politics of his country, something completely different from the divided leadership Dulles and, before him, Truman had faced.

Kissinger indeed had already experienced a taste of Assad's steely ability to make tough decisions. In the midst of Black September, 1970, when King Hussein was forcibly crushing a Palestinian uprising against his regime that had erupted with the hijacking and blowing up of four airliners on Jordanian soil, Assad's predecessor decided to send Syrian troops into northern Jordan to protect the Palestinian fighters from Jordan's regular army, the Arab Legion. Hussein had turned to Nixon and Kissinger for protection from potential Syrian air attacks. However, then Minister of Defense Assad would not commit the Syrian air force to an attack that could threaten the rule of an Arab leader whose land bordered Israel, nor did he wish to be forced into a confrontation at a time not of his own choosing. Consequently, in the face of mobilization by both Israel and the U.S. Sixth Fleet to protect King Hussein and his regime, Assad broke with his president and continued his climb to the top position in the Syrian leadership. Therefore, at their December 1973 meeting Kissinger knew he was facing a leader who had already experienced his toughness and who was prepared to deal with him mano a mano.

Syria wanted to play a role in the international arena, but was wary of the ante that it would have to pay to sit in on the game. That ante was to talk with the United States and, through it, to Israel, giving the latter for the first time Syrian Ba'athist acknowledgment, if not outright recognition. As Kissinger later wrote about the Syrian prime minister of the day, "He could not quite make up his mind which was worse: to be left out of the negotiating process or to participate in it."[4]

One of the obstacles to negotiation was that before 1973, Syria had refused to have a politically negotiated settlement with Israel. But after the war, Assad, not deceiving himself about the military balance, even if he did overemphasize the American factor in Israeli military superiority, had begun to see negotiation in some form as his only hope of regaining the Golan Heights and other Israeli-occupied territory. He came to the conclusion that a disengagement agreement on the Golan Heights was a necessary evil.

Kissinger wanted to create an agreement between Israel and Syria that would be similar to the Egyptian-Israeli agreement he had just brought off. He also wanted Assad to commit to attending the upcoming Geneva Conference to pursue a more stable peace. But Assad wanted territorial assurances from Israel before he would commit Syria to any further negotiations.

And on the Israeli side, before they would commit to the Geneva negotiations, they demanded the names of all Israeli prisoners of war in Syrian custody, and Red Cross inspection of their condition. Israel's emphasis on the return of POWs and MIAs, and even of the bodies of slain soldiers, turned out to be not just a complication in all subsequent negotiations, but also a pathway to negotiation, as it defined an area in which Israel was the party seeking Arab action, when negotiations so often focused on how much territory Israel would relinquish.

This was the window through which a third party engaged in unofficial diplomacy could enter the picture most easily and effectively. Israel wanted its people back and was willing to go to great lengths to explore any possible opening to their recovery, even the use of unofficial parties like me. These confidential talks about Israeli POWs and MIAs also opened contact with more secret and often security-related elements of both Israeli and Arab regimes and leadership, access that otherwise would have been foreclosed. Once that access was gained, if it was used carefully and with utter confidentiality, and no exploitation, it could be a unique opportunity to develop trust and confidence that could then be extended to other issues more directly related to the conflict and its resolution, or at least its management.

Kissinger knew he was facing an impasse, and so he proposed a five-step process to get both the Israelis and the Syrians to Geneva.

1. Syria would inform Israel of the number of Israeli prisoners of war it held.
2. Syria would send a list of the names of the prisoners of war to Washington.
3. In exchange for the list, Israel would submit a disengagement plan to Washington.
4. The Red Cross would be allowed into Syria and, in exchange, Kissinger would submit the Israeli disengagement plan to Assad.
5. The negotiating process would begin.

Beginning in early 1974, Kissinger was given, first, the number of Israeli prisoners of war and then a list of their names, to forward to the Israelis. Israel then duly presented Syria with ideas for disengagement. Throughout the process, Kissinger shuttled back and forth between Damascus and Jerusalem, but he could not get the Syrians and Israelis to agree on the territorial withdrawals.

Israeli internal political problems complicated Kissinger's mission. Moshe Dayan, who had been a key figure in the Egyptian disengagement plan, no longer wanted to serve in Golda Meir's cabinet and preferred not to be involved with the Syrian disengagement. This could have been fatal to the plans, because Dayan was known to have resisted Israeli occupation of Syrian soil even in 1967, believing the trouble it would cause in the international environment would far outweigh any advantages inherent in holding the territory. Luckily, he was persuaded to remain in office and make a trip to Washington to begin negotiations. Assad agreed to send his negotiator to Washington once the Israelis had arrived.

By May of 1974, Kissinger was afraid the negotiations would collapse, but he kept on shuttling, and after about five weeks of step-by-step negotiations, the Israelis and Syrians reached an agreement that was not very different from the Egyptian-Israeli disengagement agreement.

One of Kissinger's strengths throughout the negotiation was that he understood the emotional side of the issues. For example, he was constantly aware that he had to present Israeli ideas to Assad not as fixed positions but as examples of Israeli thinking. This way, Assad would not have to reject anything and was saved from being presented with an insulting and humiliating demand. Kissinger's understanding of the way power worked in the Arab world, the importance of prestige there, was crucial to his achieving what he did. This is something that was lacking in most or all of the U.S. interactions before Kissinger and under George W. Bush, who did not pay attention to the dominant subjective dimensions of the conflicts.

Kissinger's personal appreciation of the importance of stature, both to himself and to Nixon, helped him understand how these image issues could help or hurt in handling Assad's first experience as an international actor and the tension within an Israeli leadership still in shock from the Yom Kippur surprise. It may be that Kissinger's coming from the Vietnam War and Watergate helped him enter deeply enough into the internal complexities of Israeli and Arab political life and recognize the need for their leaders to emerge from the process enhanced in their stature and not humiliated for their concessions and scorned by their internal political rivals.

OIL CRISIS

By the early seventies, the United States had chronically overutilized its domestic oil resources and overestimated how much oil it had in reserve in the ground in America. The U.S. need for imported oil had grown steadily since the days of Eisenhower, and the Middle East oil producers began to gain the upper hand in price negotiations. With the beginning of the 1973 Arab-Israeli War, OPEC raised the price of oil by 70 percent and began cutting back production. OPEC said that it would resume normal production levels after Israel withdrew from the occupied territories. The United States airlifted supplies to Israel and asked Congress to approve $2.2 billion to cover the costs. The Arab reaction to this money being spent on Israel was volcanic. For the first time, Saudi Arabia felt that it had to support Arab demands with its oil resources, and it declared a total embargo on oil exports to the United States.

Many of the producers asserted that restoration of oil production and an end to the embargo were linked to a disengagement agreement between Syria and Israel. They thus caught themselves in their own trap: an agreement with Syria would take months, and most of the producers were eager for such an agreement so that they could resume normal production levels. So the longer the United States took to create one, the more the double-edged sword of the oil embargo cut into the flesh of the producers, too.

As the embargo wore on, Syria was the hardest of all Arab countries to convince as it wanted to maintain the oil squeeze on the United States until Syrian-Israeli disengagement agreements were completed. The other leaders in OPEC convinced the Syrians that the oil producers could not hold out that long, and desperately wanted to cash in on the elevated oil prices. All of Kissinger's work was dependent on the Arabs lifting the oil embargo put in place in 1973, because the American consumer was losing patience with long gas station queues and gas shortages, and the Nixon administration and its successor under Gerald Ford could not absorb another major source of domestic criticism beyond Watergate.

During Kissinger's work with Syria and Israel, Egypt and Saudi Arabia secretly sent their foreign ministers to Washington, where they were able to de-link the disengagement proposals from the embargo. The embargo was to be lifted on March 1, 1974, and the disengagement could then proceed unencumbered by this nonterritorial issue.

THE PEACE PROCESS WITH SYRIA AND ISRAEL

President Carter, in his turn, also believed that Syria was a critical figure in the Middle East and that Assad's involvement was essential if there was to be peace with Israel. In 1977, Carter invited Assad to an international conference. At the proposed Geneva Conference, the U.S. president promised comprehensive peace between Israel and the Arab world. Assad wanted to negotiate as a united Arab delegation; Israel insisted on separate bilateral talks with each Arab party. Eventually, Israel got what it asked for, but it took more than another decade and other crises for James Baker, acting on behalf of President George H. W. Bush, to be able to obtain President Assad's promise to send a senior delegation to the Madrid Conference, the replacement for the Geneva Conference that Kissinger had tried to organize. Some speculate that this move was a way of excluding Syria from the talks. Eventually, peace was made only with Egypt. Syria viewed this as the United States once again going back on its promises and trying to cleave the Arab world to Israel's advantage.

The Reagan administration brought us back to the cold war in full force. Whereas Nixon and Carter had worked with the Soviets to some extent, Reagan tried to form a Middle East defense pact against them. The U.S. view of Syria also changed. Whereas the Nixon and Carter administrations had seen Syria as part of any peace process, the Reagan administration saw it only as a Soviet satellite, and any victory over it counted as a victory over the "Evil Empire."

It can be argued that the United States' being so vocal about anti-Soviet alliances, and so adamant that Syria was a Soviet client state, gave Israel the unofficial go-ahead to invade Lebanon in 1982. After brokering a cease-fire agreement, the United States failed to enforce it, as Israel crept into Syrian territory. America also lost credibility with the massacres at Sabra and Shatila after it promised the safety of Palestinians following the PLO withdrawal. Although these massacres were directly perpetrated by the Falangist Christian militias, the Palestinians and many other international actors blamed Israel for creating the conditions for the slaughter, or even encouraging it. Later, an Israeli commission of inquiry attributed indirect responsibility to Israel's defense minister, Ariel Sharon.

The May 17, 1983, agreement between Israel and the short-lived Lebanese Christian government ending the Lebanon conflict was an affront to Assad and Syria. Secretary of State George Shultz did not visit Syria while negotiating the agreement. He wanted to deliver it to Assad as a fait accompli, but instead Assad delivered a fait accompli of his own in the brutal form of major terrorist attacks on the U.S. embassy in Beirut and on the Marines stationed in Lebanon. These attacks were carried out by the new force of the Shiites of Lebanon organized as Hizbollah, allied with Khomeini of Iran and cooperating with Syria. Hizbollah represented a transformation of the politics of Lebanon as it became the militant vanguard of what was now the largest demographic group in Lebanon, and would not let Lebanon settle back into its Christian-led pro-American and pro-Western diplomacy. George Shultz had hoped to consolidate political cooperation between Lebanon's Christians and Israel's Jews, but instead found that Israel's invasion of Lebanon had uncovered a new radical Islamic force that had put an end to the old Ben-Gurion vision of Israeli-Lebanese cooperation.

The Reagan Plan, which spelled out America's determination to bring about political agreements about the occupied West Bank between Israel and Jordan and Syrian withdrawal from Lebanon, seemed to engage all of Israel's neighbors except Syria, who saw it as aiming to encircle Syria and isolate it. But nothing ever came of the plan because Begin rejected it, King Hussein backed away from it, and Reagan simply dropped it.

Under the first Bush administration, the relationship with Syria improved slightly. Both countries supported the Taif Agreement to end the Lebanese civil war and define Syrian presence in Lebanon. Bush sent the diplomat Ed Djerejian to Syria to find common ground, but the United States and Syria still could not cooperate on a Middle East peace process. The U.S. administration wanted to work on an Israeli-Palestinian resolution before an Israeli-Syrian one; Assad thought that both had to be done together. He did not try to derail the U.S. efforts, but he did nothing to help advance them, either.

When the Soviet Union fell, Assad demonstrated his astute political sense by quickly turning toward the United States, the only remaining superpower. He did so in the context of Saddam Hussein's invasion of Kuwait. Assad, who had spent many hours trying to talk sense into Saddam, had a deep contempt for the Iraqi leader's regime for its reckless attack on Iran and, now, its violation of elementary Arab solidarity by invading and seizing a neighboring Arab state. Syria knew it had to move closer to the United States, and Assad decided to send a contingent of Syrian troops to join the American-led effort to push Iraq out of Kuwait, although he did not permit the troops to enter Iraqi territory. This participation in the first Gulf War, albeit limited, was Syria's initial stab at reconciliation, and it succeeded in bringing the United States into a decade-long attempt to broker a Syrian-Israeli peace based on Israeli withdrawal from the Golan Heights that has yet to bear fruit.

CONCLUSION

It was apparent from the outset of the cold war that the Soviet Union understood the feelings of nationalism in the Arab world. While the Soviets may not have truly cared about aiding nationalism, they knew how to use it for their own purposes. The United States feared Arab nationalism for its overthrow of conservative regimes previously under the thumb of British or French imperial power, and that it would turn radically toward the left and embrace the Soviet Union. Throughout the fifties, the United States never could quite make the distinction between nationalism and communism. This was the conceptual reason why it was so unsuccessful in the Middle East in that period.

Contradiction is the key word for the Eisenhower administration's interaction with the Middle East. Because the United States had competing interests and did not develop a full strategic plan (but instead tried to solve individual problems piecemeal), its policy was full of contradictions that always led it into trouble.

One of the biggest problems in the Middle East was that instead of their being able to develop into neutral, independent states, the countries there were pressed by the United States into aligning themselves with East or West. The most dynamic regimes, which represented the popular excitement over Arab nationalism, however flawed that conception might be, did not choose the United States. In fact, the forced choice actually pushed the Arabs more firmly into the Soviet camp. They could not choose the United States as an ally because of Israel and because of the implication of the legacy of colonialism in U.S. alliances with the former colonial powers. So even though the United States had a much greater claim to anti-imperialism than the Soviets—who were more and more firmly asserting their control over Eastern Europe and many Asian Islamic republics—it was America that was tarred with the imperialist brush. And its postwar economic glow, so attractive to the Europeans, was blinding to many Arabs.

Sadly, it can also be said that the Arab autocratic regimes tended to have a certain admiration for the autocratic system created by Stalin. They were attracted both to the idea of a one-party system and to the cult of personality, which fit their image of how an all-powerful leader should rule. The American system of checks and balances and especially its powerfully independent judiciary did not play well with Arab military leaders who had inherited power from monarchies. Arab nationalism also was attracted to economic centralization rather than private-sector entrepreneurship with its creation of multiple centers of economic power. It would take generations of reeducation and reorientation for those preferences to change in a democratic and free-market direction. Those generations are still in the future.

The American approach to the Arab world has too often been about specifying whom the United States opposes while remaining quite vague about whom it supports. In the fifties, the United States knew that it opposed communism, but it was not clear what kind of nationalist element it could endorse. Could the United States have avoided this political choice and simply determined that it was going to be a force for economic development, leaving the Arabs to figure out for themselves how to work with it? It is true that at the time of Eisenhower it was very difficult to imagine how to reconcile Ben-Gurion with Nasser or even how to dampen their mutual fears and antagonisms. Only fifty years later the United States was in a position to benefit from the existence of a temporary, wide consensus agreed upon by George W. Bush and the so-called Quartet of the United Nations secretary-general, Russia, the European community, and the United States on what was called a road map that was formally accepted by Israel, the Palestinian Authority, and key Arab states. This consensus delineated a path of negotiations that would lead to a democratic Palestinian state living side by side in peace with Israel and came to include the Beirut Arab Summit Resolution of 2002, which broke the taboo by saying that once Israel had fulfilled all its Resolution 242 withdrawal responsibilities, all Arab states would recognize Israel and live in peace with her. How long this consensus will last depends on whether it will be implemented before further military confrontations between Palestinian armed factions and Israel or Hizbollah and Israel fatally undermine the consensus.

Even more basic, if the United States had helped the Arabs ensure better relations among themselves, with more focus on shared development goals and improved governance, many of the sources of tension among the Arab states would not have evolved into serious problems, including undermining leaderships and encouraging violent internal opposition. Instead, the approach derived from the French and British has been to try to divide each state from the others or even to pit one subgroup within a state against another. This has made it still more difficult to reach consensus on social reform and has perpetuated the failure of these societies to find their structural equivalent to the multicultural and multiethnic modus vivendi of the Ottoman Empire. There is no good reason why there cannot be a concept of an Arab national state with pluralistic attitudes toward its citizens' loyalties and with each citizen having his due voice in the national government and a proper role in national development. It is not acceptable that unity can be achieved only under dictatorship and domination by one subgroup over all others.

As for the intervention of external forces, such intervention will lead only to more bloody confrontations unless those forces first take up the intensive work of repairing the rent social fabric of both Israel and the Palestinian national movement. Forcible external attempts at transformation, followed up by attempts at nation building and mending the social fabric, are inevitably doomed to failure. The hard work of building up a political culture of acceptance and tolerance, and even of respect, cannot be undertaken successfully on the heels of invasion and occupation, which consolidate deep divisions within a society. Building up after blowing up is hardly a recipe for a civil society coming together to forge a nation into a cohesive state, and yet America has tried this again and again.

LEBANON AND ISRAEL

The summer of 2006 witnessed a moment of transition in the focus of Middle East conflict. Ever since the outset of our story at the end of World War I, the Israeli-Palestinian problem—or, as it was originally termed, the Zionist conflict with the Arab inhabitants of Palestine—has been a principal focus of conflict in the Middle East. That problem, seething for a century, became almost the sole conflict once Egypt and Jordan made peace treaties with Israel, and Saudi Arabia initiated a resolution at the 2002 Arab Summit, in Beirut, which pledged each Arab state to recognize and make peace with Israel once it had met the basic conditions of UN Resolution 242. Of course, many other conflicts had come and gone over the years—between Saudi Arabia and Yemen; between Morocco and the Polisario; Syria's seizing of Lebanon and holding her for two decades; Iraq's claim on Kuwait; its invasion of Kuwait, and its long war with Iran; local border conflicts among the Gulf Emirates; the Tunb islands seizure by Iran; the Egypt-Sudan conflict over sovereignty and the boundary between them; and Libya-Chad issues, to name just those most often mentioned. The enumeration serves to remind us of how conflict-ridden the region has been.

Notwithstanding the absence of a directly negotiated peace agreement between Israel and Lebanon, Israel's withdrawal from Lebanon in 2000 left the hope of at least a continued de facto quiet border between those two countries (although the ongoing conflict between the societies—Israeli Jewish society and Hizbollah-led Shiite society in southern Lebanon—was left unresolved). But there was a loose end: though the border had been officially approved by the United Nations, it was not accepted by Hizbollah. Hizbollah insisted that Israel withdraw from Shebaa Farms, a small area where the borders of Israel, Syria, and Lebanon converge. This border area would have to be assigned to either Lebanon or Syria.

In 1974 the United Nations had drawn up disengagement lines between Israeli- and Syrian-controlled territories to be patrolled by a UN peacekeeping force. These lines designated Shebaa Farms as Syrian territory. The United Nations studied post-1966 maps submitted by both the Lebanese and the Syrian governments, which confirmed that the Shebaa Farm lands were inside the Syrian Arab Republic. Regardless, Hizbollah continued to assert that Israel's occupation of Shebaa Farms was a continued occupation of a part of Lebanon, and as such a justification for Hizbollah's continued attacks against Israel as a legitimate form of resistance. Syria preferred to stay out of the argument by saying that the issue would be resolved by Syrian-Lebanese agreement at an appropriate time, referring to a time when Israel would withdraw from all of the Golan Heights. Once the civil society of Lebanon arose in mass demonstrations after the assassination of the Lebanese prime minister Rafiq Hariri, allegedly at the order of top Syrian officials, Hizbollah could maintain its armed conflict against Israel only by dint of its completely unrecognized claim that Shebaa Farms was still Lebanese territory. This, they avowed, justified their maintaining a separate armed force at least for as long as the Lebanese army continued to be ineffectually weak.

With all the focus on the renewed conflict in Gaza as the summer of 2006 arrived, there was little opportunity for Hizbollah to bring attention to their own grievances in southern Lebanon. When Hamas kidnapped an Israeli soldier near Gaza, the idea was ignited in the minds of Hizbollah leadership to do the same along its border with Israel, to remind Israelis and indeed the whole international community of the unresolved issues of Shebaa Farms and the Hizbollah-Israel conflict.

The import of the kidnapping of two Israeli soldiers on Israeli territory was amplified by the contemporaneous rising of tensions between the United States, France, and the rest of Europe, on the one hand, and Iran on the other, involving complaints to the UN Security Council that Iran's nuclear program was a violation of its commitments under the Nuclear Non-Proliferation Treaty and calls for the imposition of sanctions against Iran. This connection of local with international issues led to the widely accepted view of the war between Hizbollah and Israel as a proxy war for the anticipated much larger U.S.-Iran confrontation.

Some even went so far as to draw an analogy between the Hizbollah-Israel war and the Spanish Civil War of the 1930s. Just as the Spanish Civil War was a prelude to World War II, so the Hizbollah-Israel war might prefigure the much wider cataclysm of a war of the West against Islam, with Islam under Iranian leadership and the United States as the dominant force leading the West. Some even thought of this as a cultural-religious war between Islam on the one hand and the Judeo-Christian West on the other, an embodiment of the clash of civilizations that had been predicted after the end of the cold war by Samuel Huntington, an American international relations professor. His essay on the subject, "The Clash of Civilizations," became a flashpoint for a growing disaffection of Arab intellectuals from the United States; they interpreted the Huntington essay as an opening shot in that war rather than as a prediction of something to be forestalled. Huntington's concept was seen by Arabs as a call for a war of ideas and cultures and not as an intellectual analysis.

The Hizbollah-Israel war that so damaged Lebanon was a turning point not only in diverting regional and world attention away from the Palestine problem, but also in that it marked the change from war based on nation-state rivalry to war arising from conflict involving religion and society. Although in the 1920s the Palestinian Arab leader Mufti Amin al-Husseini brought religious tension to the service of

Palestinian Arab nationalist hostility toward the Zionist enterprise, the religious element was not dominant in the consciousness of the two peoples. With the explosion of fundamentalist extremism and the rise of religious fundamentalism among Muslims, American Christians, and Israeli settler Jews, the religious dimension of the conflict was painfully obvious even to those who had moved far from the religious roots of their collective identity.

Indeed, from the perspective of the account in this volume, the Lebanon war brings the story full circle. The collapse of the Ottoman Empire meant that the Arab lands of that empire were no longer under Muslim rule and brought an end to the caliphate. Now, ninety years later, the idea of rule by Islamic law and even the idea of the revival of the caliphate have become part of the radical Muslim counterrevolution against secular nationalism and have given new energy and cultural meaning to anti-imperialism.

The early phases of post–World War I mandatory control by Britain and France of Iraq, Syria, Lebanon, and Palestine exacerbated ethnic and religious rivalries, which are now expressing themselves in more and more brutal violence. The British decision to form one Iraq by forcing the Shiites, Sunnis, and Kurds into a single political entity created the condition for rule by dictators, who forced unity by their swords and ensured compliance by filling their dungeons with the recalcitrant. As these powerful dictators fade, or are forcibly removed, lacking a basis of consensual shared rule, they instead fight for control with no holds barred. In Iraq, Shiite and Sunni kill one another by the truckful, even in their places of worship. In Lebanon, Shiite population growth has rendered the Lebanese modus vivendi between Maronite Christians and Sunni Arabs irrelevant, or at least defunct, as the Shiites having only a tertiary role in the political organization of the country can no longer be accepted. Hizbollah, which has become the dominant military force, controls southern Lebanon, controls the Shiite population, and has made Lebanon an active participant in the Arab struggle against Israel and—most of all, as it is currently constituted—ungovernable.

Thus the heritage of post–World War I mandatory rule has turned more and more sour for the United States as the successor external power, and the internal regional system can no longer function without a major restructuring.

President George W. Bush emphasized the need for democracy, but democracy will not be a solution if all the emphasis is on nation-state governance. There must be a reeducation about ethnic pluralism and religious mutual respect, not only about Islam, Judaism, and Christianity, but within Islam between Sunnis and Shiites, and between the various versions and styles of each. Moreover, the patterns of dominance of one group by another require transformation to a system of division of power, shared rule, and control of independent militias, anomalies that emerged from the struggles against colonial rule and other forms of external domination, and that make decent society impossible to achieve.

The changes will not come from foreign imposition, although foreign powers can play a catalytic role in bringing about the end of brutal authoritarian rule. We now have to create a relation within and among societies with the modest tolerance of the Ottoman Empire, but without empire and without supremacy of Muslims over all other citizens. We can only hope that in this phase of regional development, with the dangerous potential for generating new international conflicts, Israel and the United States will become innovative allies not in imposing yet another generation of dominance, but rather in dedicating themselves to a new depth of communication and a profound emphasis on education. Such effective education is the greatest priority, given the huge age bulge of young people in these Arab and Muslim countries who must find a fulfilling and productive way of living their adult lives that trumps their desire for revenge against those they blame for their plight. We need to put decency at the top of the social agenda, treating all groups and individuals as full participants with equal dignity in the social, political, and religious life of their nations. No longer should we see America reaching for control over all this complexity, control that is anyway beyond its grasp. American leaders and American communities must extend a hand of friendship and cooperation and, as President Obama has already said, we can hope that we will find an unclenched fist.

The religious dimension, even since the Khomeini Revolution in Iran in 1978–79, had become front and center—and not only because of America's declaration of a war on terrorism, and not only because of the great tensions engendered by the American occupation of Iraq, but also because of the awareness of a more militant and aggressive search for power and leadership by Shiite Islam in its long-standing competition with Sunni Islam and by the upsurge of Salafi perspectives within Sunni Islam. Iran started to seek regional power after the long and devastating war against Iraq. Instead of rebuilding Iran to face Saddam Hussein again, Iranians seemed to be preparing to face American power. They also began to deploy the Revolutionary Guards on a wider front, helping to build and train Hizbollah into the strongest military force in Lebanon and as a weapon of confrontation with Israel. Iran also began to get more deeply involved in the Palestine problem by arming the Palestinian Islamic jihad, the first Sunni Arab faction to celebrate the Khomeini Revolution as a major event for all Islam, not only the Shi'a. Its propaganda turned against Israel in a bid to become the most strident Muslim voice against the Jewish state. This reached its apogee with the election of President Ahmadinejad, who repeatedly called for the complete elimination of Israel. Its most dramatic surge toward regional power was its nuclear development program, which was assumed in most of the region to be aimed at making Iran a nuclear power, even though Iran persistently claims that its nuclear program is for energy production and even though it was the U.S. president Gerald Ford who first provided Iran, when the shah still ruled, with its first nuclear silo in 1976. Iran was extending its influence through religion-based anti-American and anti-Israel propaganda and through sponsoring guerrilla and terror operations in key areas of the Mashreq (the Fertile Crescent and Greater Syria), until then seen as part of the zone of Sunni dominance. It was also working to strengthen a coalition of Shiites extending from Iran to Iraq and from Iraq to Lebanon.

This regional war and its "clash of world cultures" characterization, which had gone beyond Huntington to become a widespread subject of controversy and discussion, gave a new importance and perceptual prominence to the Israel-U.S. relationship, making that relationship the subject of much sharper discussion, debate, and analysis in these two countries and within the whole international community. It seems to me that the explosion of controversy over the 2006 Lebanon war, and especially within Israel's political and military leadership, and the controversy over the 2009 Gaza War, within both Israel and the United States, opens the rare possibility of a serious reshaping of the approach to strategic cooperation between these two allied states for the first time in decades.

It is possible that important elite elements in both societies will seek to refocus their approach to the Middle East crisis toward reducing the motivation for armed conflict among both Arabs and Israelis and away from treating violent conflict as inevitable every few years. Such a joint effort at a reduction of hatred would require the creation of more effective communication between Islamic societies and peoples, especially Palestinians, on the one hand, and Americans, Israelis, and other Western societies, on the other hand. This will require a reorientation of the approach to national security away from the hardware of military power to the intellectual and emotional dimensions of "soft power"—that is, trying to influence each other through communication and understanding rather than by force. On all sides, there needs to be a mobilization of the deepest intellectual and spiritual resources with which these societies are so richly endowed to this reimagined challenge to national security.

Is it possible to bring forth mutual respect between the adherents of these different faiths? Is it possible for them to start to think of each other as being created by the One God rather than to descend to an inevitable clash of civilizations? Many of the elite in both the United States and Israel are not satisfied to have their life experience and roles in the world defined by war against Islam and against terror, though they are ready to fight when that is seemingly the only way of preventing the undoing of their civilization and values. Most Arabs would be happier if their children grew up emphasizing productive participation in their society rather than being overwhelmed by angry and even militant provocation of conflict.

Could it be that the next stage of the special relationship between Israel and the United States is to move it beyond a bilateral security alliance to a joint civilizational mega-project in intergroup and intercultural relations that would turn the next century away from terrorism, counterterrorism, and unbridled mutual hatred, and toward a major attempt at expanding the boundaries of empathy? This Israeli-U.S. project could be the first step in a wider reconciliation of the West with Islam and in making the three Abrahamic faiths focus more on what they share than on what separates them. Both the United States and Israel have seen themselves as bastions of modernity and havens of cultural openness, but they have not been able to overcome their sense of superiority over others, which has had particularly conflict-escalating ramifications in their relationship to Arab nations.

A parallel American and Israeli immersion in interreligious and intercultural dialogue would have to be encouraged by government, but carried out primarily by civil society. It would not be possible at this stage, if at any stage, for Israeli and American officials to be welcomed to deep and extended exchanges and communications across these charred boundaries, but it is possible to imagine civil society initiatives that would be fascinating and spiritually enlightening to all sides and that would promote peaceful mutual acceptance, rather than the hostility and contempt that are becoming the defining characteristics of relations between the world of Islam and the Western civilization of which America and Israel are central exemplars.

Such an initiative would also require significant openness within Israeli, American, and Arab society, of groups and subgroups now mostly isolated from one another. Americans who have crossed racial, ethnic, and religious boundaries would have to work together to produce effective communication teams that would seek to form bonds of understanding with their Arab and Muslim counterparts. Religious leaders would have to hone their skills and devote themselves to speaking of the common values of Islam, Judaism, and Christianity.

Learning to communicate across loyalties would be a major breakthrough for Arab societies and essential for new relationships between the Arabs and Jews of Israel. This should help to close the gap between the secular and religious elements within these societies, as well as across them, especially between the newly mobilized fundamentalists and their fellow citizens who insist on keeping religion out of the public square.

It may be that human societies can learn nothing from history except how to repeat our own worst mistakes, but there is a counter hope that the war between Israel and Hizbollah will turn out to be not a prelude to World War III but instead a warning—a jangling alarm—that galvanizes us all to prevent the devastating mistakes that led to war in 1939 and the failure of communication that devolved into war in 1914. If our alliances of war can be transformed into alliances for reaching out to create effective communication, if we can begin to devote even a small percentage of the prodigious resources that go into war preparation and prosecution to an effort to reduce the hatred and motivation for war and terrorism, perhaps we can turn the summer of 2009 from a dangerous turning point into a staging ground for new hope.

CHAPTER 7

THE CRISIS OF LEGITIMACY

The first half of this book describes and briefly analyzes the story of the emergence of the U.S. relationship with several key countries in the Middle East throughout the twentieth century. It shows how World War I did not end in the Middle East with the implementation of an effective system of legitimate government, but instead with British and French imperial control through mandates that left a legacy of distrust, dependency on outside forces, and wounded dignity in many of these countries. A mandate was supposed to be a training ground for democracy. Instead it became a life-and-death struggle between the imperial power and emerging nationalism. Positive enthusiasm for creating one's own state was overwhelmed by the negative destructive solidarity of hostility to the foreign occupier. The mandate idea was a false start in the modernization process and in the political and economic development of most key Middle East states.

These experiences of stunted national identity formation were related to an overemphasis on national identity informed by negation—that is, identity constructed by the struggle against outside control, especially by the mandatory power—rather than by the affirmation that comes from the excitement of building one's own nation-state. In the decades between World War I and the end of World War II, a pattern emerged in the Middle East in which modernized trade, commercial relations, critical thinking, scientific inquiry, and multicultural understanding took on the odor of betrayal of one's own culture or core identity rather than the attraction of entering the world market of ideas and commerce as a respected equal among equals.

The rulers and regimes that emerged from this bitter struggle against European control and European culture and values helped to foster an identification with the authoritarian powers in Europe, fascist and Communist, that had challenged the democratic capitalist powers that had dominated the Middle East, especially Britain and France. A dangerous model of dictatorship and militaristic nationalism was thus created. So Arab nationalism—with an indigenous cultural emphasis on obedience to authority and a model of secularism that rejected democratic values of respect for the individual and for human rights in favor of group solidarity—reinforced a tendency toward government dominated by a single person or single family or tribe. These charismatic autocrats ruled by fear and coercion rather than by developing procedures that would generate popular legitimacy; nor would they provide the type of concrete economic and social achievement that could give de facto legitimacy to their rule.

Out of this struggle against Western models and democratic modes of governance, with their limits on power, and absent the principles of rule of law that would check the arbitrariness of the ruler and militate against the corruption of his clique, Arab nationalism evolved into one-party rule and/or military dominance. The process of government change became limited to extended charismatic strongman rule or a succession of coups d'état, with no consensually accepted procedure for the peaceful transfer of power. The unintended consequence was to drive opposition underground and into extreme ideologies.

These regimes could not focus on education and health and good governance; nor ensure economic development and societal inclusion of subgroups, with equal access to power, the fruits of public life, and the benefits of social respect and dignified status in society; nor create opportunities for upward mobility or even sustained gainful employment. Rather, these regimes perpetuated and strengthened ascribed status through tribal and family ties, nepotism, or corruption. The military became the critical channel of mobility for those without inherited status or the "right" religious and ethnic group membership.

By leaving these countries to American control not only without helping them build effective state structures but also by working hard to fragment them even further, France and Britain inadvertently ensured that the American period of attempting to dominate Middle East affairs could not succeed. The United States had just a few decades of experience as a major power, which had prepared it to deal with other strong, well-organized states, but not at all to manage weak, disorganized, and fragmented societies. The British gaffe in so deeply alienating Iran from the West is now a monstrous problem for the United States and Iran alike. The French bringing such deep divisions into the life of Syria and Lebanon primed an explosion now waiting to happen, but in fact recurring every few years in the faces of Americans, Israelis, Syrians, and Lebanese. That it is so easy for many Europeans to look with contempt upon U.S. and Israeli behavior vis-à-vis Lebanon and Syria and U.S. behavior vis-à-vis Iraq and Israel/Palestine simply goes to show that long historical experience does not ensure an accurate perspective on the present and future.

Starting in the 1950s and '60s, as the British and French had mostly withdrawn from their imperial ambitions in the Middle East, the United States assumed more and more of the role of resisting the possibility of Communist penetration and of preventing the fall of the remaining pro-Western regimes. Largely inexperienced in world affairs, it had nonetheless managed the difficult processes of inclusion of many ethnic and religious groups. The United States succeeded in achieving a position of power and wealth based on individual initiative, entrepreneurship in agricultural and industrial development, the emergence of systems of management, and sometimes regulation of commerce and trade that, together with a strong legal system, had prevented dominance by the culture of corruption. The United States had developed a system of public education at the elementary and high school levels and a mixture of public and private universities that kept the American people at the forefront of science and technology, which pushed the American economy to the vanguard of world economic development. It was a nation intensely proud of its national identity as a constitutional democracy with a strong independent judiciary and a vital (basically) two-party political system. And besides, America had learned to use military power to defeat any challenges to its system from within and from without. It was this experience of military superiority that America came to rely on in international affairs whenever it could not persuade others to adopt its approaches to governance and economic development.

This inauspicious incompatibility of nation-state structure made for a problematic beginning for America's relations with many Middle East countries as the successor to Britain as the hegemonic power. Moreover, the United States did not have an approach to foreign policy that could deal effectively with the varieties of subgroups that made up the Middle East. It did not deal well with the religious factor and did not understand countries lacking effective state apparatuses and where citizen loyalties lay with tribes, ethnic groups, and religion and not primarily with state and nation. It was turned still more hostile by its deep-rooted fear that the Middle East would become a battleground theater of cold war competition and an easy mark for Soviet machinations. At the start of this saga, at the close of World War I, there was a special expectation among people of the Middle East that the United States would prove to be a new kind of Western power, an expectation fed by the high rhetoric of Woodrow Wilson as America entered the world scene—though Wilson had no vehicle for implementing his inspiring proposals. The United States just might be the power that could appreciate the desire of colonized peoples for self-determination and freedom from colonial rule. These peoples hoped for a United States that would use its power and wealth to bring to them an opportunity to shape their own destinies consistent with their cultures.

The requirement to acknowledge the poorness of the fit between, on the one hand, the European model of the nation-state and, on the other, the structure of society in the Middle East—which grows out of the Ottoman Empire but has not yet transformed into a system of effectively governed nation-states with relatively well formed conceptions of national identity—calls upon the United States to formulate a foreign policy operating simultaneously in two very different dimensions, at two contrasting levels.

One foreign policy approach must address the Arab aspirations still far from fully realized for effective, modern nation-states whose citizens identify primarily with them. The second dimension, the second level, is a foreign policy directed at societies whose people retain their primary loyalties to their religious community, ethnic group, and even their tribe. We will not manage the region effectively—assuming we need and want to manage it—as a center of turbulent change and a potential or real threat to national security by treating it as if it were made up of effective nation-states; and it does not help us to define them as failed states, and as such concretize further our condescending attitude toward these countries and peoples.

Instead, we need a conceptual framework that describes these peoples and countries in ways that show respect and give us an effective handle on how to deal with them in their diversity and particularity. Maybe there could be a politics in which we respected the local leadership but, at the same time, were realistic about their present social and political structures and understood where they hoped to head as they evolved into nation-states. Thus we would treat them as partners in an exchange, so they could benefit from the new technologies and knowledge base in the advanced elements of the world system, especially the United States and Europe. And we would do this not as their masters, but as their mentors.

A major unrealized hope for Arab nations has been that an advanced Western society would provide wealth and opportunity and a framework for them to utilize and develop human resources in order for their people to become active and productive parts of the world making history, and not just the subjects of a history made by others. This should become possible with the cooperation of—not military domination by—a prominent Western power that developed a relationship of dignified partnership rather than hegemonic control over the local societies.

Unfortunately, America's foreign policy system, based as it is on the beliefs and perceptions of its own elites and its own public opinion, never learned much about the diverse world it was so deeply affecting, even more by mythic image than by strong interaction. The American Senate rejected Wilson's internationalist ideas of multilateral security and self-determination, and the King-Crane Commission was more a pretense of listening to the Arab national voice than a reality of dealing with it in political or cultural and religious terms. The commission was especially misleading in its failure to grapple seriously with Zionism, which had already become a significant force in American policy making and had a Christian religious base of support long before it had Jewish advocates. It would have been very significant if the commission, instead of sidestepping the issue of Zionism, had pointed to it as a major task of American foreign policy thinking after World War I. How could America's championing the creation of a Jewish state be made compatible with the Arab quest for self-determination? Even if the Arabs started out with a strong rejection of the way in which the Western victors in World War I dealt with the Ottoman Empire, the United States and others should have made it a priority to engage the Arab leadership in intense discussions toward calming down mutual hostilities between Zionism and Arab national movements.

Part of the problem for the United States in the Middle East was precipitated by the violation of expectations. America could never have fulfilled such lofty hopes without the Arabs' mobilizing their own energies for change and development. But this would have required healthy self-esteem in Arab society, to legitimize the importation of ideas and technologies, and the adoption of a new Muslim style of openness in learning, political participation, and pluralistic respect for internal ethnic, religious, and cultural diversity, and respect for the diversity and richness of the world system and its many peoples. In other words, the new Arab and other Middle East nation-states needed to inherit from the Ottoman Empire its zest for diversity rather than the autocratic, centralizing, monocultural emphasis of many of the nation-states that succeeded the Ottoman Empire.

If the criticism of the United States after Woodrow Wilson was making lofty promises that it could not fulfill, as the century wore on the criticism evolved into the notion of the United States being the master of double standards. The United States would advocate humane universal values but would apply those values primarily to improve its own society. In international affairs, the United States defied those values to advance its own interests of power and wealth and to support its favorite regimes, no matter the evils of which they were guilty. Early twentieth-century Arab experience is exemplified by the realization of the exiled Ibn Saud in Kuwait at the turn of the century, when he came to understand that the Western powers would support you for as long as they benefited, but would unhesitatingly abandon you when they perceived their interests somewhat differently. So, while America may have perceived its struggle against communism as a defense of the interests of the Arabs and their faith, the Arabs, especially the nationalists among them, saw this struggle as simply another round in the great European game of jockeying for position, with little attention invested in the fate of the peoples used as pawns.

More recently, there have been three main dimensions to America's post–World War II engagement in the Middle East:

1. The Middle East is a geostrategic region, located to the immediate south of the Soviet Union and bestriding key access points between continents: Africa and Asia, Europe and Asia. This would include the waterways from the Mediterranean to the Indian Ocean, through both the man-built Suez Canal and the intermediary natural bodies of water such as the Gulf between Iran and Iraq. In the post–cold war period the old geostrategic emphasis has changed. The Soviet Union, ever tempted to expand southward toward warmer waters and the oil sources that fueled Western expansion and wealth, is no longer at the core of world politics. But geography changes more slowly than empires,

and the region remains at the transition point of continents and civilizations.

2. The Middle East is the repository of the greatest concentration of fossil fuel reserves at a time when the West is consuming more energy than ever before and confronting a thirsty competitor for the product for the first time since these fuels became central to economic life. The meteoric growth of the Chinese market and the political instability of the oil- and gas-producing countries make the Middle East an area of continuing primary strategic concern. And yet the Middle East is a less successful part of the trading and commercial-industrial world than any other major region. It lags in literacy and economic growth, and has low rates of adoption and integration of information-age technology (except for the recent adoption of the technology of mass communication, especially satellite television). There has been too little dissemination of the individual communication technology of the Internet or even of cheap, reliable, and easily accessible telephones. Still, mass communication technology is so far a mixed blessing, since it has been used more to broadcast animosity toward the outsider than to provide educational content or promote curiosity for wider learning.

3. Instability in the Middle East is related to several interconnected phenomena, including the failure to establish strong bases for government legitimacy in the postcolonial period. This has led to violent opposition to many regimes, both as an extension of anti-imperial struggles and as a product of the struggle between autocratic, corrupt government authority and self-righteous opposition movements claiming the mantle of national consciousness and/or the imprimatur of religious truth and orthodoxy.

For many years the United States provided strong political support and bolstered the military defense of conservative Arab regimes, disregarding the status of individual freedom and education of the youth in those societies.

After the Soviet invasion of Afghanistan ended in 1989, the United States armed and afforded strong political legitimacy to the Arab volunteers in Afghanistan who fought against Soviet takeover of that country. They were a new generation of angry young Muslim radicals from a number of Arab countries, including Saudi Arabia, Egypt, and Algeria, forged into a hard core of well-trained religiopolitical militias easily mobilized to violence against targets not congenial to American interests. The threshold for violence in these regions had been lowered sharply by the long and bloody Iran-Iraq War and by the murderous violence given great popularity and appeal by the Palestinian military struggle against Israel, especially as directed against Israeli civilians. There was also the model of the Algerian revolution of the fifties and later the brutal Algerian internal upheaval of army versus fundamentalist terrorism, and the wars of Yemen and Saudi Arabia. All of these and many other armed conflicts contributed to a highly volatile political culture of authoritarian leadership and armed militancy of opposition forces. This itself was a strong disincentive to private and public foreign investment in economic development. It also diverted young people from education for employment and from peaceful, nonviolent political movements and toward the expressive and largely self-destructive politics of armed rage.

The strong opposition of the United States to the nationalist movements in the Arab and Muslim world of the fifties and sixties had several unintended consequences that incubated America's problems in the region today. The inability of the secular nationalist movements to create a firm foundation for legitimacy of governance in their states left a dangerous vacuum for their successors. Once the wave of unity attempts abated without success, the Arab emerging elites and peoples turned to more traditional forms of commitment and loyalty, especially those that were religious-based and in opposition to the nation-state structures and their leadership. The Arab peoples saw their regimes as corrupt when viewed against the standard set in the Koran of a just and justice-seeking society.

Internal limits on the education and the narrowness of ideological training of the first nationalist leaders were primary reasons that national institutions were weak, nondemocratic, and too easily corrupted. Furthermore, nonaligned politics gave a clear direction that these independent states did not wish to be satellites of either American or Soviet power. But it did not give them a blueprint for governance that could bring about modernization or a culture that could integrate the variety of tribes, linguistic groups, ethnic groups, religions, and provinces, which prevented the emergence of a real national solidarity and cohesion. Loyalties remained very localized. Divide-and-conquer did not perpetuate colonial rule much beyond the end of World War II, but it did leave these societies deeply divided. Rulers turned instead to control by secret police, corruption, and other methods that only pushed legitimate, effective governance further and further into the future.

The failures of Arab nationalist movements and their leaders have left the Arabs without a unified or even effectively cooperative regional bloc of states. Even the formerly perennial crowd pleaser of opposition to Israel and to the American-Israeli nexus is not what it used to be, since Egypt and Jordan have made peace with Israel and other Arab states have much moderated their rejection of her. Now even that issue produces as much division as agreement, which has strengthened the forces opposing modern nationalism and played into the hands of the fundamentalist religiopolitical forces trying to maintain an unreconstructed rejection of Israel and unrelenting armed struggle against her.

Still, the basic problem left with the Arab states after World War I has remained unsolved. The Arabs have not evolved a method of choosing leadership that encourages responsible governance and allows for new leaders to emerge from a large pool of talented people and to come to power without violence or major disorder and without opening the door to foreign intervention. Changes have happened by hereditary succession both within the monarchies and in some of the Arab republics, but this does not solve the problem of consent of the governed and does not ensure the selection of the best person for the job, or a change at regular intervals rather than waiting for succession through ineluctable biological process.

CHAPTER 8

ISRAEL

As we review the saga of America in the Middle East, it becomes more and more clear that a large group of people in that region began hearing about the United States in a way that corresponded to America's best self-image. American missionaries and educators spread an idea of shared humanitarian values and positive contribution to the life of the region through their teachings and benevolent approach to the people under Ottoman rule. However, over time and particularly in the last decade, the region has turned very sour toward the United States, its actions, and its policies.

The clearest example is the extreme vilification of America in the propaganda of Al Qaeda, especially the words of Ayman al-Zawahiri, the main deputy of Osama bin Laden. But he is by no means alone. Many others share that animus toward the United States, and are obsessively hostile not only to what America has done but also (say some American leaders) to the very essence of what America is. They have a vengeful desire to do harm to the core of the United States and to tear it down from its pedestal of world leadership. It is very important to the people of the United States and to those in the region to begin to reverse this hate-filled perception of a failed relationship, one fated to deteriorate even more and grow ever more hostile.

The relationship between the United States and Israel should be the exception to that sense of failure, and a partial antidote to it, given the shared belief in democracy and given that Israel is democracy's best (many would say only) exemplar in the region. Moreover, Israel is the most determined Middle East ally of the United States, and the country that most affirms American leadership and expresses clearly its appreciation for a world in which the United States is the dominant power, seeing it ultimately as a source of good. However, a complex struggle has been waged in American government circles and wider American civil society over the years since President Woodrow Wilson about the policy of the United States toward Zionism and about the creation of the state of Israel and its bolstering as a military power. This unresolved problem needs to be fully worked through so that a key part of America's Middle East foreign policy is supported by a broad American consensus in which the full range of the American people can feel proud and which they see as contributing to their national security and dignity.

It is possible to trace the chronic divisions about Israel in U.S. government circles through successive presidents and their advisers, who often had competing views. In Wilson's case, there was his friendship with Cleveland Dodge, his Princeton Arabist classmate, and with Louis Brandeis, whom Wilson appointed as associate justice of the Supreme Court, the first Jew ever to be appointed to the Court. Brandeis became a leading figure in American Zionism and strongly encouraged Wilson to meet Chaim Weizmann and become an early supporter of Britain's intention to issue a public statement of support for the Zionist project of a Jewish homeland in Palestine. This statement developed into the Balfour Declaration, which Wilson supported against the strong objections of Secretary of State Robert Lansing.

Roosevelt made his historic detour to the Suez Canal on his return from his final wartime summit with Stalin and Churchill in Yalta, to meet with Arab kings to try to persuade them to accept an influx of Jewish refugees to Palestine from war-ravaged Europe. He wanted to both resolve the problem of the Jewish refugees and ensure a steady flow of oil from Saudi Arabia to Europe and NATO to maintain the momentum of the Marshall Plan to rebuild European industry.

President Truman struggled with these issues throughout his first term and into his second while a battle raged between the State Department Middle East specialists under the leadership of Loy Henderson, who saw American support of Israel as imperiling American oil interests, and Truman's White House advisers David Niles and then Clark Clifford, who saw Israel as an essential bulwark against the Soviet Union and as the fulfillment of a long-held dream of Western Christians of the restoration of the Jews to their ancestral homeland, the birthplace of Jesus.

Moreover, President Truman accepted the argument that the Holocaust was irrefutable proof that the Jews needed and should have a homeland in which they were sovereign rather than continue to be subject to the often draconian dictates of host powers. Eisenhower was so focused on the struggle against Soviet communism and enjoyed so much popularity that he could ignore the Jewish lobby and reject the joint British, French, and Israeli campaign against Nasser and reverse the seizure of the Sinai in 1956–57. However, seeing the region wholly through cold war eyes, he could not resolve the long-standing conflict in America over Israel and the nature of American-Israeli relations.

Kennedy tried to improve American relations with both Egypt and Israel. His hope was dashed, however, as Nasser preferred the expansion of "Arab socialism" into Yemen to any rapprochement with America, and Israel looked to Kennedy to meet its defense needs rather than for a peace initiative.

Johnson was too preoccupied with the war in Vietnam to go out of his way to fulfill Eisenhower's promise of freedom of passage through the Straits of Tiran, and thus was unable to stop the rush to war between Israel and the Arabs in 1967.

After the 1967 War, the gap between Israel and the Arabs was beyond America's capacity to bridge. Nixon and Kissinger resupplied Israel with matériel in a unique airlift after the shock of the Arab success in the first few days of the 1973 War, and then used the intense public focus on the region after the war to promote the Israel-Egypt and Israel-Syria disengagement agreements. Those agreements introduced the modern peace process launched by President Anwar Sadat of Egypt and Prime Minister Menachem Begin, leading to the Camp David Summit in which President Jimmy Carter personally mediated a peace agreement between Egypt and Israel. (He also mediated an agreement on autonomy for the Palestinians, but that has produced only thirty years of, so far, failed attempts at achieving Israeli-Palestinian peace.)

Ronald Reagan changed his secretary of state in the midst of a war in Lebanon in which Israel surrounded the Palestinian leadership in Beirut. The replacement, George Shultz, then launched the negotiations that led to the abortive Israeli-Lebanese agreement of May 1983. Meanwhile, terrorist attacks on the American embassy and then on the Marines stationed in Lebanon introduced the United States to terrorism from an Islamic group, this time Hizbollah, the Shiite Lebanese militia fighting Israel's invasion of Lebanon.

Shultz was wary of King Hussein's nonresponsiveness to Reagan's peace initiative after the end of the summer of Israel's invasion of Lebanon. He refused to go out of his way to advance an initiative of Prime Minister Shimon Peres and then Defense Minister Yitzhak Rabin to reach an understanding with King Hussein of Jordan to reinforce the Jordanian Hashemite presence in the West Bank by convening an international conference. That conference, it was thought, would provide a Soviet-American umbrella under which Jordan could reassert its presence in the West Bank, giving itself standing to represent the Palestinians in a negotiation with Israel. The Palestinian response to this attempt to circumvent them was a factor in the outbreak of the first Palestinian intifada, in December 1987. It signaled the end of the period of minimal armed resistance to the Israeli occupation, and led to Israel's moving to talk to the PLO, first through American mediation by the Baker Five Points and later under the umbrella of the 1991 Madrid Conference, promoted by the first President Bush and his secretary of state, Jim Baker, and the secret Israel-PLO talks in Oslo in 1993.

The United States was still not comfortable with negotiation with the PLO, which it continued to see as a cold war ally of the Soviet Union. Only after Israel and the PLO reached an agreement on their own did President Bill Clinton invite the two sides to Washington, which led to the famous White House Lawn handshake between Yasser Arafat and Yitzhak Rabin.

The assassination of Prime Minister Rabin in November 1995 by an Israeli religious extremist short-circuited the peace progress. It was a great shock to Israeli society, but also to the Palestinians and to President Bill Clinton, who tried to redeem the situation by creating a unique moment of closeness in Israeli-American relations when he bid goodbye, in Hebrew, at Rabin's graveside with the words *"Shalom, haver"* ("Goodbye, friend"). He and King Hussein of Jordan, who had just signed a peace treaty with Rabin, both eulogized the Israeli leader. In this way, Clinton was able to demonstrate that the contradiction in U.S. relations with Israel and the Arabs could be overcome in the context of making peace, a lesson that still requires fulfillment by successor leaders of the United States, Israel, and the Palestinian people.

Clinton worked hard to fulfill Rabin's vision of peace with the Palestinians and hosted Arafat a number of times at the White House to demonstrate the importance he attributed to the Palestinian-Israeli relationship and the peace process. However, he did not succeed in moving the Israeli prime minister of the time, Ehud Barak, to put the same emphasis on that relationship until it was too late and it had exploded in all their faces into a new round of violence. Arafat was never fully enough convinced of his historic opportunity to create a Palestinian state to engage in effective negotiations that would include his own concessions under Clinton's leadership at the Camp David summit. Thus Clinton failed where Carter succeeded.

George W. Bush decided to renounce Clinton's legacy and severed the U.S. relationship with Arafat. From the outset of his presidency, Bush zeroed in on regional problems in the Middle East and not on the Israeli-Palestinian problem. He was especially incensed by Saddam Hussein's refusal to comply with the UN Security Council resolutions that specified monitoring of Iraqi weapons programs and severely limited them. Bush and his team were very concerned with energy supplies and, unlike most of their predecessors, did not focus sharply on the relationship with Saudi Arabia, but looked instead to the huge Iraqi reserves as part of a solution for a steady supply of oil at moderate price. There was little effort expended on either conservation or seriously reducing vehicle size and gas consumption. Indeed, the high-consumption SUV was a hallmark of the Bush years. So the United States was again more dependent on imported oil and found itself at war in one of the largest oil-reserve countries and entangled in problematic relations with Saudi Arabia and other Arab oil-producing countries, both because of American military presence in the Arabian Peninsula and because Bush was not working very hard on the issue of Palestine. And all the while the violence between Israel and the Palestinians was reaching new levels of viciousness.

Most of all, globalism was beginning to bite deeply into the sense of life satisfaction in the region, and the feeling was growing that its regimes were not serving their people in bringing them into the new worlds of opportunity fully enough or fast enough. As a result, opposition to the regimes and to their major international supporter, the United States, was waxing hotter and, in an age when nationalism and socialism were no longer the sources of excitement, Islam became the focus of oppositional intensity.

George H. W. Bush had prevented the Saddam Hussein Scud attacks from drawing Israel into the first Gulf War against Iraq and then led the way to the Madrid Peace Conference that brought Syria and Israel into negotiation, and eventually Israel and the PLO, too. After attending the funeral of Prime Minister Rabin following his traumatic assassination, Clinton devoted much of his foreign policy energy to a failed diplomacy of peace between Arafat and Prime Minister Barak. George W. Bush focused on the effort to force Saddam Hussein out of office in Iraq, but he also advanced the Roadmap for Peace as a new approach to Arab-Israeli peacemaking with new international involvement, including Britain, the United Nations, the Russians, and the European community.

In a world of some two hundred sovereign entities, it is not easy to single out certain dyads in international relations that have special closeness and that mean a great deal to the states and people on both sides of the relationship. For the United States and Israel, their relationship has been filled with intensity and been marked by decisions that have affected the lives of their peoples any number of times. The relationship has been strong and meaningful for the whole of the life of Israel, and for a long part of the life of the United States as a force in world affairs. Indeed since the entry of the United States into World War I and the Balfour Declaration, the idea of a Jewish state was moving from an ideological notion of a minority of Jews to a factor and then a force in the history of the Middle East and of American relations with the region.

Throughout most of this time the relationship has had strong support from U.S. presidents, but was also the subject of considerable controversy in professional diplomatic circles, where there was concern that a U.S.-Israel relationship would be costly to U.S. interests, as it would perturb American relations with the Arab states and peoples and even threaten oil relationships with Saudi Arabia and other key Middle Eastern suppliers of oil on the international market

Yet few international relations are more intense.

Even before the idea of the Jews reestablishing a commonwealth in the Holy Land became popular among the Jews of Eastern Europe, the Protestant American practice of personal Bible reading and study created a powerful religious link between the Old Testament stories of the Hebrews in the Promised Land and the New Testament revelations in which the return of the Jews to that Promised Land was a necessary precursor to Armageddon and the Second Coming of Christ. In this way, Zionism emerged as a religious force in American Christianity even before it generated a strong political lobby among Jews and others for a future Jewish state in Palestine. It was not lost on some social engineers that the idea of Jews returning to the Promised Land represented at least a partial solution to the flood of Jewish immigration to the United States, which some argued had become more than American society could easily absorb. What had begun as a reflection of the depth of America's religious life and especially its biblical literalism now became an important domestic component in legitimizing American imperial ambitions to control the Middle East region.

The special relationship that has come to exist between the United States and Israel was for forty years a rare area of proud bipartisan consensus in American foreign policy. However, in the post–1973 War period, the harsh impact of repeated American travails in the Middle East and the intractable conflict between the Palestinian national movement and Israel, including the growth of Palestinian military and terrorist movements and Israel's harsh repression of them, have made the story of Israel and America much more gloomy and have deprived it of much of its fairy-tale excitement. It is no longer a David-and-Goliath story, or a rags-to-riches story, or even a story of America's redemption of oppressed war refugees.

Some of the consensus has eroded, and it has become clear to many Americans that even if they continue to take pride in the role the United States has played in the firm establishment of Israel, they have by now an uneasy feeling, if not misgivings, about how much the relationship was forged on military assistance and buildup. U.S. support has enabled Israel to become the leading military power in the Middle East, much as the United States is in the world system, and with some of the same attitudinal consequences. The image of the two countries is no longer primarily based on the values they uphold in common, but rather on actions and policies that perpetuate injustices and inequalities through the application of superior force.

Therefore, issues that divide Americans over the use of U.S. military force have now also divided the once bipartisan consensus for the support of Israel. This division still leaves the majority clearly in support of Israel, but the most highly educated Americans tend to raise more questions and express more ambivalence about Israel than the majority of less educated Americans. For some, the issue is Israel's not living up to its democratic standards in relation to its Arab citizens, about one million of the six million Israeli citizens. However, for most who are concerned about Israel, and America's relationship with her, the issue is more the plight of the Palestinians in the West Bank and Gaza and the measures taken to suppress their resistance to occupation.

The Arab citizens of Israel do not have the full benefits of the economic, educational, and social advancement of the country, and they are not yet included as potential candidates for the highest ranks of Israeli government. It must also be said that ultra-Orthodox Jews are not fully integrated into the modern dimension of Israeli society, but in their case it is largely self-exclusion. In the United States, there has been a long-standing problem of racial inequality. However, in 2008, the American people shattered a major measure of exclusion by electing an African American to be president. The election was not only a numerical victory: the widespread excitement and enthusiasm for Barack Obama, even though the country was going through very difficult challenges, showed that the American people had moved beyond previous patterns of exclusion and now understood that the best of their values required equal opportunities for leadership and economic benefits for all its citizens. In the next few years, we will come to know how this decision changes American society and whether it reduces the vulnerability of the United States to the accusation of a double standard. With the United States having taken this historic step, it becomes still more important for Israel itself to take the steps it can to permit the Palestinian people to achieve their own self-determination and for the Arabs of Israel to become fully equal citizens in the state, as complicated as that is, given that they share a national identity with Israel's most inveterate adversary, at least as of now.

Some Americans are often upset by the suspicion that their close relationship with Israel is a causal factor in Arab hostility toward the United States, up to and including terrorist attacks of Islamic radicals against U.S. citizens.

The difficulty of overcoming animosity between the Arab world and America, on the one hand, and the still deeper hostility between the Arab Muslim world and Israel, on the other, is a result not only of difficult experiences in their past and present relationship. Deep underneath these present difficult political conflicts, there is a competition among the religious cultures they each represent. Christianity and Islam have had years of intense conflict since the Roman Empire declined and Islam began to spread very widely and very rapidly. The problem reached its nadir in the Crusades when the political hierarchy between them became intertwined with the religious conflict and they fought each other for control of Jerusalem and the Holy Land. Judaism preceded both of the other Abrahamic faiths, but never attracted and rarely pursued the huge number of converts that flowed to either Christianity or Islam. The sense of competition between Judaism and Islam can be traced mythically as far back as Ishmael and Isaac being sons of Abraham with different mothers and both of them claiming to be the main protagonist of the great biblical saga of Abraham's near sacrifice of his son. Each is sure that the text points to his own progenitor and, of course, Christianity sees that moment as the prefiguring of the crucifixion. From this source, and from other sacred texts, the three faiths share many of their deepest values, including the oneness of God and their shared belief that all of them are part of God's creation. They also came to share the view of Jerusalem as a holy city for each and as the place for their redemption. In other words, they argue and compete about the deepest things they share.

Finally, Israelis and Palestinians compete about who have been the most victimized people in history.

Concern about who is closest to God, and who has suffered the most from the evil that men do, places heavy obstacles on the path to reconciliation, and these obstacles will not be cleared by weak claims of secularization. What is required is not only careful negotiation of political agreements but also mutually respectful communication about their religious and cultural heritage, each and all of them.

The political story of the U.S.-Israel relationship begins with American support for the Balfour Declaration of 1917, the encouragement given to Lord Balfour for this historic act of making the first diplomatic step of major power recognition of the idea of the Jewish people reestablishing a political presence in their ancient homeland. First, before the official British government approval and sending of the letter, President Wilson indicated his support for the initiative. Later, he made that support public, encouraged by Justice Brandeis, among others, and inspired, among various factors, by his own reading of the Bible.

Cleveland Dodge, a Princeton classmate of Woodrow Wilson, was a strong supporter of Arab nationalism. When Wilson was president and facing the decision to support Zionism, he found himself in a conversation with his old friend Dodge. Dodge, however, did not recognize that he had a unique opportunity to express his opposition to this important decision of the president. Instead, he was focused on the Ottoman oppression of the Armenians, not aware yet of the importance of the Zionist threat, as Arabs would come to see it. Earlier I explained that Dodge was an active participant in Protestant American missionary interests in the Holy Land and in the wider Ottoman lands. So the president was at the earliest stages in touch with the variety of American civil society commitments on different sides of the issue. However, he never delved very deeply into these Ottoman Empire succession issues. As soon as Wilson became deeply engaged in the Paris Peace Conference, he was devoted to the League of Nations idea and focused on the peace agreement with Germany; he did not concern himself much about the future of the Ottoman lands, including the Palestine area.

Just how many of the themes of America's involvement in the history of the emergence of Israel were presaged from the very beginning is quite remarkable. First, the array of American civil society interests in the Middle East was brought to bear on presidential decision making again and again throughout the history of this issue. Second, U.S. presidents' personal faith repeatedly affected their weighing of alternative policies as they strove to make global political and strategic factors consistent with their religious commitment about the Holy Land and the revival and security of the Jews in it. Third, attitudes toward the Jewish state were heightened by a sense that America could not easily be the refuge of the masses of Jewish refugees and impoverished people flowing in from Eastern Europe following World War I. Finally, Wilson was the first but not the last to struggle with the relation between other strategic priorities and the issues involving the Jews and, later, the state of Israel.

A painful point in the twenty-first century is that while the fear that the United States would be called upon to send troops to defend Israel has mostly passed—as Israel has become strong enough to protect itself, with the help of highly developed American technology, often ingeniously adapted for use in the Israeli security arena—it has been replaced by a fear that the Islamic world's hostility to Israel intensifies hostility toward the United States.

What is needed now from the United States seems no less difficult: for it to help Israel solve its problem of the occupied territories before it permanently erodes the democratic and Jewish character of Israeli society. These two special characteristics, which have been at the core of the relationship between the United States and Israel, are both being seriously challenged by demographics and the ethics of the occupation. The prolonged occupation has produced serious divisions within Israeli society and paralysis on major actions imperative for Israeli national and economic development. In the context of this protracted struggle, there has emerged among some elements in the American elite, including some Jews, an abiding pessimism about whether Israel can ever find its place in the region. The United States therefore cannot content itself with fulfilling only a strategic role in guaranteeing Israel's long-term survival. It must help create the intellectual, moral, and even spiritual conceptualization of the meaning of the Israeli state.

The United States and American Jews have both tried to stay far away from the intense and often vicious internal politics in Israel, but now the struggle in the Middle East requires a clear indication from the United States of the need to end Israeli domination of Palestinian life and to help the Palestinians develop a system of responsible, authoritative government that can truly be a partner in a peaceful future with Israel, and not in the radical Islamic movements of terrorism that so roil and threaten Israeli and American society.

The negative side of removing the problem is often exclusively emphasized, but there is an inspiring side, too: America would benefit from a sense of achievement at solving a world problem that has escaped solution at least since the French Revolution, and would be playing an important role in Western civilization. Europe was never able to solve the problem of Christian-Jewish relations fairly and justly or ensure a dignified life for its Jews. That is one of the core reasons why the United States has been so much better at maintaining a trusted relationship with its own Jews and the Jews of the world, and especially with Israel. By solving the problem of Israel and the Palestinians, the United States would show that it had the staying power to remain loyal to long-term friends with long-term problems. It would demonstrate that this peculiar positive aspect of American history—its history of the welcoming of the Jews to America as full citizens, which goes back to George Washington and his visit to Newport, Rhode Island, followed by the special role that the United States has played in the establishment of the Jewish state and its security ever since—could be a way to resolve the issue, rather than, as many have charged, be a source of the problem.

It could show that the problem is better handled by a country with a good trusting relationship with Israel than by one that spent so much intellectual and political energy condemning Israel and dressing her down for her failures with the Palestinians. This issue relates deeply to the more intense presence of Christianity in contemporary America than in a secularized Europe. That religious dimension of resolving the problem could be especially inspiring for American Protestants, as well as for others in the United States who are adherents to one or another of the Abrahamic faiths and would be inspired to see those faiths act in the spirit of their loftiest values rather than as violent rivals with one another.

CHAPTER 9

THE ISRAELI-PALESTINIAN CONFLICT

BEFORE THE CREATION OF ISRAEL

The Israeli-Arab conflict has never been separate from the complex flow of modern history: it grew out of major international historical developments, and, in turn, they shaped it. Geographically, Palestine is at the intersection of Asia, Africa, and Europe. Culturally, it is the birthplace of two of the three Abrahamic religions and is of central religious significance to all three; it has been shaped by Jewish history, Arab history, and European imperial history.

The conflict there is first an intercommunal struggle between the indigenous Palestinian Arab people and the growing community of Jews coming to revive their national historical dream after centuries of dispersion in Europe, Asia, Africa, the Middle East, and, most recently, the Americas. At the same time, it has also been a primary arena in the struggle between the north and the south, and between East and West in the long cold war.

It has its foundations in the experiences of the Jews of Europe in the latter half of the nineteenth century and of Arabs in Syria and Palestine under the waning Ottoman Empire, and in the ideologies of both Zionism and Arab nationalism. The intense social and political transition and turmoil of the late nineteenth century gave rise to direct conflict between these two ideologies and the movements they spawned through the upheaval of World War I and that flared into violence during the British mandate over Palestine between the two world wars.

There are many strains of Zionism, and Arab nationalism has had many different versions, ranging from the idea of one Arab state over the whole of the Arab Middle East, to the idea of Greater Syria, to the idea of Palestinian nationalism with its focus on defeating the Zionist idea and creating an independent state in the whole of Palestine. Yet, despite their many incarnations, the two movements are still in search of a version of each that can coexist with the other. They still have to find a way to the modernization processes of internal development out of which they each began, and to put aside the obsessive focus on building a foundation for their own nationalism on the rubble of the other's.

Their internecine struggle, the overidentification of their expatriate communities with one side or the other, and the alignment of rival international interests have intensified their conflict to the point that they have not been able to create and live out their two narratives as linked by anything other than mutual hostility. They have not been able to see themselves as part of the same joint struggle to transition from the premodern empires from which they emerged to modern national states that could be partners in economic, political, and social development, rather than sworn existential enemies. Their histories have always been written as apologia for one side or the other, with heavy emphasis on the tragedy of one at the hands of the other, and not as an indivisible world historical phenomenon in which they were both swept up.

World War I is traditionally understood to have been motivated by the growing struggle between Germany, the rising military and industrial power, and Britain and France, the dominant imperial and naval powers, and to have had its flashpoint in the troubles in the Balkans—that region at the margin of East and West, where Christian-Muslim conflict, represented by the Austro-Hungarian and Ottoman Empires, respectively, was played out for centuries—which culminated in the assassination of Archduke Franz Ferdinand of Austria-Hungary in Sarajevo in the summer of 1914. Too little attention has been paid to the links between the European power struggle that led to the collapse of the Hapsburg and czarist empires and the demise of the Ottoman Empire, which left room for the meteoric rise of the new quasi-imperial United States. The lives of both the Arab peoples of Palestine and the wider Middle East and the Jewish people of Europe and the Arab countries were profoundly disrupted by these events. They were forced into a clash from which neither they nor the new world power system has been able to extricate them in all the intervening years.

The decline of the Ottoman Empire left the indigenous people of Palestine with a highly confused political status and a contradictory set of identifications and loyalties. Their economic condition was unclear; they had undergone an only partially understood land reform, and attempts at educational reform had not been integrated. A strong wind of Western modernization had penetrated the Arab elite in Palestine, Greater Syria, and Egypt. The Palestinian Arabs found themselves caught between the gradually growing irrelevance of their loyalty to Istanbul and the caliphate and the forces of change represented by emerging Arab and Syrian nationalism. That nationalism had strong echoes of the European nationalism penetrating their lives through the modern Jewish nationalist movement of Zionism, an analogous movement in that it also reflected the way modern nationalism impinged on a traditional religious society.

Zionism was not only a political movement to create a Jewish state but also a remarkable struggle to forge a new culture of self-reliance, solidarity of manual and agricultural labor (to replace the traditional culture and solidarity of an ancient religion), and emancipation from the Pale of Settlement and ghetto that Europe had become. Its engine of change was a modernized Hebrew language with all of the literary and artistic expression of a modern, partly secularized national culture. The Palestinians were trying to adjust from their role as inhabitants of a province of the far-flung Ottoman Empire, with its traditional education and an economy under reform pressure both before and even more so after the Young Turk Revolution in 1908. The new regime gave priority to Turkish nationalism and downplayed the shared Islamic identification of both Turkish and Arab subjects of the empire. The Ottoman Empire was trying very hard in its last decades to institute reforms to improve the economic situation and educational level of its Arab subjects, as well as to implement major changes in the central Turkish elements of the empire's structure that had led to the Young Turk revolt and the assertion of Turkish nationalism. The rise of Turkish nationalism became yet another layer of complication that the indigenous peoples of the provinces making up Palestine needed to absorb in very little time. But it was a major, though distant, element of the same story of imperial decline that was to have the sharpest impact on the lives of Palestinians.

In sum, the Arabs of Palestine were by no means able to assimilate the waves of rapid and fundamental change that marked the last phase of Ottoman suzerainty and the emergence of the British imperial mandate over Palestine. That mandate had a triple contradictory set of commitments: first, making Palestine the focus of the Jewish quest for a homeland; second, making Palestine the focus of Arab national self-determination; and third, all the while, ensuring that the needs of the empire were served as the highest priority.

The heaviest concentration of Jewish life at the end of the nineteenth century was in the regions governed by the failing Russian czarist empire and the troubled Austro-Hungarian Empire. The early stages of modernity in those lands resulted in a substantial growth in Jewish population, particularly as the rate of infant mortality fell steeply while the birthrate remained high. This population increase was contemporaneous with a gradual impoverishment of the Slavic peasantry and the growth of an exploited urban proletariat, both groups only too willing to identify a scapegoat for their troubles. This combination produced a recrudescence of anti-Semitism in Russia, including the pogroms in which Jews were targeted for brutal, "spontaneous," and often officially sanctioned attacks, from which authorities did nothing to protect them.

The rising nationalism across Europe was an affirmative expression of national, ethnic, and linguistic solidarity coupled with a fervent rejection of the multilingual, multireligious, and multicultural life of the empires from which these nations wished to secede. The Jews suffered from no longer having a secure, well-defined place in a multicultural environment, but they also themselves developed a modern nationalist consciousness in which they sought national autonomy or even statehood. They also wanted to revive their traditional biblical language of Hebrew, even though not a single person alive used it as the vernacular, and to create through it a new literature of art and national pride. The combination of external oppression and rejection and a new sense of cultural and national potential produced the vivid ideology of Zionism, and the beginning of emigration from the ghettos of Europe to Palestine and the much larger emigration to the West, especially to the "Golden Land," America.

This Jewish nationalist revival, bringing the power of modern secular nationalism together with traditional Jewish solidarity of religion and peoplehood, produced a powerful movement with political and world historical implications. The Zionist Jews were so different from the traditional religious Jews who lived in small numbers in the holy cities of Palestine—such as Tiberias, Safed, and especially Jerusalem—that it was impossible for the Palestinian indigenous Arabs to find a category of analysis that fit them, and so they borrowed from other times and contexts the ill-suited rubric of "colonizers." The Jews, of course, did not have an imperial cosmopolitan center, so the danger they represented was not domination from a metropolitan imperial capital but displacement from the very land itself. The Arabs also could not find an analytic formulation that helped them develop a strategy for stanching the Zionist enthusiasm and the flow of Eastern European Jews to their land, or for reversing the support of this movement by the British Empire, which had assumed authority over Palestine after the Paris Peace Conference. Nor could they do any better when the British gave way to the American colossus that was to follow when the United States inherited Britain's role in the Middle East.

At the same time, the energy and excitement of the Zionist movement made it impossible for its leaders to accurately assess the implications of its growth for the life of the indigenous Arab people or the fierceness with which the Arabs would resist Zionist encroachment. The Jews did not understand what was happening during the decline of the Ottoman Empire, including the emergence of Arab nationalist aspirations in Palestine, Syria, and other Arab lands.

The Zionist Jews and the indigenous Palestinians made very different decisions about how to deal with the British, decisions that had profound effects on their separate societies. The Jews developed an elaborate cultural and political framework for organizing their nation-building process, including democratic elections for their governing body. The Arabs refused to create a parallel body and thus left themselves with rule by an appointed religious political figure, who stymied the development of wider participatory institutions and declined to practice the art of diplomacy and incremental advance of their interests.

In order to maintain their claim of the fundamental illegitimacy of a Jewish communal presence in Palestine, the Arabs developed a strong preference for rejecting any and all Zionist claims. They practiced the art of propaganda, but succeeded in sowing fear among their own people more than in persuading outside audiences. They turned their politics toward armed resistance, even while the British imperial power had more military experience and the Zionists had more energy and skill in creating their own military capability. It was not until more than eighty years after the Balfour Declaration that the Palestinians began to understand that more effective governance and democratic representation would serve their national interest. Several times, when the tide of imperial or international policy turned in their direction, they could not find a way to shed their habit of rejection in order to benefit from the advantages a changed international situation was offering them.

Neither side was ready to accept the existential reality of the other, or the pragmatic necessity of coexistence if they were not to spend the next hundred years killing one another and obliterating their own hopes. It is only now, after they have tried for so long all the nonsolutions that involved breaking the will and eradicating the social and economic basis of the other's society, that they may, just may, be seriously ready for a coexistence that is not simply a code word for control and domination. However, since the conflict began in an international context as a world conflict, we should not forget that the solution will require a reorientation of the international community from the position of backing a chosen side to the essential role of facilitating peaceful agreement for long-term coexistence and for recognition of each of these nations as a full member of the international community of nations. Otherwise, we can look forward to still more years in which the two peoples blow each other up in a conflict that threatens the peace and security of the international system.

Most of the notable Arab families living under the Ottoman Empire felt an allegiance to that regime. They believed they had to defend the empire because it was the last stronghold of Muslim sovereign society in the Arab world. But during the revolt of the Young Turks in the first decade of the twentieth century, distinctions were drawn between Arabs and Turks. Arabs were disturbed by the privileging of Turks over them, which was becoming the sociopolitical norm under the new Young Turk regime. The Arabs began to realize that despite their devotion to the new regime of the old empire, they would never be treated as full and equal citizens in it. They came to believe that if they were ever to realize their national aspirations, they would need their own countries. The breakdown of the Ottoman Empire therefore uncapped a great burst of energy of Arab nationalistic enthusiasm.

Ironically, European Jews were faced with similar problems. No matter how secular or assimilated they became, they were not accepted as equal, full citizen members of the states in which they lived. Many Jews who had moved, whether physically or intellectually, beyond the confines of the traditional Jewish miniworld of small, self-enclosed communities—the *shtetlekh*—found they were not accepted in their new identity of national citizen in countries such as Germany and France, or even in the newly independent Poland between the wars. The Jews trapped in this quandary, mostly secular, proved to be a fertile ground for turning the theoretical ideas of Jewish nationalism into the beginnings of a political movement. Moreover, increasing violence toward them in Europe stimulated stronger support for the idea of a homeland, support that developed into an organized lobby working for a Jewish state in Palestine.

Palestinian society was overwhelmed. As so often before, Palestine was yet again a focus of so many neighboring political actors and so much global change and turmoil. It is only too understandable that it became a cauldron of conflict among many forces and peoples entering a new historical set of challenges after World War I. Indeed, that war created, in many ways, the necessity of thinking in world historical and cultural terms and of no longer settling for regional analyses that separated European culture and history from those of Islam, the Arabs, and the Persians. World War I brought the three monotheistic religions of Judaism, Islam, and Christianity into a new dynamic, historical relationship, one they have yet to comprehend enough to turn into an opportunity for growth or for deepening of each through understanding and communication with the others. Instead, the religions, their adherents, and even their reformers have understood this shared history as an inevitable renewal of a more extreme and deadly version of medieval religious war and Crusader conflict. They are engaged in their own internal and inward-looking struggles with modernity, and they learn little, if anything, from one another.

World War I also brought into a new, sharper focus the importance of the Arab regions to the British Empire. Not only did Britain come to see that the key strategic link to India was through the eastern Mediterranean and the land bridge of the Middle East from both Europe and Africa through to Asia, it also accorded much greater importance to the major seaports on the edges of the Middle East landmass: Haifa, Alexandria, Aden, Bushehr, Kuwait, and Basra. Britain's decision in the 1880s to gain control of the French-built Suez Canal and turn it into a strongpoint of the British raj led directly to a strategic rationale and *irrationale* to deny Egypt national independence after World War I and again after World War II. It was precisely at those critical times when Egypt could have used a kick-start to create a sound basis for economic development and social solidarity before the emergence of the struggle with Zionism and the state of Israel. This would have prevented the rise of Egyptian independence simultaneously with the explosion of the conflict with Israel and the first defeat of Egypt's national army by the military power of the new Jewish state.

Thus, the modern Arab state, unencumbered by mandate or colonial control, could emerge only in a period when the British position in the region was deeply eroded by the cost of waging World War II and imperial overstretch, and, more immediately, while the Palestinian conflict with Israel was erupting. This confluence of historical processes magnified the perception of that conflict's role in the emergence of these newly independent Arab states and indeed made of Israel a much greater perceived impediment to Arab nationalism and the emergence of the new Arab states of Egypt, Syria, Jordan, and Palestine and even Iraq and Lebanon. Israel became even more intertwined in the history of colonialism and imperialism by having the emergence of Arab independence so closely juxtaposed with the emergence of Israel, and the waging of war with it.

The complex interactions of world historical events and the emergence of Zionism and its conflict with the Palestinians have been so intricate and multidimensional as to defy a simple and objective, historically accurate analysis. Instead these interactions are generally described using simplistic blame theories that serve the propaganda needs of whoever is using them. Indeed, the parties involved in the conflict often try to exclude themselves from the world processes and histories that accentuated and exacerbated it. Arabs insist that the tragedy of the Jews in World War II, the Holocaust, has nothing to do with them, and Israelis too often refuse to see the links of imperial history to their own behavior.

It was clear at the end of World War I, with the collapse of the czarist and Hapsburg empires, that one of the postwar problems to be faced was the social and political homelessness of the Jews of Eastern Europe, including Russia and its hinterlands. Massive Jewish emigration to Western Europe and America had reached a nativist-perceived political and social saturation point, and it was ostrich-like for the Arab world to imagine that the problem could be approached without taking into account the other moving parts in the international system. None of the Western European states was in a stable sociopolitical situation after the massive bloodletting of the war; and Poland could not be changed culturally and politically fast enough to become the peaceful long-term future home for even its own millions of Jews. Indeed, the fact that aspiration for a better life was leading some Jews out of Europe, and not only to the United States, was no doubt a relief to the social planners of the European states facing their own adjustment problems after the Great War.

For Europe and for the Jews, Zionism was an idea whose time had come, and therefore Wilson was not acting out of a failure of moral insight when he focused on war refugees, Eastern European minorities, and the problem of the Jews in Eastern Europe, all of which combined to encourage his early support for the Balfour Declaration. The European powers and America, however, showed a lack of imagination in failing to perceive that a new problem, from which they would not soon be freed, was being created: the Arabs, already burdened by a surfeit of change and struggling to absorb the disappointment of the deferral of their independence to yet another generation, could not assimilate the influx of European Jews into their society and political system. The major practical problem was that by declaiming the Balfour Declaration and the idea of a Jewish homeland in Palestine, the British were imposing by fiat a potentially huge intervention that they could not support financially, or enforce by military power just at the time when they were demobilizing most of their military forces.

The British faced strategic overstretch following World War I. They needed to cut their overseas and military budgets. At the same time, they were expanding their empire into the Arab world. Without adequate planning, they had taken on the new responsibility of balancing the promised development of the young Jewish community of Palestine with the growth of the national consciousness and resistance to encroachment of the Arab inhabitants.

STEPS TOWARD AN INEVITABLE CONFLICT

The first major victory in the Jewish struggle for a homeland came in 1917 with the issuance of the Balfour Declaration. The British foreign minister, Lord Arthur Balfour, composed a letter to Lord Rothschild, the head of a prominent Jewish family in Britain, promising British support for a Jewish national homeland in Palestine. Lord Balfour was careful to specify that the Jews would be given a homeland but not control over Palestine, a fine distinction that would become the subject of much debate. The letter was also careful to mention that this homeland "shall not prejudice the civil and religious rights of existing non-Jewish communities in Palestine." The most crucial item of note in this clause is that the indigenous Palestinian population is addressed by negation only, by who they were *not* (i.e., "non-Jewish communities") and not as a distinct people.

The Balfour Declaration further promised to protect the "rights and status of Jews in any other country." This phrase was born out of the concern of non-Zionist and anti-Zionist British Jews, who feared that Zionism would undermine their great struggle to achieve equal rights for Jews in their new countries. This was true especially for some who had achieved a high status in British life. The implications of Zionism for Jews in Western countries was never again dealt with in such direct diplomatic language, and though the importance of Diaspora Jews has only grown, the diplomatic process has not found a way to bring their leadership into a role of appropriate responsibility in this worldwide struggle. Of course, part of the explanation for the removal of this issue from the formal agenda of the Zionist-Arab conflict is the great, even overwhelming, success of the Zionist agenda in Jewish Diaspora life, but this is only a stronger reason to make this Jewish Diaspora actor a positive part of the process of managing and even resolving the conflict, rather than a player with great influence but little responsibility.

With the issuance of the Balfour Declaration, Chaim Weizmann, the leader of the Zionist movement during World War I, felt that the promise of a Jewish state would now come to fruition, but Britain later distanced itself from the Balfour promise. By the time of World War II, Weizmann allowed that the British had made many promises with regard to control over Palestine and therefore could not and would not keep all of them.

However, the Balfour Declaration did not stand alone. Its interpretation was rendered more ambiguous by the revelation of two previous agreements into which Britain had entered. The first was an understanding reached in 1915 in a series of letters between Sharif Hussein, emir of Mecca, and Sir Henry McMahon, a representative of the British government in Cairo. Sir Henry had sought to enlist the help of the Arab leaders in the struggle to defeat the Ottoman Empire, in order to avail Britain of both their military help and their legitimization. In exchange for this assistance, he proposed that the British would support postwar Arab independence, even if the lands were under British influence. Many believed that this promise included support for the Palestinians' right to their own homeland in Palestine or as part of Syrian independence. So by the time the Balfour Declaration was written, there was a strong and justifiable Arab assumption that the land of Palestine had already been promised to them on the condition that they help end Ottoman control. However, the maps and territorial designation of the correspondence left many uncertainties, especially about the future of Palestine.

In 1916, the British and the French negotiated another agreement, Sykes-Picot, named for its French and British framers. It was a classic imperial division of the spoils, kept secret until revealed by Bolshevik revolutionaries who rejected the implicit assumption of Russian acceptance of this imperialistic bargain. The arrangement was that after the defeat of the Ottoman Empire, Britain and France would each assume control over designated parts of the newly liberated territories. France was to have some form of suzerainty over coastal Syria and Kurdish lands in Turkey and Iraq. Britain would control part of Iraq, from Basra in the south through Baghdad, the ports of Haifa and Jaffa, and vaguely designated areas of Syria, which might or might not include Palestine. The disposition of Palestine was left vague, such that France and Britain would have to negotiate again—though the next time would be after British military victories in Palestine and Syria.

The uncertainty over Palestine played an important role in Britain's determination to sponsor Zionism and thus ensure British and not French centrality in the future of Palestine. Sykes-Picot became for the Arabs the arch-symbol of nefarious Western dealings with them, and would play a core and problematic role in the division of the land after World War I. I personally recall the deep anguish of Jordan's King Hussein during the American-led war to expel Iraq from Kuwait in 1991, as he struggled to digest what he saw as the return of the Sykes-Picot mode of imperial redesign of Arab lands and borders more than seventy years later. Pacing in front of photographs of his ancestors, he said that they had been the recipients of empty promises and the victims of imperialistic machinations.

After World War I, the League of Nations gave Britain a mandate over Palestine. Mandates were meant to be the transitional stage between colonial direct rule and national self-determination, but as is so often the case in these interim arrangements, the goodwill that was presumed to be the basis for the process was swamped by the conflict between impatient nationalism and persistent imperial imperatives. Instead of serving as peaceful transitions to self-determination, mandates became stumbling blocks in themselves, as it seemed necessary to maintain them by force of arms against nationalist uprising. Creating enough consensus among the local people and building institutions of broad self-rule by popular assent proved beyond the capability of the powers that ruled and the peoples they dominated.

Mandates dissolved into intense intergroup conflict: local peoples fought against the mandatory authority, and various local factions vied for control of the benefits of the mandate and of the movement for self-determination, a goal that this internal conflict served only to delay.

In the 1920s the British tried to establish a local government in Palestine that would include both Jews and Arabs. Many of the indigenous Arabs, including some leading families, realized that if they did not cooperate with the British to create a government, they could lose their chance to govern. Sizable numbers of Jewish immigrants were settling in Palestine, and the Arabs knew that it was in their interest to gain power and be recognized as the rulers while they still had a majority. But as they were about to reach agreement with the British over the joint Jewish-Arab governance of Palestine, an important nationalist religious figure emerged: Mufti Haj Amin al-Husseini. He insisted there could be no combined government, and felt that to accede to such a British-sanctioned government with the Jews would be to accord them undue legitimacy and status in the land. Whatever the justification for Husseini's position, the permanent damage he did was to prevent the emergence of a nascent representative agency for the Palestinian Arabs, an institution that could have learned to govern and manage the affairs of the emerging national community parallel to the emergence of the Jewish governing body, the Jewish Agency.

The painful irony for the Palestinians is that this decision left the Jewish community of Palestine and the Jewish Agency as the sole example of successful implementation of the Wilsonian mandate theory. Whereas the Jews were able to use the mandatory period to set up a full range of effective governing institutions that facilitated their eventual self-determination, the Palestinians ended the mandate bereft of leadership and with no effective structure with which to face the enormous crisis of the 1947–49 War. The result was the crushing of their community and the tragic refugee problem still unsolved some sixty years later. This preclusion of institutional leadership and insistence on individual leadership amounted to a one-man veto over all decisions of national importance for the Palestinians and set a pattern that continues to undermine Palestinian quality of life, standing in the world community, and status in any negotiation.

To strengthen his case and his control within Palestine and throughout the larger Muslim and Arab world, Husseini started to reframe the political dispute as a religious war. He declared that the Jews coming to pray at the Western Wall were "trespassing" on sacred Muslim soil. The Ottomans had struck a "compromise" that permitted the Jews to pray at the Wall, but forbade them from bringing anything that would make the activity of prayer resemble a claim to permanent ownership stake, even if the objects were clearly only adjuncts to the religious service: no chairs; no *mechitza*, or wall separating the sexes; no table on which to rest the Torah, and so on.

Husseini's prohibition instigated a great deal of violence between the Jews and Palestinians, and eventually led to the most serious violence of the first decade of the mandate, which in 1929 included a massacre of Jews in Hebron. Neither the Jews nor the Arabs ever forgot this massacre, but instead of its serving as an object lesson that would ensure that such brutality would never be repeated, it has been replayed in a series of terrible Hebron events in which Jews and Arabs have behaved at their worst and shown that the way of religious extremism is accessible to both communities.

Through his proclamations and his holy war, Husseini gained much respect and power over the Palestinians. When Ataturk, the new leader of modern Turkey after World War I, did away with the caliphate, the Muslim people were left without a supreme earthly ruler. By turning the battle over land into a religious fight, Husseini placed the conflict in a new context. His actions gained him the needed fame and power, and he became the dominant personality among the Palestinians for the next decade, leading them into more and more violent resistance and fewer and fewer chances of realizing a good life.

Palestinian society (and traditional Arab culture) was based on tribes and clans. In the 1920s and '30s, there were two main Palestinian political elite families, the Nashishibis and the Husseinis. They both opposed Zionism, but held different views on how to express that opposition most effectively and on how to deal with the British. There was no fully legitimate organized political structure in Arab Palestine. Leadership was gained through intensity of opposition to the Zionists, and based on incitement to violence and chaos and on infighting among the Palestinians without regard to its damaging economic consequences: greater destitution for the poor and more dependence on Jewish jobs and largesse.

Nor was Jewish solidarity monolithic by any means. Groups within the Jewish Agency believed that a more aggressive Jewish posture against both the Palestinians and the British was necessary. As a result, the Irgun was developed as a splinter group of the Jewish Agency's officially designated self-defense authority, the Haganah, becoming a terrorist organization that caused a great deal of trouble for the inhabitants of Palestine. It aroused great resentment of Jewish behavior among not only British government officials but also many people independent of government. The British had made the decision to accept the cause of Zionism, but the means of opposition adopted by Zionist zealots such as those in the Irgun withered that support.

As the violence worsened in Palestine, the British began to realize that they did not have the manpower, supplies, or financial resources to get bogged down in tribal wars there, nor did they have the will to prevail. In order to find a solution to the crisis, they established the Peel Commission of 1936–37, a group of experts sent to investigate the region and led by the British diplomat, Lord Robert Peel. The commission explored issues of economy and education and other topics affecting the local populations. In the end, they had one important recommendation: Palestine had to be partitioned and each people had to have its own land and state. The commission recommended that Jerusalem be placed under British control. This marked the first time the world started talking in official terms about two states in the region of Palestine.

But the idea of any Jewish-held part of Palestine was rejected by the Arab leadership and accepted only conditionally by the Jews. The leader of the Jewish Agency, David Ben-Gurion, was so focused on maintaining or even increasing the flow of Jewish immigration to Palestine that he thought the Jews should accept partition and then bring in enough European Jews that the Arabs would be outnumbered and would eventually have to cede more land to the Jewish state.

Before another attempt could be made to find a solution to the problem of Palestine, World War II began, and the British abandoned partition and indeed rejected their Balfour Declaration commitments in favor of rehabilitating their relations with the Arabs. The Peel Commission report was so roundly rejected by the Arabs that the British did not even try to implement it, and as violence in Palestine grew again, they decided to consult with Arab leaders rather than only with Palestinians. This time the British considerations were heavily influenced by the prospect of a major war in which the Germans would attempt to outflank the British militarily by supplanting them in their appeal to the Arabs. This prompted the British decision to move toward a promise of a Palestinian state and a severe limit on Jewish immigration.

The British spelled out their policy in their White Paper of 1939. This marked the effective end of Balfour's promise and led to Ben-Gurion's decision to move the center of Zionist international politics from London to America. In the Biltmore Program, adopted in 1942 at the New York hotel of the same name, Ben-Gurion openly declared the goal of a Jewish state as the official program for Zionism after the war. The move of the international center of the political struggle to America was a critical shift for the history of the U.S. relationship with the Middle East and for the importance of American Jewry to the struggle.

WORLD WAR II

The beginning of World War II brought new challenges for all the parties in the Middle East. Some Arabs in Palestine believed that taking up arms with Germany could be an effective way to remove British colonial rule. This unfortunate decision marred their credibility with the rest of the international community and definitely lost them ground with the British at a critical moment. Husseini's decisions first to move to Baghdad, where there was a short-lived pro-German regime, and then to spend the war in Berlin and link his case to Hitler's notorious Jew hatred, were colossal, self-destructive examples of expressive politics dominating pragmatic, strategic thinking. Those decisions further demonstrate how Arab politicians failed to understand how their story was linked to the world story, whatever they imagined about their separateness of fate and destiny. However opportunistic such decisions can be in their origins, their consequences can extend much deeper and much longer, and this was certainly true of Husseini's Berlin sojourn.

As the war clouds loomed, the British decided it was now expedient for them to align themselves more closely to the Arab side in the conflict. Through their White Paper, their statement of British policy vis-à-vis Palestine that would align them with Arab interests going into the war, they instituted a rigid quota on Jewish immigration into Palestine, knowing that anything less would not mollify Arab hostility and Palestinian suspicion of their motives. Sadly for the British, even this gesture, which so alienated the Jews, was too little, too late for the Arabs. They could not forget the brutal British suppression of the 1936 Arab Revolt, which they saw as representing Britain's true agenda.

The White Paper created a significant dilemma for Ben-Gurion and the Jews. Without a strong Britain leading the fight against Germany, the very existence of the Jews was in danger; yet at the same time the Jews wanted to fight against the British and their White Paper policy. Ben-Gurion is known to have decided to "fight the White Paper as if there is no war, and fight the war like there is no White Paper." The issuance of the White Paper began to destroy the relationship between the official Jewish organizations and leaders and the British.

During this period, Chaim Weizmann, the initial leader of the Zionist movement in its World War I days, lost control over the movement in Palestine after the White Paper of 1939. Ben-Gurion undertook political control, but even he did not have full command, as many Jews would not accept his subtle distinctions and revolted violently against the British even during the war. Ben-Gurion began to focus on building the Jewish military force to help the British defend Palestine on the Egyptian and Syrian borders, with the attendant benefit of readying his forces for the postwar showdown with the Arabs that he believed inevitable. But at the same time, Ben-Gurion was in constant conflict with Menachem Begin, the Irgun's militant leader, who planned and executed military attacks on the British troops in Palestine during and after World War II, and was the successor to Ze'ev Jabotinsky, the founder of Revisionist Zionism, the movement that rejected any compromise that did not claim the whole of Palestine for the Jewish state. The Irgun is most well known for the 1946 bombing of the King David Hotel and the 1944 assassination of the British official Lord Moyne, events that undermined what was left of the British relationship with Zionism.

It is striking that the Jews, who in the lead-up to World War I had prepared themselves for the era in which the British would make the key decisions about Zionism, now were focusing their lobbying efforts and their public diplomacy on the American scene, correctly assessing the shift in the locus of world power that would be effected by the time the war ended. The Palestinians, in the meantime, cast their lot with the Germans, and did very little to develop a relationship with the United States. Fortunately for them, both the Saudis and the Egyptians had become important to the Allies' strategic war effort. That gave the Arab side some standing vis-à-vis the United States when the war ended.

Though Ben-Gurion was helping the British fight the war against the Germans, he also realized he needed to fight the White Paper. To avoid a direct confrontation with the British when they needed all their strength to deal with the Germans, he instituted a massive project of illegal Jewish immigration from Europe to Palestine. This adventurous path served a dual purpose of meeting the need for a popular policy of rescue for endangered European Jews and tweaking the British lion's nose without clipping its claws.

In response, the British simply deducted their estimate of the number of illegal immigrants from the quota of legal immigrants, but in their relentless fight against the "illegals," they created for themselves a major public relations disaster: they sank ships carrying unauthorized refugees, resulting in significant loss of life, and shipped survivors back to European detention camps. These human rights faux pas intensified the pressure in America among Jews and others to push for Jewish refugee resettlement as soon as the war was over. Eventually, Roosevelt reached a major policy decision that concretized the difference between American perceptions of justice and British policies. He openly insisted that the British allow the immediate entry of one hundred thousand Jewish war refugees into Palestine. This demand, scuttling the British White Paper of 1939, led the British government to abandon the mandate and turn the problem of Palestine over to the newly created United Nations, which was under primary American tutelage, and abandon the hope of achieving Anglo-American agreement on Palestine.

By the end of World War II the conflicting promises the British had made regarding Palestine had created a dangerous and untenable position for all sides. The problems the British were having in Palestine, in combination with the massive losses they suffered during the war, caused them once again to try to withdraw from the area. To do this, they created an Anglo-American commission of inquiry to make recommendations on the future of the mandate and of post-mandate Palestine. They wanted to put an end to the idea of a Jewish state and to place Palestine under a United Nations mandate. But the American members of the commission were not ready to go along with the plan.

After visiting the displaced persons camps in Europe and meeting with a number of Arab leaders in the Middle East, the Americans felt that simply putting Palestine under a UN mandate, and eventually making it a state, would not be sufficient. The United States decided that the answer was to place Palestine under a temporary trusteeship, eventually create a binational state, and immediately allow the entry of one hundred thousand Jewish immigrants, something that ensured the failure of the Anglo-American Commission to achieve its goal of finding a joint solution for Palestine. The commission's report was a dead letter before its ink had dried. Now the Americans would succeed the British rather than join them.

A number of different plans were proposed for Palestine. However, the British-American gap regarding Jewish refugees showed how an issue driven by domestic humanitarian and Jewish pressure, and which could not be denied by Roosevelt, made U.S. backing of the British and leaving Palestine to them untenable. For the British, accepting one hundred thousand refugees was incompatible with any hope of keeping Arab confidence in this transition period, and so the commission failed.

Roosevelt himself had not been responsive to pressures during the war to accept Jewish refugees into America, and he had summarily turned down the Morgenthau Plan of punishing Germany after the war by forcing it to become a nonindustrial, agricultural state. Roosevelt now wanted to find a humanitarian solution for the Jewish refugee problem, and understood that it could not be an attempt to reintegrate the Jews of Europe into the societies that had so rejected them and, in many cases, had been complicit in their near annihilation. Again, as in 1919, as the winner of the war, the United States did not seek territorial aggrandizement, but the president felt that he could well afford to satisfy his humanitarian need to find a solution for some part of the Jewish problem. The Jews had been very loyal constituents. The Jewish community of Palestine had strongly identified with the Allied cause, and a Jewish state would be a dependable ally to the United States in a region that was becoming more strategically important and less politically predictable.

The British, for their part, were by the end of the war so dependent on American goodwill and economic and military power that they simply could not defy the strongly stated wishes of the U.S. president. Churchill had too many postwar issues on which he needed Roosevelt's acquiescence and assistance, including the future of Eastern Europe and southern Europe, especially Greece.

At the end of 1946, seeing the situation on the ground out of control, and with the British unable to meet minimum American demands, President Truman, looking for a more solid long-term solution, changed U.S. policy and decided that he supported the idea of partition for Palestine. Because so many options had been presented—including partition, binationalism, and an Arab federation of states that would include the new Jewish state—and because the British and the Americans could not agree on what should be done, Britain asked the United Nations to decide. (It is important to note that recourse to the United Nations was pursued only after it had become clear that the bilateral British-American formula was not achievable.) The United Nations established the UN Special Committee on Palestine, which presented two plans. One was the majority report and the official decision of the committee. The other, supported only by Yugoslavia, Iran, and India, was the minority report and was not adopted.

The majority report called for a partition of Palestine into an Arab and a Jewish state and trusteeship for Jerusalem and Bethlehem. The plan would allow 150,000 Jewish immigrants into Palestine. The minority report supported the idea of a binational state, but it would be a "federal state," where the Arabs would be the majority, but the Jews would have all the same rights.

Based on the recommendations of the majority report, the United Nations adopted Resolution 181. The Arab League rejected both the majority and the minority reports, fearing the consequences of the geographic separation that would result from the creation of a Jewish state in their midst, and the economic decline that the Jewish port at Haifa would cause for the Arab port of Beirut. And of course there was still a very strong religious objection to a Jewish state in a predominantly Muslim region.

Meanwhile, the Jews did not want to postpone their declaration of independence any longer, and in 1947 Ben-Gurion announced that their state would emerge upon the expiration of the mandate in May of 1948. During the United Nations partition vote, civil war had begun between local Arabs and Jews. This internal war was especially brutal, with grave consequences for both communities and particularly catastrophic results for the Arab community of Palestine.

Attacks against civilians were the main method of intercommunal warfare. Their principal long-term effect was a disaster for the Palestinians who fled or were driven out of their habitations in the territories assigned to the Jewish state, a de facto expansion of the boundaries of the Jewish state. Popular fear of being targeted for attack in the intercommunal fighting grew among the Palestinian Arabs, which led more and more of the civilian population to seek escape from the scene of the conflict. Thus, the combination of direct attack and a growing fear of attack produced a frenzy of abandonment and flight. For the new Israeli state, this was an enormous relief from the pressure of Palestinian presence in mixed cities such as Haifa, Lydda, and Ramleh and allowed the clearing of access routes through once heavily populated towns and villages.

The decline of law and order in Palestine accentuated more than ever the contrast between the well-organized Jewish community, with a central authority monopolizing the means of coercion, and the lack of a clear structure of authority on the Palestinian side. With no recognized, organized community leadership structure, the issue was not whether other Arabs encouraged Palestinians to leave, but rather that there was no systematic planning for providing protection or food and shelter for those who would stay as the war intensified.

Palestinians' intense propaganda about how terrible it would be for them under the Jews scared them more than it deterred the Jews or mobilized the international community. (This self-destructive and paralyzing hate propaganda was to be used by both parties in the conflict again and again.) Faced with intense conflict and rumors of atrocities, in the context of widespread Arab belief in the worst about the Jews, the civilian population fled, and no one stopped them from running or provided them with a secure and practicable alternative to flight. For the Palestinians, their self-induced panic proved devastating to their society, and there were no effective institutions or leadership to mitigate the fear.

The Arab nations jointly attacked the new state of Israel when it was declared at the end of the mandate on May 15, 1948, and the fighting that ensued has become known as the War of 1948, in Israel as the

War of Independence, and by the Palestinians as the Nakhba, or the Disaster. At first the Arab invasion seemed to be successful, but within two weeks of the outbreak of hostilities the United Nations envoy had begun to work hard to negotiate a cease-fire, and the Arab states had other priorities more important to them than Palestine. As May turned to June, the Arab armies were no longer looking quite as successful, and therefore they agreed after a month of fighting to accept a cease-fire. This gave Ben-Gurion an opportunity to regroup, replenish his arms from Czechoslovakia, and begin to turn the tide.

Fighting erupted again in July, for about ten days, during which it was clear that the Israeli army had grown larger than the combined Arab invasion force, as the Israeli side was more and more unified in its will to survive and to win the war, while the Arabs continued to be divided by their different agendas and unique domestic problems. The Israeli forces captured two very important mixed towns, Lydda and Ramleh, and expelled their Arab inhabitants. It was becoming clear that the main problem for the United Nations was going to be refugees. The Egyptians were making some progress in their fighting in the south, but even that was limited. All the other Arab armies were being pushed back. Indeed, the Syrian and Iraqi armies were forced out of Palestine entirely.

The United Nations mediator, Count Folke Bernadotte, began to despair that the UN resolution of November 4, 1947, could ever lead to peace. He started to seek other approaches and relied greatly on British ideas and logistics. Bernadotte realized that the British proposals could work only with prior American agreement. Robert McClintock, one of the American officials who in the course of the war had moved away from partition, began to consider the Greater Transjordan concept, which was the annexation by Abdullah of Transjordan of much of Arab Palestine. Bernadotte adopted this idea as an important part of his own conception, but he was assassinated on September 17, 1948, by three members of the Stern Gang, a radical anti-British, Jewish underground movement. His proposal did not long survive him.

The British tried to keep Bernadotte's plan alive, and they had

State Department support, but President Truman had other priorities. First was the preparation for the cold war and preventing Soviet influence in the Mediterranean and the Arab states. He was also facing a reelection campaign. The Israelis rejected the new boundary demarcation of the Bernadotte plan; they were not willing to yield the Negev to any proposed Arab state. The British were determined to continue to support Bernadotte's Greater Transjordan option, but the Americans would describe it only as a possible basis for negotiation, leaving it to the parties to agree on boundaries and relationships. Truman looked to a fully negotiated solution, and the British wanted no negotiations at all. Ben-Gurion used a fait accompli policy, which was to capture the whole of the Galilee and the Negev by military means, and the White House accepted that the Galilee and the northern Negev would be part of the Jewish state. The British were incensed by what they considered damage to their special strategic interests, but they understood that Truman had a different set of geopolitical priorities. Those American aims could not be served by supporting implementation of the Bernadotte plan. Truman stayed with this position of advocating Israel's claim to the Negev even after the election.

Surprisingly, Secretary of State George Marshall, who had frequently endorsed State Department reservations about Truman's support of pro-Israeli policies, now wholeheartedly supported the president. He did not want a major General Assembly reconsideration of Palestine because he feared that the bitter debate that would be provoked would leave the United States sitting alone, the target of aspersions on its actions and motives. Thus the United States refused to back a British initiative to present the Bernadotte report to the General Assembly. Attention then turned away from redesigning the partition plan to finding the road to a permanent truce between Israel and the Arab countries.

Ben-Gurion's decision to purchase arms from Czechoslovakia, a member of the Eastern bloc, reinforced anxiety in Washington that if Israel were not firmly tied to the United States early in its history, it would be a target of opportunity for the Soviet Union in what had become the beginning of the cold war, as the Soviet Union began to flex its muscles internationally after World War II. It was difficult for outsiders to assess just how left was the Israeli Left and how much credit Israeli society was attributing to the Soviet Union's role in crushing Nazism. American intelligence had first gauged the Yishuv, the prestate Jewish community of Palestine, as militarily weak and a soft target for Arab attack. The United States had feared that it would be called upon to rescue the fledgling state from annihilation. This led Truman to move to the idea of a UN trusteeship soon after the partition decision in the General Assembly. All of this showed that the official American assessment did not have a firm grasp of the nature and substance of the emerging state, and that it distinguished poorly between the new Israeli reality and long-held assumptions about the Jews and their vulnerability. Truman's decisions were made by no means only to satisfy his Jewish voters, but also as part of American postwar thinking about how to keep U.S. influence primary in the Middle East and keep the Soviet Union from making progress by playing upon Jewish leftist tendencies.

The war also brought to the forefront the idea that the Jewish-Palestinian conflict was becoming an international one and not simply a local, intercommunal permanent civil war—although it certainly was that, too. The Israeli-Palestinian conflict had already become a defining issue of the new United Nations, and a battleground of the cold war, in which the United States had begun to use the tactic that became the hallmark of voting in the United Nations: Great Powers bringing pressure and offering inducements to gain votes to their side on many issues of international divisiveness. The Zionist wish to bring Jewish history into the general flow of world history was coming to pass, but on a faster, bumpier, and more sharply cornered road than Zionist visionaries could have imagined. The Palestinian issue, as both a refugee question and a question of self-determination not yet fulfilled, was well on its way to a leading place on what later became the north-south agenda and the third world agenda.

The Jews, in both Israel and America, were not able to adjust from their role as recognized victim to being accused of visiting suffering upon others, and Israeli and Jewish politics were, for the rest of the century, seized with the relationship between Israel's victimization and its emerging power. Israel to this day struggles to come to terms with this oppressed/oppressor world image and self-image.

The Palestinian question, the Jewish question, the third world agenda, the East-West rivalry, and the wider Arab-Israeli conflict became more and more intertwined, and the conflict, more and more intractable. If the raj had been the jewel in the Crown of the British Empire, Israel became the diamond in the rough for the American era of world affairs. Its high value in American foreign policy, its strong domestic base, and the glitter of its narrative of the transformation of a suffering people into a modern, successful nation—in many ways a simulacrum of the American experience—made it a diamond. However, it was a gem that never could be polished to perfection; it had the flaw of the Palestinian problem and all the occlusions of Middle East politics.

Another problem that resulted from the War of 1948 was the creation of parallel but irreconcilable national myths based on narratives of suffering, heroism, and cruelty. The war was a brutal one for both sides. Casualties were heavy. Many Palestinians were fated to spend the rest of their lives as refugees. Jewish casualties amounted to 1 percent of the entire Israeli population, and Israel for decades suffered from the loss of that whole generation of young men and women who would have been so critical to its political, cultural, and economic development. Each side has legitimate atrocity stories to tell. These terrifying narratives became national truth.

One of the major psychological obstacles to peacemaking is the inability of either side to accept the validity of any other national story. The zero-sum game of writing history as national narrative is problematic in that it prevents the sides from truly negotiating with each other and precludes their seeing each other as they see themselves, or at least in a way that permits peaceful coexistence with a modicum of mutual respect and acceptance.

AFTER THE CREATION OF ISRAEL

As discussed in preceding chapters, the defeat of the Arab countries in the War of 1948 (as in earlier and later altercations between Arabs and Israelis) resulted in intense anger within Arab countries, focused largely on their own government officials. The question of competent leadership became a central theme among Arabs. The existence of Israel was a constant and galling reminder of the lack of leadership and the corruption rampant in the Arab world. To address this fermenting antigovernment feeling, many Arab countries intensified their commitment to Arab nationalism, an ideology that clearly went beyond the self-interest of any particular leader and promised to make the Arabs collectively strong enough both to face up to Israel and to be masters in their own house. However, because national unity was beyond the capabilities of that generation of Arab leadership and beyond popular thinking, the Arab states would undergo decades of attempted regime change, and positive transformation that never fully materialized.

The two most salient examples of this trend are Egypt, where King Farouk was overthrown by the Free Officers Corps and Nasser eventually took control, and Syria, which suffered almost two decades of governmental upheaval before Hafez al-Assad gained power. In the end, the ripple effect of nationalism and the ensuing changes in leadership caused the Palestinian problems to become almost invisible. The United States and the other Western powers became obsessed with their cold war on communism, and so they focused their efforts on fostering friendly governments in the Middle East in order to forestall expansion by the Soviet Union. The issue of Palestine was converted into a trading counter in the battles for influence in the region.

An unfortunate result of the Soviet-American competition to secure influence in the Middle East was an arms race between the Arabs and the Israelis that was supported by the Soviet Union and first France and then the United States. This arms race is most clearly exemplified by the Czech arms deal and the political battles in Egypt in the 1950s.

Thus, at first, Arab states opposed Israel as part of their competition among themselves for power. It was only as they came to realize and experience the wide dimension of the Palestinian refugee problem that the refugee tragedy became the core of anti-Israel hostility. With the creation of the refugee problem and the collapse of the Palestinian elite, the issue of Palestine could easily be picked up by Egypt. The problem was on their border, the Palestinians were their coreligionists and ethnic brothers, many Palestinians had taken refuge in Egypt, and there was a vacuum of leadership among them. Furthermore, Egypt now had control of Gaza, which contained a large concentration of Palestinian refugees, and some of the biggest ref-ugee camps.

American foreign policy toward the Middle East in the 1950s was dominated by the growing antipathy of the Eisenhower administration toward Nasser-led Arab nationalism. The Palestinian factor had moved somewhat into the background because Palestinian leadership had been decimated by the 1948 War and first on the Arab agenda was to end British imperial domination in the region. This culminated in the Suez Canal War of 1956, the main context of which was British-Egyptian rivalry over the canal. In that war, the United States was not an arms supplier, but it played an important role in ending the war and pushing Israel out of the Sinai.

Eisenhower's firmness in pressing Israel was in keeping with his insistence that there be a return to the status quo antebellum so that Britain and France would gain no benefit from their aggression. It also reflected two dimensions of his policy that have not recurred in subsequent presidencies. First, he characterized the Suez campaign not primarily as an Israeli attack on Egypt, but rather as an attempt by Britain and France to revive a type of imperial diplomacy that he considered both archaic and damaging to NATO's defense against Soviet encroachment in the Middle East. Second, he was confident enough in his strength going into the 1956 presidential election to demonstrate forcefully that he would maintain this foreign policy priority above any domestic pressures to support Israel.

That war changed fundamentally the American relationship to the conflict between the Israelis and Palestinians. The United States made a commitment that Israel would be free to navigate the international waters of the Straits of Tiran, which opened up Eilat, the southernmost point of Israel, to become Israel's Red Sea port for African and Asian trade and for receiving Iranian oil. However, preoccupied by the Vietnam War, President Johnson was not willing, in May of 1967, to make a unilateral American decision to keep the straits open on the strength of American naval power.

Even though the 1956 War was not primarily about Israeli-Palestinian relations, it was partially provoked by the Palestinian fedayeen launching attacks from Gaza against Israeli settlements and the Israeli military retaliations that embarrassed Nasser over Egypt's military impotence.

By the early sixties, Nasser had moved to gain control of the direction of the Palestinian issue by creating the Palestine Liberation Organization under the aegis of Egypt and the Arab League. People realized quickly that the PLO offered no military threat to Israel. In order to give the organization teeth, Syria adopted Fatah to try to build it into something larger. It was in Syria that a young PLO officer named Yasser Arafat formed the Fatah military organization to bring the Palestinian idea out of the quiescence of Nasser's no-war policy and into a period marked by terrorism and guerrilla warfare, launched especially from Syrian and Jordanian territory. In this way, Arafat was trying to raise the temperature of Arab hostility to Israel and to bring the Palestinians back to the world stage through the medium of another general Arab-Israeli war. His efforts to heat up these fronts provoked Israeli raids that presaged the 1967 War.

WAR OF 1967

The increased tension and violence resulting from the growth of the PLO—and particularly the active militancy of Fatah, which was more upsetting to Israeli equilibrium than militarily effective—and Israel's retaliations, which heightened the involvement of neighboring countries, leading to troubles for Jordan and skirmishes and shelling over the Israeli-Syrian border. In April of 1967 there was an air battle over Damascus in which the Israelis shot down six Syrian planes while losing none, a huge embarrassment for the Syrians.

On May 13, 1967, the Soviets informed the Egyptians that Israeli troops were being massed on the Syrian border. The accusation, implying an imminent Israeli attack on Syria, was false and incendiary. The next day, Nasser ordered his troops into the Sinai, and two days later Egypt expelled the United Nations Emergency Force from the Sinai.

On May 22, Nasser closed the Gulf of Aqaba and the Straits of Tiran to all Israeli ships and any ships bringing strategic cargo to Israel, notwithstanding that in 1957 Israel had publicly declared that any closure of the gulf or the straits would be a cause for war. However, it was not only the closing of the straits that led to war. Israeli public reaction was based on exaggerated fears of military weakness, as information about Israel's improved military status had not been passed on, even to the Israeli elite. The fear of war undermined public confidence in Levi Eshkol, who had never been a military leader and had always been skeptical about Israeli saber rattling, but nonetheless had continued the Ben-Gurion practice of being both prime minister and defense minister. After Eshkol stumbled through a speech on Israeli television, he was no longer acceptable to many Israelis as defense minister, and his own cabinet forced him out and turned to Moshe Dayan, a close colleague of David Ben-Gurion's who had always publicly and privately dismissed Eshkol as an unworthy successor to Ben-Gurion and inadequate to the task of leading Israel.

Emotions ran high among American Jews at the time. Fear was intense before the war. The excitement over the Israeli victory changed the psychology of American Jewry, first to euphoria and then to a firm rejection of all Arab demands. This caused Israel to be less ready to consider the compromises offered to Prime Minister Golda Meir that might possibly have headed off the Yom Kippur War. Johnson's decision at the end of May 1967 to refuse to act unilaterally to fulfill

Eisenhower's promise weakened the American impact on Israel in its demand that it forgo a first strike. Once it was clear that Israeli public fear had forced Eshkol out of the Defense Ministry and that the United States was not going to intervene, the die was cast.

Israel launched a decisive air strike on the first day of the June 1967 War against the air forces of Egypt, Syria, and Jordan, and land strikes as well. It was only a few days before there was a humiliating and devastating Arab defeat, and before Israel had overreached in pushing Jordan out of the West Bank and directly occupying the Palestinian living areas of Gaza, the West Bank, and Jerusalem— even though Israelis had understood before the war that the occupation of these areas might create a more profound long-term problem than they could hope to solve.

The Israelis were able to defeat the combined forces of all the surrounding Arab countries in six days. In that time, they pushed beyond their borders in the Sinai Desert and in the northern Golan Heights. The Arab world was shocked by Israel's overpowering success.

The resounding Israeli victory in the Six-Day War of 1967 convinced most Israelis that the Arab countries would now have to come to terms with the fact that Israel was a permanent fixture on the Middle East landscape. This realization, they hoped, would finally make Arab nations willing to negotiate a peace settlement with them. Israel did not recognize that the emotional impact of its victory would push the Arabs to a more visceral rejection of Israel than ever before. The expectation that military victory would translate into political progress bespoke a complete misreading of the Arab mentality.

Even before the United Nations could issue Resolution 242, the Arab League met in Khartoum and declared that there would be no peace with Israel, no recognition of Israel, and no negotiation with Israel. The Three Nos of Khartoum, as the declaration came to be called, became deeply embedded in Israeli thinking, and even today Israelis often recall that Khartoum position without taking notice of the changes of position since then, leading up to the Beirut Summit resolution that committed the Arab states to make peace with Israel once it resolved its problems with the Palestinian state and with Syria.

After the War of 1967, some members of the Israeli government believed that to ensure the security of Israel's borders they had to settle the newly conquered territory of the Jordan Valley. This plan was named the Allon Plan, after its creator, the soldier and politician Yigal Allon, who called for the creation of settlements in the valley. People today still argue that these settlements served as a buffer zone between pre-1967 Israel and its Arab neighbors.

The lead-up to the Six-Day War had weakened the control of the government of Prime Minister Levi Eshkol, and though he was opposed to the idea of settlements, he was not able to prevail over the coalition of forces represented by Yisrael Galili, Moshe Dayan, and others who wanted to start redrawing the map and who were preparing to lay permanent claim to the West Bank. Initially, though, the claim over the Sinai and Golan was intended more as a bargaining chip in the Labor Party's conception of a territorial compromise under which Israel would withdraw from the Sinai, the Golan, and parts of the West Bank in exchange for keeping Jerusalem and the Jordan Valley. It was believed that Israel needed these two areas to facilitate defense in the event of a tank assault across its narrow waist from the eastern front of Jordan and Iraq. But once Labor began this settlement policy, it was not long before other subgroups in Israeli society insisted on settling areas of the West Bank that had more historic associations than security significance. These nationalist groups could not be turned back once the settlement process had begun.

More than that, with the emergence of a series of Likud governments in place of Labor, it was not long before different security theories emerged that emphasized not the Jordan Valley but the hilltops and areas closest to Israel's narrow waist. Furthermore, Ariel Sharon, the architect of the Likud Party after the 1973 War, when he reached power as minister of agriculture and then of defense, started a much more extensive settlement program all along the length of the West Bank in an attempt to bury the Green Line separating Israel and the West Bank since the end of the 1948 War and until the onset of the 1967 War. So the Allon Plan, which would have maintained in Israel and the Jordan Valley altogether some 25 to 30 percent of the West

Bank, was not so much abandoned by Sharon and the Likud Party's settlement plan as it was massively supplemented from the other end of the West Bank. The settlement project meant that Israel was eating up the territory first from the east and then from the west, leaving in the end only about 45 percent of the West Bank for the Palestinians. This map was only reinforced by Israel's decision after the onset of the Second Intifada of 2000–2003 to build a wall of separation between Israel and the Palestinians that moved the Green Line eastward and sandwiched the Palestinians between the two maps of Israeli "security": the Allon Plan and the Sharon Plan.

For the Palestinians, the Six-Day War created a new phenomenon, "double refugees"; removed Jordan from control of the lives of the West Bank Palestinians; and revived a movement for Palestinian self-rule and self-determination. Many of the Palestinians who had left their homes in 1948 were now forced to leave their new homes in the West Bank and become refugees in Jordan. This greatly exacerbated Arab anger toward Israel and led directly to an expansion of Arafat's Fatah group and its armed struggle of resistance to Israel.

Israel gained the military upper hand quickly, but as it turned out, the myth of armed resistance was more powerful than the fact of military defeat. Karameh, a town on the eastern side of the Jordan River, became the headquarters of the Fatah military once Arafat and his colleagues were forced out of the West Bank by the Israeli army. In March of 1968, Israel decided to mount an operation to destroy this military base. However, the operation turned more complicated than the Israel Defense Forces had foreseen, and even though the Palestinians were predictably defeated, they were able to mount significant resistance and succeeded in destroying a number of Israeli armored vehicles. The idea that Palestinians had stood firm in battle against Israel and not run away, and had inflicted some casualties, helped to assuage Palestinian shame over years of inactive resistance and to make Arafat and Fatah heroes, especially for the young, who flocked to join Fatah. There was now an emerging Palestinian self-image of revolutionary guerrilla fighters, which created a sense of "I fight, therefore I am."

The Palestinians, through this fighting, declared that they were back in the historical battle against Zionism, despite the abject defeat of the Arab national armies. This helped to generate a number of other, smaller and more radical Palestinian military factions, some of which adopted tactics such as hijacking and bombing passenger aircraft. The bolstered sense of national pride created a steady flow of youthful recruits to the armed struggle that has not run dry in forty years.

At the end of the sixties the Palestinian movement adopted a leftist, Marxist style, whereas in the Second Intifada, thirty years later, their new movement spoke in an Islamicist idiom, but still gained its reputation and self-respect through acts of violence and armed struggle. Although now the preferred mode of self-expression was suicide bombing of Israeli civilian targets, yet another species of Palestinian psychological warfare.

Jordan could not tolerate for long the freewheeling Palestinian armed presence within its borders. Their undisciplined conduct threatened to turn Jordan into a free fire zone, and there was a real risk that they would undermine King Hussein's control. In fact, George Habash's Popular Front for the Liberation of Palestine believed that the Palestinian movement could topple the Jordanian king, and in order to precipitate a clash his forces hijacked four civilian airliners on Jordanian soil. Hussein became convinced that he could not allow himself to be intimidated. He decided in 1970 that enough was enough and loosed the Jordanian army upon the Palestinian forces. Syria immediately sent its troops across the border into Jordan, capturing the city of Irbid. A wider conflict loomed as both Israel and the United States prepared themselves militarily to defend the Hashemite regime.

President Nixon and National Security Adviser Henry Kissinger were persuaded that Moscow was using its client Syria and the Palestinians to bring down the pro-Western government of Jordan. They would not allow this. The United States answered Hussein's appeal for help. Kissinger approached the Israeli ambassador in Washington, Yitzhak Rabin, and together they developed a plan for Israel to launch air and armored strikes against Syrian forces if the Syrians continued their assault on the Jordanian army. Seeing that he was now backed by both the United States and Israel, King Hussein was emboldened enough to launch his armored and air forces against the Syrians. The Syrian defense minister, Hafez al-Assad, defied the president of Syria and refused to commit the Syrian air force against Jordan. Uninterested in a hopeless combat with Israel and maybe the United States, and unwilling to deepen the conflict with Jordan, he withdrew his forces to his side of the border. In the end, the result was not a regional conflagration, but only the expulsion of the Palestinian forces to Lebanon. Assad was willing to defend the Palestinian movement from destruction, but not help it destroy the Hashemite kingdom.

Once in Lebanon, the Palestinians prepared themselves to make the same mistake: they began to create a state within a state. The radical Palestinians found that the method of hijacking planes, and thereby bringing the conflict into Europe, was paying off, at least in terms of notoriety on the international scene. Within the politics of a refugee people still trying to explain away their passivity of 1948, such media attention was a great boost to the morale of the movement and to the national solidarity of Palestinians at large with their fighters, especially in the absence of any realistic chance for territorial victory over Israel. The Palestinians were well on their way to the failed strategy of emotional victories that covered up strategic setbacks. Not long after they were forced out of Jordan and into Lebanon, their military tactics provoked an Israeli invasion of Lebanon, leading to the next stage in this Palestinian pattern of fighting until they were expelled from one country after another.

The death of Egypt's President Nasser in 1970 was the beginning of a new phase in history for Egypt and Israel, and would eventually have a profound impact on the Palestinian-Israeli conflict as well as the larger Arab-Israeli conflict. The new president, Anwar Sadat, distanced himself from the previous close relationship with the Soviet Union. This break with the Soviets eventually aided Sadat in his peace initiative with Israel, but first he needed to prove himself in battle and see how far the Soviet Union would help him in war. The War of 1973 was the result.

On October 6, 1973, when Sadat's forces crossed the Suez Canal into the Sinai, they shocked the world and took Israel completely by surprise. The Israelis were able to regroup and absorb large-scale American resupply efforts. They soon repulsed the Egyptians and were eventually across the canal, but the three days of victory during which the Israelis were set back on their heels were exactly what Sadat needed at home and abroad to give him the standing to go further in dismantling the Nasser legacy and move away from war. Once the Israelis had crossed the canal, there was a danger of the utter destruction of Egypt's Third Army, which would have left Egypt naked again and Sadat unable to follow his peace plans. Under strong pressure and even under threats of Soviet and then American nuclear alerts, the United States and the Soviet Union forged a cease-fire and brought Israel and Egypt to preliminary talks at Kilometer 101 of the road between Cairo and the canal, talks that turned out to be the forerunner to the modern peace process, which has proceeded through successes and failures ever since.

One irony in all this was that to develop his relationship with the United States, Sadat first had to test how far the Soviets would support him in war. The greater irony, of course, was that to have any chance at peace, he had to go to war. Moreover, he was able to show self-restraint in defining limited goals in his crossing of the canal and the discipline not to expand those goals once he had initial success, so as not to invite disaster for his military forces if they moved into more open territory in Sinai, where they would be fodder for the American-supplied Israeli Phantoms.

Even though Egypt did not "win" the War of 1973, Sadat made a huge dent in his war of ideas. By crossing the canal, he helped Egypt cross a barrier of dignity and stop being afraid of Israel. Egyptians could feel a measure of pride in their army and their country. It was only once this barrier of dignity had been crossed that Egypt could make peace with Israel.

Sadat's restraint in war was a key to his success in getting back the Sinai through peace. If he had followed the argument of Arab colleagues, he would have insisted on the Israelis withdrawing from other Arab territories, especially the West Bank and Gaza. Instead, he stood firm on the basic deal of getting back all of the Sinai for a peace treaty, and he accepted the modest steps of the agreement in which Israel committed itself, for the first time, to accepting the legitimate rights of the Palestinians, the first stage of which was autonomy. In this way Sadat became the first Arab leader who understood how to reach his goal by avoiding exaggeration, by defining his objectives modestly, by building his own relationship with the United States even while knowing that the Americans would remain closer to Israel than to Egypt, and by breaking the rule of Arab unanimity in favor of independent one-state diplomacy.

Because of the new sentiments in Egypt, Sadat felt he was able to accept the idea of the U.S. Rogers Plan—which proposed an implementation of Resolution 242 by both sides—and the intervention of Kissinger in negotiating a disengagement agreement that called for an exchange of land for nonbelligerency and, later, peace. Sadat could then begin to make a credible case that making peace was not surrender, but was in itself an act of leadership and courage.

The case worked for Egypt, but did not convince the other Arab states. As we saw in chapter 5 on Syria, President Assad felt deceived by Sadat and betrayed by Egypt's peace initiative. As for the Palestinians, so far they have launched two armed rebellions, the First and Second Intifadas, to achieve the psychological readiness to do what Sadat did by crossing the canal. We shall see now, in the twenty-first century, whether those two intifadas, together with the Oslo Agreement with Rabin and the Sharon withdrawal from Gaza, will embolden the Palestinians finally to make their peace with Israel and will prepare the Israelis to meet the basic Palestinian needs for truly independent statehood in the West Bank and Gaza with a foothold in Jerusalem, which would be the Palestinian capital.

AMERICAN PEACEMAKING

The United States, in the person of Secretary of State Henry Kissinger, took control of the disengagement agreements between Israel and Egypt and Israel and Syria after the 1973 War. Kissinger and Nixon had ignored or at least refused to respond to Sadat's signals of his willingness to seek agreement before war was launched, but once it was under way and Israel suffered the great shock of the surprise attack and the political earthquakes that followed the war, Kissinger and Nixon realized that Arab-Israeli war had become too dangerous, not only for the parties involved but also for their sponsors and for world peace. The Soviet preparations for military intervention to rescue Egypt's Third Army and the American nuclear alert to stop the Soviets in their tracks imperiled the structure of war prevention the United States and the Soviet Union had constructed since the outset of the cold war. Middle East affairs were far too important to be left to Middle Easterners.

Kissinger's innovation was to move slowly through the process. Most other intermediaries who tried to bring calm to the region jumped straight to the end game of peace between nations. Kissinger realized that none of the parties was ready for final agreements or to make decisions on fundamental issues. He proposed to work initially only on the disengagement agreements. He wanted to extricate the parties from the war and learn enough about them to be prepared to negotiate peace later.

Kissinger's methods instituted a new way of conducting diplomatic work. His first means of reaching an agreement was called "step-by-step diplomacy," which focuses on what the parties can agree upon *today*. This might be as small as choosing the process the rest of the negotiations will follow or the venue in which the parties will meet. Kissinger realized that if they made small moves, eventually those moves would have to get bigger and would lead to talking about the final disengagement agreements.

Although Averell Harriman had foreshadowed it, Kissinger made an art of going from head of state to head of state in his "shuttle diplomacy." He started to narrow the diplomatic distance between Cairo and Jerusalem, and Damascus and Jerusalem. He spent a lot of his time traveling between all three cities talking with the respective leaders and trying to find common ground. Kissinger's unique method involved building relationships between himself and individual leaders, but never between the leaders themselves. For his time, this was an effective strategy, but its application later in the Palestinian-Israeli crisis would not be as productive.

In the end, Kissinger was able to "shuttle-diplomacy" his way to two disengagement agreements between Israel and Egypt and one with Syria, but he failed to move the Jordanian front at all. His inactivity on anything on the Palestinian front set the stage for the PLO to become the sole legitimate representative of the Palestinian people, as Jordan was unable to reestablish any foothold in the West Bank. Moreover, this omission by Kissinger left the core conflict between Palestinians and Israelis untouched until they began their own secret talks, first in Western Europe, authorized by Yasser Arafat and Prime Minister Shimon Peres, in the mid-1980s, and later in Oslo by Arafat and Prime Minister Rabin.

By the time of Oslo, the Soviet Union no longer existed and therefore the parties were ready for an all-American negotiation process again. Jim Baker, secretary of state to President George H. W. Bush, ushered the parties to the table in Madrid, but could not bring them to agreement. Thus, the Israelis and the Palestinians decided to negotiate secretly on their own in Oslo, this time reaching agreement, and bringing the leaders of Israel and the PLO to shake hands on the White House Lawn under the auspices of President Bill Clinton.

ANALYSIS OF THE 1970S

The end of the seventies was a critical turning point in the Middle East and in the relationship of the United States to the Middle East.

The War of 1973 had ended in a major escalation of Israel's dependency on the United States for arms supply and political support. The war also triggered a nuclear alert that brought the United States and the Soviet Union close to a last-minute confrontation in the cold war, just before détente took full hold. The war brought Henry Kissinger to the center of Middle East diplomacy during the tenure of a Watergate-wounded Richard Nixon and a weak Gerald Ford, and he was able to design and implement the major U.S. attempt to engineer Israeli-Arab peace in the remaining years of the cold war.

The Yom Kippur War of 1973 had accelerated the decline of the founding ruling party of Israel, Mapai, later called the Labor Party, and in 1977 Menachem Begin led his Herut Party and its new Knesset list of Likud into heading a government coalition. Begin finally became prime minister after waiting in opposition since the founding of the state.

Though Kissinger was successful in creating disengagement agreements with Egypt and Syria, his attempt to make progress on the West Bank was very much blocked by the post-1967 emergence of the Israeli settler movement and the growth of the ideology of the greater land of Israel. Even though Kissinger was dealing with a government headed by the young military leader of the 1967 Six-Day War, Yitzhak Rabin—and his number two, Shimon Peres, a close associate of Mapai's and Israel's founding leader, David Ben-Gurion—they were not strong enough in Israeli politics to buck the trend, and they begged Kissinger to forgo a disengagement agreement with Jordan. Such an agreement would have given the Hashemite kingdom of Jordan a presence in the Jericho area of the West Bank. Kissinger's acceptance of this deferment of dealing with Jordan and the Palestinians had dire consequences, not only for the future of American Middle East policy, but also for the Labor Party. By the time Kissinger had turned to the idea of a Jordan-Israel disengagement, this issue was no longer a matter of strategic and military considerations alone. It had become an ideological divide that Rabin and Peres feared to cross.

The strategy of Ben-Gurion and Mapai going back to at least the forties was to create an alliance with the Hashemites against Palestinian radical nationalists. Now, in the seventies and eighties, it was becoming clear that Labor could not sustain this coalition with concessions that would keep the Hashemites at the center of Palestinian-Israeli politics. Kissinger's acquiescence to the Israeli internal political need to defer any step that might affirm a Jordanian claim in the West Bank was reinforced in 1985 by Secretary of State George Shultz, when he refused to support the agreement reached between Shimon Peres and King Hussein in London to create an international context in which Jordan supposedly could engage in discussions with Israel.

Once the opportunity for this disengagement agreement passed, the opening for King Hussein and Jordan to play a core role in the Palestinian-Israeli future was foreclosed. In other words, the tactical decision of Kissinger, Rabin, and Peres to skip over Hussein in this 1970s round of negotiations put an end to the strategic option preferred by both Labor leaders and Kissinger of reestablishing a Hashemite presence in the West Bank. It also accelerated the strategic change to make the PLO the sole negotiating partner that could represent the Palestinians. This was the option that would prove so difficult for both the United States and Israel, who emotionally could not stand the PLO, its armed struggle, its covenant, or its leadership. Moreover, when they finally overcame their resistance to reaching an agreement with the PLO, both the United States and Israel would eventually be forced by their publics' attitudes to break off talks and let the Palestinian issue degrade again into violent and self-destructive confrontation.

This decision of Kissinger and Rabin, urged on them by Peres, ensured that Labor's path would be hard and muddy. Rabin, Peres, and their successor, Ehud Barak, would spend the next twenty years with Yasser Arafat at the Palestinian helm. All three of them were trying to create a no-Jordan solution for the Palestinian takeover of the West Bank. This solution had a dual purpose: to prevent more Palestinian violence against the Israelis and to keep the demographic balance so that there would be more Jews between the Jordan River and the Mediterranean than Palestinians. However, the settlement policy that they pursued, and which was intensified by Likud prime ministers, had made reaching a solution much more complicated because of an ever-increasing population of Jewish settlers on more and more West Bank land and over a wider and wider definition of Jewish Jerusalem. These settlers saw themselves not as a bargaining chip in negotiations but as the hard-core vanguard of the whole Zionist enterprise and therefore, from their point of view, not subject to negotiation or withdrawal.

The 1973 War therefore led Egypt and Israel in very different domestic directions. Israel was in the throes of ending the longtime political hegemony of its founding and ruling party, the Mapai, and the emergence into political centrality of the immigrants from Morocco and other North African lands who had been outside of leadership roles until the end of the seventies. There was strong resentment of the power and wealth that had accrued to the institutions of state socialism, and demands for a more market-oriented economic system, a weakening of the central role of the kibbutz in Israeli social life, and an end to the dominant role of the Histadrut (the labor union federation and its associated enterprises) in Israel's economic life and social welfare and health delivery. The perpetuation of long-term control of the country by the old-time socialist elite had led to corruption, and this contributed to the desire to rotate party control away from the founding leadership. It led also to an aggressive attack on old quasi-socialist statist ideas of the Israeli economy in favor of free enterprise and economic and currency reform in directions more sympathetic to the preferences of American Jews and more aligned with the American capitalist model. It also gave birth in Israel to the Gush Emunim movement, a new hard-line religious Zionist ideology and movement that demanded accelerated settlement activity and strongly rejected the Labor Party post-1967 idea of territorial compromise in the West Bank.

Egypt, meanwhile, was tired of Nasserism and its political and economic practices, and was moving toward a breakdown of the rule of the Arab Socialist Union and the evaporation of fantasies of confronting Israel head-on by conventional military means. This change of direction swept across Egypt with the emergence of Anwar Sadat, first in his expulsion of the Soviets, ending their military control of Egypt and opening the country to foreign presence and capital, and then, most decisively, when he changed the course of Egyptian political and economic history by moving to end war with Israel. Under much pressure from an Egyptian middle class tired of having its promising young men waste away their productive learning and earning years in extended military service, which would probably end with yet another military thrashing by Israel, Sadat sought to move to end belligerence with Israel.

Egyptians were through with being denied freedom of speech, or any other freedoms, for that matter. The most apt example was the popular celebration in Cairo when Sadat for the first time allowed Egyptians to own private cars and to drive their Fiats (the only car make available) with reckless abandon. Leaning on their horns as if they were holiday noisemakers—as Swiss do with their holiday hammers and Americans do with their Fourth of July fireworks—and racing around the wide Nasserist boulevards without regard to lanes or speed limits or pedestrian crossings were Egyptian expressions of freedom and a celebration of change that was keenly felt and not enough understood outside the country.

This driving craze—driving without having learned to drive—was the best predictor of popular response not only to the opening up of some minor personal freedoms, but also to Sadat's decision to break out of the cycle of war and go to Jerusalem to declare "No more war."

There was a mass outpouring on the streets when Sadat returned from his momentous trip, but Israelis and many Americans interpreted it as a sequel to the forced rallies organized under Nasser and paid for by the secret police. They could not discern the powerful emotion underlying the Egyptian sense of having been liberated from the enormous frustration, fear of death, and social control, all wrapped up in Arab military dictatorship, and supposedly all justified by perennial war with Israel. In fact, the deeper function of maintaining the centrality of conflict with Israel for Egypt had been to feed the insatiable desire of Nasser and his successors to control their people by filling their minds with propaganda supporting the regime against any demands for change or the end of institutionalized corruption.

The purported need for a state of constant military readiness in Egypt had been used as an excuse for the denial of freedoms or free economic activity. It explained the failure of the country to achieve economic growth and overcome the impact of the population explosion. What Sadat did not realize until, for him, too late, and what has been the hard imperative of Mubarak's long presidency, was that peace and the nascent relationship with the United States brought a whole new set of expectations from the Egyptian people for a better quality of life, at first economic, but in many other sectors, too. Mubarak would have to struggle to maintain the peace agreement even when it was not extended to the Palestinians, and at the same time bring the peace dividend that Sadat had overtly promised and that had been built up in the popular mind as the expected result of these new policy departures.

Prime Minister Begin—flush with the new excitement of winning an election after failing for thirty years, and eager to show that his government not only was not going to lead to war, but was capable of bringing peace—chose the path of withdrawal from all of the Sinai. But he could not bring himself to move much on the Palestinian question. Any move to withdraw from Judea and Samaria would have been a challenge to the very ideological basis of his party. Even an acknowledgment of the Palestinian people as a legitimate national movement would have shaken his core constituency. Moreover, to yield ground to the Palestinians would have conferred legitimacy upon a Palestinian national political movement that Begin had always seen as spurious, real only as a negation of Zionism and not as an authentic national movement worthy of self-determination.

Thus the furthest he could go was to reach back to his own post–World War I memory as a young Polish Jew. That memory was based on the ideas of autonomy for minority groups that emerged in

Eastern Europe partly as a response to the Wilsonian insistence on the rights of minorities in the newly created states after the fall of the Austro-Hungarian Empire and the Russian Revolution.

Begin did his very best in responding to the insistent Egyptian demand on behalf of the Palestinians, but for him to go beyond that limited Polish conception of autonomy for minority groups to making Sadat an Arab hero by moving to a real national agreement with the Palestinians and not just the Egyptians would have required a very different relationship between Begin and the United States. It would also have required a very different Israeli view of the importance of Sadat's success as an Arab leader for the future of Arab and Middle East relations with both the United States and Israel.

America had never had an adequate understanding of how essential settlement of the Palestinian issue was to the stability of the region and to U.S. status in the Arab states. The United States did not have a firm enough grasp of the changing winds of rising militant Islam and declining secular nationalism to understand what Sadat's failure to go beyond his monumental Egyptian success to an even greater Arab success would mean in the regional context only a few years later. The United States began to have an inkling of what might have been when it encountered the bubbling up of Islamicist extremism first in the Khomeini revolution, then in the jihadist assassination of Sadat, and then in the burst of violence by Hizbollah against the American embassy and U.S. Marines in Lebanon. Further indications were the gradual stagnation of Egypt's opening up of its economy and society as it entered a bitter war against its own fundamentalist extremists, who were ruining tourism with terrorist attacks on foreign visitors to Cairo and Luxor. The forlorn hope that Begin would accept a full-blown Palestinian solution of self-determination was decidedly a bridge too far.

As the situation developed, sadly for Begin and even more so for Sadat, 1977–79 was not only a period of breakthrough for Egypt in making its own independent decision about war and peace, but also a time in which the alliance of Israel with Iran and the shah came to a crashing end and in which the emergent contemporary militant political Islam replaced Arab nationalism as the wellspring of the deepest hostility to the United States and Israel. For Israel, it was a period in which withdrawing from all of Sinai and freeing itself from the straitjacket of the old Labor slogan of Territorial Compromise—actually a code phrase for the retention of some, but not all, of the Arab territory captured in 1967 in return for Arab agreement to make peace— had become a viable option. The power of the Palestinian issue and the enormous impact of the post-1967 Israeli settlement in the West Bank began to undermine the sense of achievement of Carter and Sadat very soon after Camp David.

The bitter struggle over President Carter's demand for a settlement freeze in the West Bank and Gaza began as soon as Begin traveled to New York from Camp David to brief the American Jewish leadership. The Israeli leader demonstrated that the new religious fervor of the Israeli settlers and the new reinforced territorial ideological basis of Likud, in its post-1977 role as the dominant party of Israel, were leading inexorably toward holding on to the territories and precluding any resolution of the Palestinian problem.

The settlement drive of the eighties and nineties made the idea of incremental progress toward Palestinian self-government seem like a transparent ploy, deceiving no one but some of the Israelis themselves. This new movement of settlers defined the line of battle between Palestinians and Israelis, among Israelis, and between Israel and the United States. It became a determinant of the inability of Israel and Egypt under the leadership of the United States to translate the Sadat initiative into a wider acceptance of Israel through a solution to the Palestinian problem and the inclusion of Israel in the politics and economic life of the Middle East. It also helped lead to a temporary ostracism of Egypt from Arab politics, which although short-lived, was intense enough to ensure that the Sadat initiative was not to be a harbinger of a new age of Egyptian leadership in the Arab world.

This well-organized rejectionist front of the Arab states, including

Iraq and Syria, was the sharp riposte to Sadat for his breaking the taboos about Israel. The attachment among the Arab states to their fiction of the nonexistence of Israel seemed a matter of fundamental principle even more than an objection to a tactical approach of going it alone, since there was no hint that these Arabs would have gone along with this break in policy toward Israel if it had been offered in a multilateral context. It was also true that Sadat's dramatic approach to public diplomacy on international television and his explicit statements in the Knesset regarding the acceptance of Israel and "No more war," which had such an obvious impact on the Israeli public and even on the government's political behavior (at least in the realm of Egyptian territorial withdrawal), was not something Arab regimes were ready for their citizens to know, to learn from, or to press them to emulate.

It was only years later that the impact of failing to reap the full benefits of Sadat became clear in the context of the gathering energy of the Khomeini Revolution and its anti-American animus. Sadat and Khomeini represented two alternative paths to major change in Middle Eastern society and politics. While Khomeini could not export his revolution to the Sunni world overtly, he exported it indirectly by energizing the emergence of Sunni Islamicist politics and sullying the reputation of the Sadat approach of reconciliation with Israel and partnership with America. It was the Islamicist assassination of Sadat and its immediate follow-up in the Israeli invasion of Lebanon to crush the Palestinian revolution and Arafat's movement that turned the tide most drastically. The 1982 Lebanon War gave a huge boost to the Iranian-backed Hizbollah movement of the Lebanese Shiites in southern Lebanon. This movement, closely allied in both religious and political terms to the Iranian Revolutionary Guards as the cutting edge of the Khomeini foreign policy, helped to inaugurate the power of terrorism. It detoured American policy from its preferred path of building a new peaceful alliance to one of pursuing military defeat of the terrorist movements and their state sponsors.

The missed opportunity to further the progress of the Sadat breakthrough by beginning to mend the historic breach between the

Palestinians and the Israelis has had long-term consequences in the growing power of Islamicist political radicalism. It is this radicalism—not stopped when Arafat and his Fatah still had control of the PLO nor while King Hussein of Jordan still had a role in the politics of the Palestinians—that has so negatively impacted American security and the chances of success of the major peace efforts over the last twenty years. The once smaller leftist Palestinian movements were waning as Soviet power was waning, their energy and enthusiasm giving way to the new energy of religiously inspired politics and violence. Israel built more and more settlements and made it clear that occupation was not a short-term story and, in fact, would be reinforced by a whole new wave of construction and military activism after Lebanon.

This strategic choice of Israel and the rejectionist front's venom against Sadat, Israel, and the United States boxed in Sadat's successor, Hosni Mubarak. All he could do was hold on to the formal elements of the peace treaty with Israel and to the solemn promise of no more war. Neither a warmer nor a wider peace was possible in these circumstances. Moreover, Egypt was in a domestic struggle with its own extremists, who effectively exploited the anti–Coptic Christian feelings in certain parts of the country and tried to capitalize on then-outmoded suspicion of foreigners. This attack on foreigners boomeranged on the terrorists and gave the Egyptian government the strong support of the many people who lived off the tourist trade, one of the few sectors of the Egyptian economy that had grown directly as a result of peace.

The Reagan administration undermined its own clear message that Pax Americana was the best way for post-Nasserite Arab society to develop by its failed policy of seeking a separate Lebanese-Israeli peace without prior consultation with Syria. This left the field clear for pro-Khomeini Shiites to develop Hizbollah into an effective anti-Israel guerrilla movement that both became a conduit for the entrance of the Iranian Revolutionary Guard into Arab-Israeli politics and provided Syria with its preferred choice of an indirect military weapon with which to pester Israel and sap future peace efforts. The Reagan administration also encouraged Saddam Hussein's reckless militarism as he launched war against Khomeini's Iran. Moreover, the Sharon-led policy of expanded settlements and of trying to replace the PLO with a collaborationist Palestinian leadership (the Village Leagues) made it clear that the Sadat initiative did not have the momentum to extend peace beyond the bilateral Egyptian-Israeli agreement.

Still, Sadat's initiative not only decisively changed the military balance between Israel and the Arabs in conventional threats, it also was a major ideological step that wiped away in one action the Three Nos of Khartoum, which had been the Arab watchword since 1967. But Sadat's initiative could not be a full success because the failure to solve the Palestinian problem when Egyptian peace energy was alive gave a decisive advantage to the other alternative for the Arab future—Islamic militancy and a revival of underclass politics—just when a middle class was emerging among both Egyptians and Palestinians. The stridency of that militancy drowned out the middle class's call for change, moderation, and an end to conflict.

When Cyrus Vance and President Jimmy Carter tried to create a Geneva Conference for the Middle East, Sadat knew it would not work and decided not to wait any longer for the Arab consensus to emerge. He was determined to do what he knew was right and was what his people most needed. He undertook a unilateral, independent peace initiative, finally doing overtly what Syrians had accused Egypt of doing for years—that is, cozying up to America and undercutting Arab unity in its fight with Israel.

The power of charismatic national leaders such as Sadat derives in large measure from their self-identification with the nation and their conviction that they have a deep bond with the fundamental, even if unspoken, desires of their people. Such leaders have a profound sense that only they can bring those desires to fruition by dramatic leadership decisions that break with convention to meet the needs of the people and change their lives for the better.

This self-perception of Sadat made an indelible impression on me in a series of meetings in which he did not speak of himself as the leader of Egypt, or even as its ruler, but *as* Egypt. In his mind he *was* Egypt. This conflation of the nation and the person gave him the confidence to break the taboos of his society, but also allowed no space for voices that spoke of their country and their people differently. I remember him sharply rebuking me for listening attentively to and reflecting the views of leading Egyptian intellectuals of the time. He said, "They are not Egypt. They do not know what Egypt is. They live only in the cities. They do not know the life of the village, where I was born." He was totally deaf to the growing criticism that was beginning to take on a more extreme Islamicist cast, and which eventually felled him.

Sadat believed that a leader should not waste his energy on a large number of trivial matters, but should prepare himself for one major decision that will decisively improve the life of his people. A leader had to learn everything there was to know about the environment for that decision and the apprehended impediments to its success, and to pursue it with all the energy and fiber within him. Ending Egypt's involvement in war was that decision for Sadat.

He was convinced, as he said to me sharply on more than one occasion, that he knew what Egypt was and that his critics were mostly Cairo-born and did not understand the "Egyptian village"—of which he was a native and in which his mental processes were still embedded—or the mentality of rural Egyptians. Sadat believed that Egyptians and their beliefs could be explained largely by their origins. He felt that the same was true of Israelis, and was persuaded that he could do much better with Israelis born in Israel than with those born abroad, especially in Eastern Europe. He placed Moshe Dayan and Ezer Weizman, defense minister of Israel when Sadat flew to Jerusalem, in the native category and decided that it was with them he could work best. He pressed me to be a personal interlocutor between him and that generation of Israeli leadership.

DYNAMICS OF THE PEACE PROCESS

The peace process has been deeply complicated by the strong mythic levels of hostility, reinforced again and again by acts of violence and viciousness that multiply popular animosity and deepen the cultural roots of the enmity. Fundamentally, Israelis and Palestinians persist in their respective claims to be the sole authentic indigenous people of the land of Israel/Palestine, and in seeing the other's claims as unfounded.

In recent years there have been important instances of leaders and other spokespeople who have broken this taboo by accepting and internalizing the legitimacy of the other. They have acknowledged that no military victory can decide the conflict, since both peoples are deeply attached to the land and to their national existence upon it, and they neither will nor even can give up that commitment.

Those who have not yet crossed the Rubicon to a true acceptance of the other are given much encouragement in their refusal to do so by the perceptions and actions of their coreligionists, the Arabs of the region and the Jews of the Diaspora. For these cousins, identification with the conflict becomes a core aspect of group identity. This element of self-definition by negation of the other is especially persistent for them because they are far from the lively experience of almost daily encounter with the other and the importance of shaping a self by affirmation of a new culture in a new historical era, which in the long run erodes the hard focus on rejecting the other. For a long time the Arabs were able to play out their participation in the emotions of the conflict through Pan-Arab institutions and regional journalism and literature. However, as Arab leaders began to lose their absolute control over their masses and over the concepts and ideas that passed through the minds of their groups, the people needed to express their empathy and anger more directly through street demonstrations and through the emergence of radical opposition parties and Islamic movements. Now there is often a wide gap between state leadership and the street in the emotional volatility produced by the identification with the conflict and its violence. For the Jews in the Diaspora, identification with the conflict is expressed often by financial support of Israeli society and by advocacy of Israeli foreign policies with their own governments. A good example of the more traditional form of Arab identification at a distance was the creation of the Arab Boycott Office, which in the final analysis has done more to limit the Arabs in international trade than to have a major effect on Israel's economy. Israelis have simply found ways of doing business with the Arab world through third parties and offshore subsidiaries based in countries with which Arabs do business. For Israel, the main effect of the boycott has been to reinforce a Jewish sense of victimhood even as Israel has become the most powerful military state in the region and a highly developed Westernized economy. This gap between perception and reality is often confusing to non-Israelis and even to those Arabs who try to reinforce the boycott while remaining angry at the consequences.

A prime example of this negative identification with the conflict on the Jewish side is the emergence of the Jewish lobby for Israel in the United States. When Israel was a struggling emerging state, this political advocacy was very helpful to Israel in a hostile environment. But once Israel achieved a moment of opportunity to break out of isolation and ostracism toward peaceful inclusion in the life of the Middle East, many Diaspora Jewish institutions could not shift their consciousness from the negation to the active search for peaceful interaction. At this point, that negative identity threatened to become an obstacle to Israel's most cherished goal, the end of the conflict.

Arab intellectual elites have been among the most persistent and hostile actors in the war of ideas against a Jewish nation in the Middle East. This role of poisoning the atmosphere about the Jews and Judaism has proven to be even more persistent and pernicious than the attempts of Arab intellectuals to provide logistical and even financial support to Palestinian military organizations.

On its side, Israel has been buoyed up continually by the awareness of its strong moral and political support and substantial funding from world Jewry. The diplomatic importance of this role has attracted attention in moments of particular stress, and through the many American vetoes cast at the United Nations Security Council against resolutions condemning Israel. At moments of crisis, such as the Partition Resolution in 1947 and the decision to recognize Israel in 1948, these external forces are more sharply noticed. Diaspora Jews, especially those in America, have seen themselves as a counterweight to anti-Semitic strands of world policy and to an oil lobby for pro-Arab and anti-Israel positions that they perceived as powerful, though it is perhaps less powerful than they imagined.

Unfortunately, neither Arab states nor American and other Diaspora Jewry have been able to transition from the period of total conflict between Arabs and Israelis to the more complex situation in which some Arabs, beginning with Egypt, are willing to recognize and make peace with Israel and in which many Israelis and many Jews are more than willing to accept an independent Palestinian state living side by side in peace with Israel. The zero-sum view of the conflict has not been superseded in large elements of the Arab and Jewish worlds. And global diplomatic efforts have not yet been effective in giving these important external communities the role of contributing to peace rather than the distinction of standing in its way as loyalists of their favored party.

Arab states do have to pay a price for their actions. Their accountability comes within the international system that, however limited in its defense of the two-state solution, still has countries, especially the United States, that will be critical of Arab ostracism of Israel.

American Jewish leadership suffers from its lack of accountability to anyone but its own limited constituency. It is an unelected leadership that is, for the most part, unchallenged by a largely supportive American Jewish communal press. However, it is in some measure held indirectly accountable by the Israeli press and Israeli government leaders, although those critiques are rarely systematic. Israeli leadership principally seeks signs of group solidarity and loyalty from the Diaspora leaders, and not indications of political acuity or helpfulness in pursuing peace. In fact, negative reaction in Israel to Diaspora independent peace efforts is expressed mostly by not treating them seriously. Diaspora leaders who "behave" are greeted with more access to the leadership of Israel and higher attendance by Israeli leaders at American nongovernmental meetings.

Though the American Jewish community would like to see itself as advocating for a close relationship between Israel and the United States, it would not tolerate any serious systematic critique coming from the U.S. government, even though it expects to be treated as a very serious partner in America's role in the region. There is therefore no context for a legitimate political public discussion of the role and positions taken by American Jewish communal institutions, and indeed no public scrutiny of or debate over American relations with Israel that is not subject to the litmus test of anti-Semitism. Though anti-Semitism certainly still exists, and there can be no doubt that some anti-Semites make their critique on bigoted grounds, there needs to be a legitimate, open, and uncensored public discourse on all the important issues regarding American Middle East policy and its relation to the Israeli-Palestinian conflict. The issues are too important, both to U.S. national security and to the structure of American multiethnic society, not to consider carefully how the American Jewish community should conduct its business about Israel and a U.S. role in the region.

The Arab American and Muslim American communities have faced a very difficult environment in the United States since 9/11. They have seen many examples of racial profiling; they have seen visas for friends, family, and colleagues in the Arab world become much more difficult to arrange; and they have had to live through a substantial U.S. war with an Arab country in which thousands of Americans and tens of thousands of Iraqis have perished. However, the combination of all these difficult factors only makes it clearer that the Arab American and Muslim American communities share with the American Jewish community the intense intertwining of their domestic comfort in the United States with the relationship of the U.S. government to their respective communities of identification in the Middle East. It is important first of all that the codes of conduct in the Middle East of pursuing the Israeli-Palestinian conflict and the

Arab-Israeli conflict not be imported to the United States. The norms in the region permit and sometimes even encourage not only outbursts of violence but a constant din of recrimination and stereotyping, and a steady drumbeat of contempt and incitement to hatred.

The dangerous trend we are now facing is the intensification of religious themes such that Americans are perceived as particularly hostile and disrespectful toward Islam as a great faith. Too easily in the Muslim world extremist expressions of animus against America and hatred for Israel can be heard in public forums, on television and radio, and in mosques. Some Arab efforts are now being directed at increasing the quality and quantity of the study of Islam in U.S. universities. However, these efforts will not be effective unless they deal with the relationship between respect for Islam and respect by Muslims for Christianity and Judaism. The American university system, and the educational systems in general, must be encouraged to educate for tolerance and, beyond tolerance, respect for Islam as a fierce advocate of monotheism and a strong advocate, in its sacred texts, of social justice. It is essential that the climate in world society not so easily accept the ubiquity and frequency of attitudes and expressions of contempt between Islam and Christianity, and Islam and Judaism.

The Jews, Christians, and Muslims of the United States need to prevent such language and expressions from polluting public discussion of these sensitive issues, especially in the media and in the primary schools, high schools, and universities of this nation. It is important that the norm of discussion include respect for the other and for the other's right to express what he or she believes without risk of sanction or of group labeling and stereotyping.

We need to think about how we can enhance the quality of teaching about these subjects. Moreover, current education on the content of the several faiths, though necessary, is insufficient. There must be an atmosphere of sensitivity, positive curiosity, and mutual respect, all grounded on a basic understanding that world society either will have this element of respect or will continue to deteriorate into reciprocal hostility and greater violence between America and elements of the Muslim world. We cannot found effective and peaceful international relations on a bedrock of popular anger, resentment, and vituperation.

The communities of identification with parties to the conflict should prepare their leaders to meet in America with people of the other community to educate themselves about other perspectives and inculcate a norm of pluralistic acceptance and inclusiveness as the American way. We have to try to develop a culture of communication in the United States that encourages face-to-face contact across groups and offers opportunities to meet leaders, teachers, and intelligent men and women from the different societies involved. The American context must become one in which the norm is openness of discussion, civility, and variety of contacts, rather than lack of civility, separation of communities of communication, and reluctance to be in close contact with members of the other group.

One particular responsibility must be assumed more frequently and openly by Muslim Americans and Arab Americans: to talk and write to people in the media in their countries of origin or identification about what is good for them about living in America and about the norms and practices of pluralism that prevail here.

These attitudes about the communities that identify with the direct parties to the conflict were much sharpened through the years of the two Palestinian intifadas as violence and confrontation became a matter of daily, or at least regular, live news coverage. Israeli society was gradually learning that the conflict could not be resolved by unilateral military action, and the Palestinians were realizing the limits of guerrilla warfare, even when intensified by suicide bombers; but outside the arena of direct conflict, anger and resentment at one or both parties became harsher and more anguished. Still, those who expressed themselves in the most militant tones, without empathy for the other side, garnered disproportionate attention, as the news media found it more interesting for their audience to hear polarized polemics rather than the more hesitant and measured voices of people reaching out in an attempt to bridge the gap.

Until the more intense confrontations of the First Intifada, it was common for discussions among Jews, and not infrequently among Arabs, to assume that the future of the territories was Israel's decision to make, and to see the occupied Palestinians as too weak or too passive to play much of a role in determining the future. Sadly, it took stone-throwing and violence for Palestinians to shed their passivity, and for Israelis to realize that there was no chance Palestinians would simply surrender to Israeli wishes and to annexation.

In many Arab states, with people more and more preoccupied with their own local development and governance challenges, the din of television, broadcasting, and violence rearoused Arab domestic public opinion. This political awareness included contempt for their own governments for their impotence in the face of Israeli power and for their inability to bring the United States, with whom many of them allied themselves, to stop the oppression. However, gradually elites in many Arab countries began to recognize that anger and resentment were not policies and that only a peaceful settlement could change the dynamics. More Arabs had intentionally or accidentally encountered Israelis during travel or at international conferences and had reduced their fear and increased their willingness to understand how engagement might be more effective in changing Israeli attitudes and policies than boycott or quarantine.

Political negotiation was necessary to replace the futility of an entirely military approach to the conflict, but a purely political process would not be enough. There would have to be reconciliation through the resocialization of the peoples and the humanization of the other. And it is in this process that communities of identification in the diasporas would be especially essential. Civil societies and their institutions would have to become mobilized to encounter each other, learn about each other, and teach each other that hope was a better driver of change than perpetual fear. Since these communities of identification hold important levers of cultural and religious identity, they could be more effective in a phase of reconciliation than they were in the phase of war, when, not carrying the weapons themselves, they enthusiastically cheered on their favorite gladiators.

CONCLUSION

Jews and Palestinians each feel a wounded dignity stemming from historical humiliations and deprivations. Israeli sovereignty and the success of building a modern state have done much to establish a firm foundation for Jewish dignity. The Palestinians would have to reach a stage of successful, independent, and free national statehood to be able to replace humiliation with dignity and to establish national pride on the basis of building their own society rather than negating Israel's. Establishing a basis for dignity for each people would bring a readiness to acknowledge the need for the dignity of the other and the legitimacy of the other's claim to national statehood.

Still, the dispossessed, the refugees, and the bereaved would not be able to feel the full benefits of this statehood, and it would therefore be important to find ways to represent them in the communal memory and in the saga of national revival. It is clear from the epic poetry of the pioneering Hebrew poet Haim Nahman Bialik, who bemoaned Jewish passivity in the face of vicious pogroms, that developing the capability of self-defense was essential for regaining self-esteem for both Jews and Palestinians. The achievement of defense forces became a critical part of the Jewish view of what Zionism could mean for changing Jewish self-perception of weakness and vulnerability. For the Palestinians, credibility for achieving positions of political leadership continue to rest heavily on a record of active participation in armed struggle, first in the revolt against the British and then that against Israel. It is necessary for both peoples to come to separate national dignity and national leadership from national aggression. Whatever its origins in the history of the conflict, it will be difficult to achieve reconciliation while dignity rests so heavily on success in perpetrating brutality against the other.

It is especially important to acknowledge that popular mass participation in the national saga was for many people possible only through the military route. Palestinian peasants played an important role in the emergence of Palestinian nationalism through revolts, and on the Israeli side no institution was more effective in consolidating a unified national identity from the multitude of Jewish Diaspora cultures than the Israel Defense Forces. Thus, a peace process will have to include new mechanisms for inclusion of the impoverished or marginal subgroups of the societies. The main hope in the election of Hamas to run the Palestinian Legislative Council and to form a new Palestinian Authority government is that the Palestinian street will no longer have to fight against its government's attempts at peaceful settlement because the government now represents the street and the masses much more than previously.

However, the rise of Hamas also points to the need for greater attention to the roles of Islam and Judaism and the relationship between them as a factor in either's inhibiting or facilitating conflict resolution. On the international scale, Palestine was a powerful wedge dividing the United States from the Arab world, but it was also true that the conflict in Palestine made American communication with the Arabs more essential, and their mutual relationship required each to exert influence over their preferred ally in the conflict. It is essential to have a realistic assessment that the close U.S.-Israeli relationship is one of the key levers to a possible change in Israeli readiness for peace, and that the Arab states' relationship to the Palestinians should become an effective, subtle lever of change on Hamas and the Palestinian Authority. The coordination of these two very different forms of influence is one of the challenges to peace diplomacy that must be met in the coming years. Without the United States establishing a firm trusted partner relationship with one or more Arab states to that end, the peace process will continue to stumble.

CHAPTER 10

FROM THE WAR OF IDEAS TO THE PEACE OF IDEAS

The post-9/11 war against Al Qaeda, which led to a war in Afghanistan and a war against Iraq, could not be concluded in a satisfactory manner by military means. Though terrorists need to know that they will be hit hard anytime they emerge, and must learn that democratic nations are strong enough, in will and in military capability, to overcome their vulnerability to terrorist attacks, the long-term war will be one not of guns and bombs but of ideas. Because the enemy is not an organized military force that can be defeated in one pitched battle, or even in a series of battles, it is necessary to diminish this enemy's appeal—to drastically reduce the popularity of its total war approach to conflict with Israel and/or the United States, which recruits highly motivated youth and turns them into killers willing to target civilians.

A war of ideas is being waged among competing views of what is the good life for a young Muslim in the twenty-first century. What are the evils that must be eliminated to make that life as good as it can be for the millions of young Muslims, especially Arab Muslims? In the relations between the West and the world of Islam, and especially the Arabs who inhabit that world, a vital element of the definition of "the good life" is a sense of feeling respected and living with dignity. The first step for those in the West who monitor and indeed affect that struggle is to learn how to listen to and talk with these young people and their elders. We must shed our habit of talking down to them. By showing them respect and giving them equal standing, we can help them be more confident and freer to talk forthrightly with each other. Then, if we listen carefully, we will be able to hear with critical empathy. Perhaps then they will be able to talk with us more openly and honestly. This means a genuine interaction, no longer with the colonized addressing the colonizer. The present discourse is a form of strategic communication, designed not to share one's authentic feelings but rather to propitiate, deflect, and/or delude the other.

If we can communicate mutual respect, they should be able to talk to us from within the framework of their faith and from within the aspirations of their future, and maybe this will reach more deeply into our souls, so that we can begin to put aside the dialogue of stereotype and hegemony. We might learn to express our deeper commitments, demonstrating our inner life rather than our power and wealth.

We have to hear more clearly the voices of their faith and learn to respond with the voices of our several faiths, or our lack of faith. Only with such communication will we be able to uncover the truth of our shared humanity and begin to rediscover the culture in which we can all live with respect for each other under the One God, and put aside the distorted glass through which we see each other with so much anger, fear, and resentment.

If we are able to start a dialogue based on this sense of shared humanity, we might be able to move beyond their perception of us—that is, the United States—as an oversize brute power that is so large it occludes their view even of each other and threatens to render them indiscernible. Our light is seen to outshine all others, sacrilegiously intruding on their sense of the sacred. This anxious self-awareness, in which many young Arab people become preoccupied, by the social comparison between the size of America's impact on contemporary history compared with that of their own culture, generates in some of their youth a desire to create events of spectacular visibility, the kind of visibility that manifests in stunning acts of defiant violence and terrorism. They defy their invisibility by erupting into our line of sight. For them, better to be hated and feared than to be ignored and dismissed.

The main positive contribution of the administrations of the two presidents Bush and President Clinton to the saga of U.S.–Middle East relations was their common decision to make the Middle East the central focus of American foreign policy and national security during a period when political Islam was emerging as a major force of world instability. Their doing so was a greater-than-ever challenge to the emerging identity of a modern Middle East, even more than Nasserism during the Eisenhower administration.

This turning of American strategic and foreign policy attention to the Middle East should have given the United States an opportunity to complete and correct the work left undone by Woodrow Wilson when he entered the post–World War I world reorganization scene. Sadly, he did not have enough of a grasp of either domestic American politics or the complications of European conflict and imperial power rivalries. Thus, he could not make a lasting contribution to the solution of the problems of Ottoman Empire succession. Indeed, he created expectations that would not be met, which only made the possibility of success of the mandate approach even less likely. Eisenhower and Dulles tried to turn the Middle East in a more America-friendly direction through the cold war rivalry with the Soviet Union, but they could not harness the strong nationalist excitement of their era, and before long they were in trouble in Iran, Egypt, and Syria. They did make a false start, though an interesting one, on the Arab-Israeli conflict with the Alpha and the Omega efforts. Overall, Eisenhower's administration made the United States more the target of the Arabs' nationalist anger than their champion or friend.

Now, after the administration of George W. Bush, the United States has been designated the primary target of the new ideological excitement, generated this time not by socialism or nationalism, but by an Islamicist search for power and glory. Its passionate hatred is directed intensely toward the United States, with special focus on

America's use of military power, which is resented for its strengthening of what are seen as corrupt regimes not completely enough Islamic. These regimes of course use their own power to suppress Islamic revolution, and often do so with deadly success. Moreover, U.S. power is considered the critical buttress to Israeli power and its ability to continue to occupy Arab land four decades after the 1967 War. Finally, Islamic fundamentalists see American dominance as forcing a regional order upon these Muslim majority societies that they cannot tolerate, or even integrate, into their traditional worldview.

Eisenhower and Dulles hoped to recruit Arab enthusiasm to the fight against communism. They ended up only focusing Arab nationalism against America as its most powerful foe. Now the United States is again failing to find an idea that can compete with the anti-American ideas of Bin Laden and Islamic radicalism. Instead of proposing a competing vision, America has generated, through its overwhelming use of military power, an intense boomerang effect that has succeeded in making those anti-American ideas even more powerful, and more central to the new wave of ideological fervor.

The United States has focused its attention on regime change through force-fed democracy. This was to be the solution to the genuine problem of finding a source of legitimacy for these new, independent Arab states. Such legitimacy was supposed to have been the result of this imposed democracy, which was to fill the vacuum of legitimacy that emerged from the lack of widespread loyalty to the regime and consent of its people. Moreover, such legitimacy would have provided the basis for a true national solidarity. Such an attachment to the state as a source of pride and development could have come to outweigh the attachment to tribe, ethnicity, region, and religion that had won the deepest loyalty of the masses. There has to be a true transformation of these weak states from having a leadership remarkable for its corruption or repression to one identified for its provision to the people of a sense of pride and of the economic and educational benefits of a modern nation-state.

At the same time, America has shown no openness to what it has learned or come to respect in the enthusiasm of Islamic Arabs for their religious culture and their sense of solidarity with other Arabs. The ability of the Arabs to maintain cohesiveness across national boundaries at a time when their overall culture had low status in the world should be seen not as a threat to the West but as an admirable quality of cultural maintenance. We have not given enough attention to understanding and relating to the internal struggles of the Islamic and Arab worlds so that they would be perceived not as the target of American wrath but as a fellow human community, to which Americans could and would offer a hand of friendship and cooperation as they struggle through the difficult early stages of economic and social development. We need to understand that trying to dominate them has turned out to be only the guarantee against our being a leader in facilitating their pursuit of their own solution to governance legitimacy and competence in modernity and development policy. Successive U.S. administrations chose a partial slice of the problem on which to focus, and each failed to resolve their particular slice. Saddam Hussein wanted to lead the Arab world into the post–cold war period and toward an unrealizable desire to reduce Western superpower hegemony. Afghanistan insurgency had been part of the cause of the decline and demise of the Soviet Union. Now Saddam wanted to lead a process that would bring the world from two superpowers—not only to one, as in Afghanistan—to none.

The Bushes, each in his own way, emphasized the need to confront and defeat militarily this Saddam regime and his stale resurgence of the worst version and distortion of Arab nationalism and militarism. George H. W. Bush successfully put together a widely based coalition to eject Saddam from Kuwait. He used the influence he earned to launch a major effort at dealing with the Arab-Israeli problem, but the sequence left unsolved the future of security in the Gulf region. He retained a large American military presence in Saudi Arabia, which lingered long after the twin troubles of the Iran-Iraq War and the war to eject Iraq from Kuwait. The problems remained: first, the lack of strategic security in a Saddam regime defeated but unchastened in its approach to the world; second, a Saudi regime internally threatened by its courageous military decisions unaccompanied by parallel decisions to prepare its own society for the future, and for the presence on its territory of the American military; third, an Iran emboldened by the removal of its threatening enemy's military capability, without any solution to the underlying Iranian alienation from Pax Americana and its fear that Pax Americana would turn into threats against the mullah regime of Iran.

George W. Bush went much further with his military confrontation of the Saddam regime, without gaining a single Arab ally. (Bush Sr. had had great, even remarkable, military success and yet enough self-discipline to refrain from conquering an Arab capital.) The war itself and the massive American military presence in Saudi Arabia, combined with Saddam's propaganda barrage, reinforced old Arab nationalist resentments and stereotypes. These included concerns about Israel, and about the United States as lead player in defending Israel and as the representative of neo-imperial control of the Arab world. Most problematic for the security of the region's regimes were perceptions of America as the power behind hated and corrupt Arab governments. This barrage of anachronistic Arab nationalist rhetoric was a catalyst for the explosive anti-American reaction a decade later among Islamic radicals, who had learned to link traditional passion for Islam to the anger stoking anti-imperialism and anti-Zionism. It mattered little that America's approach to the Middle East had shown itself under Bush Sr. to be far from imperialistic in its motivation: he resisted the temptation to conquer and occupy Iraq, and launched a major effort at implementing UN Resolutions 242 and 338, which arguably failed because of his weak relationship with Israel, rather than from weakness of resolve.

By the late nineties, Islamic radicals had come to understand how their power could be maximized. They would have to claim to advance not only the religious cause but the nationalist one as well. They would have to pose as the most virulent opponents of foreign control and the strongest advocates of anti-imperialism.

The Islamicist cause was strengthened by a combination of the successful emergence of Hizbollah in driving America from Lebanon through terrorism and the growing power of Hamas in Palestine. Hamas appeared as a noncorrupt Palestinian leadership, aggressively willing to ensure that no Palestinian would be killed without an Israeli being killed immediately after. Often these acts of violence were carried out with great visibility and drama—by blowing up Israeli cafés, restaurants, and buses in the heart of Jerusalem or Tel Aviv. Here was a Palestinian movement devoted to making Israeli life miserable. In my most intense discussions with Hamas leadership, they strained to show that they had learned that Palestinian masses cared little for their search to reestablish the caliphate; what the masses did care about was that Hamas was a major force toward ending Israeli occupation. Unlike the widespread caricature of PLO leaders, Hamas leaders did not cavort in European five-star hotels.

Perhaps the most damaging to Arab politics of Saddam's rhetorical flourishes was his denunciation of Arab oil wealth as just another example of regime corruption and misuse of public resources. What had been a promise to turn oil into a means of jump-starting an era of Islamic resurgence was, in Saddam's view, just another example of regime abuse of Arab national resources for personal gain. Saddam's rhetoric was not effective enough to bring forth Arab support for his invasion of Kuwait, but it was strong enough to intensify hatred of Arab regimes among many Arabs. His rhetoric fostered hatred that was key to the later success of Bin Laden and other Islamic ideologues and political revolutionaries. His words linked resentment against the Saudi and other Arab regimes (especially that of Egypt) to the easily aroused hatred of Israel, and to renewed anger at the United States. This combination of factors exploded against the United States during the George W. Bush administration, and the American people were not equipped to grasp the real connection.

The Bin Laden and Al Qaeda phenomenon was in part the unintended result of the Reagan administration's policy of developing professional Arab terrorists to fight an anti-Soviet action in Afghanistan. Beyond Afghanistan, an anti-American animus in Saudi Arabia and elsewhere grew out of the half-defeat of Saddam in the first Gulf War, followed by ill-designed sanctions that victimized the long-suffering Iraqi masses and only furthered Saddam's central-ized control of all economic power in Iraq. Legitimate commerce was replaced by smuggling and a corrupt Oil-for-Food Program that en-riched Saddam and his cronies and crushed the small but important Sunni middle class of Baghdad. Many Arab commentators saw the United States and even the United Nations as insensitive to the starva-tion of children in Iraq, and concocted a conspiracy theory in which America kept the despised Saddam in power while destroying Iraq's middle class and impoverishing and weakening a great Arab state.

Saddam's rhetoric and his use of Scuds against Israel had an espe-cially distorting impact on Palestinian political realism. Not since Sa-dat's crossing of the Suez Canal had Palestinians seen an Arab leader carry out and implement threats against Israel and succeed in inculcat-ing fear in the usually unruffled citizenry of Tel Aviv. This played very well among the Palestinians, given their incendiary mix of exis-tential despair and fantasies of redemption by a military defeat of Is-rael. Saddam made them believe for a moment that there was indeed a military answer to Israeli power in the region, a fantasy that rein-forced the disgust for Palestinian politics in large parts of Israeli soci-ety and areas in the Arab states. Saddam's call to arms made Arafat a still weaker leader than he otherwise might have been going into the negotiations sponsored by the United States in Madrid. Arafat had alienated the Gulf Arabs by his and his people's support for Saddam, which had led to the expulsion of the Palestinian exile community from Kuwait, the Palestinian community that had been the most pro-ductive and successful of the Palestinian diaspora. This was costly to Arafat, both diplomatically and economically, in his relationship with Gulf Arabs. It lost him his most uniformly supportive exiles. He also lost the respect of many in his own elite, who saw his behavior in the war as a foolish indulgence that had visited yet another catastrophe upon his people, this time in Kuwait, and had left the people of the West Bank and Gaza bereft of political support at the war's end.

At the same time, the great enthusiasm for Saddam and his illusion of power among Palestinian communities in Jordan was too strong for King Hussein to ignore. Whether the king believed it himself or simply felt that he could not distance himself so completely from the popular feeling of his countrymen, he played along with it. Old memories of lost Hashemite glory in the Gulf were aroused in him, and he chose to follow a policy consistent with his family's traditional belief that to invite foreign forces to resolve an inter-Arab dispute was a shameful failure that could only increase the level of foreign control in their lives. Paradoxically, this very popular defiance of American leadership gave King Hussein the maneuvering room to make the peace with the Israeli prime minister Rabin in the early nineties that broke his dependence on a never-to-happen prior Syrian peace initiative, an initiative he would still be waiting for in the grave. Thus King Hussein was able to use the break with the United States that took place after the Saddam invasion of Kuwait to free himself from the self-imposed Jordanian straitjacket that would not permit Jordan to make an open peace with Israel until the Syrian regime had made one first. But he now felt that he had enough idiosyncrasy credits[1] from his defiant stance to the United States in 1990 to allow his independent initiative for peace while Rabin was still in power.

Meanwhile, Arafat had weakened himself further by seeming to endorse Palestinian enthusiasm for Saddam's missile aggression against Israeli citizens. The Scud attacks rekindled the attraction of the old strategy of focusing on hurting Israel rather than having Palestinians reach for their own strategic goal of self-determination. This further complicated Arafat's difficult task of making the epic compromises necessary to fully implement the Oslo Accords of mutual recognition between Israel and the PLO. He could not definitively break from the Palestinian tradition of employing violent resistance to Zionism as an essential tool of Palestinian politics and advocacy, even when that tool was becoming ever more self-destructive and even when the international community, including the United States, had moved this issue to the top of its agenda. By the time Arafat's successor, Abu Mazen, had declared the end of armed struggle, Fatah had become too weak to transform that decision into a peace agreement with Israel.

This virtual addiction to the politics of violence against Israel was

rekindled by Saddam and reinforced by the new Islamic fundamentalism. It deprived the Palestinians of the chance to take full advantage
of Israeli willingness, for the first time in history, to make a peace
agreement with the Palestinian national movement. The full authority
of the United States was behind the idea of such an agreement, and it
fell squarely within the context of international law and UN resolutions. After all, such resolutions had been supported by the Arab
states and the Israelis, and indeed by the PLO itself. After the Kuwait
war, Arafat was told in no uncertain terms by his colleagues in the
nonaligned movement that they wanted this problem solved, that the
solution contained within Resolutions 242 and 338 was possible, and
that they were sick and tired of this issue dominating the UN agenda.
Still, Arafat could not bring himself to set aside the rusty and ineffective tools of his youth to rise to the new stature of international
statesman, even though he had been invited to do so at the most distinguished levels.

In this way, the forceful efforts by President Clinton during the
last year of his second term could not succeed, and Clinton's presidency ended with a new explosion of Palestinian-Israeli violence.
Clinton's focus on the Palestinian question had left the Saddam-Iraqi
issue to fester and erupt when George W. Bush, Clinton's successor,
decided to avenge the terrible attacks by Bin Laden on New York and
Washington by crushing Saddam Hussein in Iraq.

This rekindling of old attitudes by Saddam and Hamas had also
distanced Arafat from the support of many in the Palestinian elite.
They knew that new approaches were needed to take advantage of
the Rabin era in Israel and of the post-cold-war era in international
politics. Arafat, instead of integrating the new Palestinian Westernized elite into his brain trust, saw them becoming more and more
alienated from him and his outmoded style of tribalistic leadership.

Indeed, it is one of the sad aspects of American political and
diplomatic intelligence of these post-cold-war years that the United
States could not grasp the relationship between its Gulf security initiatives and Israeli-Palestinian issues. Saddam's invasion of Kuwait
was closely linked to the collapse of the Baker Five Points initiative of

1988, which was designed to bring about a Cairo-mediated Israeli-Palestinian dialogue. This idea failed in early 1990 and drove Arafat away from his dependence on Egypt and into the arms of Saddam and back to terrorist attacks on Israel. Saddam felt more confident of Arab support as a result of the breakdown of Israeli-Palestinian diplomacy. In turn, he offered Arafat and the Palestinians the seductive fantasy of an Arab military equalizer.

This linking of Gulf issues with the Palestinian issue emerged again sharply with the outbreak of the Second Intifada in 2000. Israel's evident military superiority and success in the repression of the Palestinians became a backdrop to a renewed wave of Arab hatred of Israel and the United States. This time the impact of the intifada was magnified by the Arab satellite media penetration of "the Arab street." In the heyday of Arab nationalism, the preferred term for discussing and describing the Arab populations of these newly independent Arab states was "Arab masses." This term, borrowed from socialist and Communist rhetoric, did not give much analytic understanding of Arab society. As the Arab middle class, including the intelligentsia, became a more noticeable stratum in the post-Nasser era, it became important to distinguish between this middle class and the lower strata of Arab society, who were far more populous and far less educated and independent in their thinking. This class included the many rural people and the large influx to the cities of the poor, who created the extensive slums and zones of abject poverty. Populations exploded in many of these countries, especially Egypt and Iran, and migration from rural areas to cities in search for a viable source of income created a large population no longer integrated into the organic communities of a small farming village. It began to be clear that the state leaders were losing their monopoly over what the people knew and how they came to know it. It also became more clear that this stratum of society, with its capacity for mobilization and its responsiveness to radio and television, had become an important force in Arab politics, a force that could no longer be expected to passively accept the actions and words of the leader. "The Arab street" responded to the events around them with an emotional intensity that precluded a strategic balance between their anger and rational assessment of the consequences of harsh or precipitous action against the object of their anger. So, for example, an Egyptian president or a Jordanian king would carefully weigh, at least in theory, his emotional reaction to some disappointment with the United States against the knowledge of his dependency on a good relationship with the United States. "The Arab street" felt free to declaim its indignation and anger and often even resented the leader's balanced approach. In this way the image of the Arab leader as authoritarian dictator required emendation because "the Arab street" now had to be part of the leader's calculation and could be a genuine constraint on that leader. The state was no longer a strong state and the leader was no longer a strong leader. Society was more divided and leaders could much less easily make decisions that would be implemented by all of their people. During the periods of the intifada, the broadcasts from Arab satellite television provided immediate and continual depictions of Palestinian defeat and suppression and Israeli military dominance, thus provoking the anger in "the Arab street" against Israel and the United States, but more and more frequently against their own leadership for its inability and even unwillingness to confront Israel militarily.

This time there was no fantasy that Saddam could even the balance. The Palestinians pursued a no-holds-barred campaign of terror against Israeli citizens. At the same time, the broadcast of the Palestinian story left no likelihood that any Arab state or coalition would even think of helping the United States deal with the broken Iraqi military power. The Arab priority was to face down Israeli military superiority. The absence of any determined American opposition to Israel's use of force precluded the United States from having any chance of gaining Arab support in opposing Saddam. It also left the scene open for a renewed paroxysm of anti-American hatred. This gap in American understanding of how the widely broadcast Palestinian defeats could prevent any Arab empathy for America's worries over Saddam also led to the demise of the effectiveness of Colin Powell as U.S. secretary of state. Powell had been sent on the fool's errand of mobilizing the Arabs against Saddam while offering no respite to the Palestinians. Eventually, this left him with no authority and no credibility, especially when he vouched for the existence of Saddam's weapons of mass destruction, which never did materialize.

At the same time, the Palestinians themselves were desperately seeking a military means of destabilizing Israel and equalizing a highly uneven battlefield. Saddam had aroused a generation of Arabs, and Palestinians in particular, by his fantasy of mass destruction. The Palestinians transformed this fantasy into a reality through the eruption of mass terrorism. Saddam had revived an obsolete idea that there could be a magic Arab bullet that could penetrate the heart of Israeli power and sense of superiority. However, Iraq could not, under Saddam, undergo the deep structural changes that would have made it a real threat.

Saddam wanted to prevent the emergence of the age of a single world power, when that world power would be an America allied with the Jewish state of Israel. He wanted to end the problem of Arab poverty, and especially of rich states and poor states (at the same time as he was impoverishing his own people), by forcing a sharing of the Gulf's oil wealth with the masses. He wanted to challenge Israeli hegemony in the Mashreq with the development of superweapons, including weapons of mass destruction, to be delivered by missiles. He succeeded in none of this. He only aroused in elements of the Arab world their failing hopes, and their antidote was greater hatred than ever. His pretensions helped to delay for decades the real progress that would have come from decisions for peace and the determined efforts to educate both boys and girls that must underlie any hopes for development. Saddam had successfully indoctrinated another generation of Arab intelligentsia with the belief that its problems were externally imposed, and he led that intelligentsia to again specialize in blaming external enemies for Arab underdevelopment.

In this post-Saddam decade, the Arab intellectual has had at his disposal the powerful new tool of enhanced international telecommunication. This tool, however, was at first not used to lift the masses with new, inspiring ideas. These modern technologies were not used to generate excitement for education, critical thinking, or a new religious depth of rethinking of universalizing the powerful message of the Prophet. Instead, the Arab world wasted the tool by using it to deepen and spread hatred, to blame others and keep Islam a religion of internal obedience and not a passion for shared justice in society and in the world system. In this turn of the kaleidoscope, a full generation after Nasser and Khomeini, it has meant that Islam, and not secular nationalism, would become the dominant idiom, only deepening the problem of educational and scientific underdevelopment in the Arab world.

The short perspective of time in American society, where each presidential administration is seen as a separate historical era, only foreshortens the ability to link phenomena and understand them in sufficient depth, rather than as personal foibles of particular presidents. We emphasize so much the distinctions among the presidents—Reagan, Bush Sr., Clinton, and Bush Jr.—that we cannot see how the problematic world relationships we suffer over the years are linked. The defeat of Saddam in 1991 and the arousal of the rhetoric of Arab nationalism to a new shrill intensity in the Saddam form were the true links of Al Qaeda to Iraq—not the operational link that the George W. Bush administration heralded.

The popular belief core of hostility consisted of hatred toward America and Israel, and contempt for Arab regimes. On the American side, the link is the overconfidence that conventional military power can undermine such beliefs and defeat such forces. We have not been able to replace these core beliefs with a systematic approach to strengthening the moderate alternative version of Islam and of Arab societal development and improved governance. The sharp focus in the Arab world on dramatic acts of terror or on a frantic search to acquire weapons of mass destruction was a destructive detour. The remarkable effort of the Madrid Conference, with its multilateral framework of peace talks, could not move as fast as the pace of violence. Thus the slow accretion of new ideas in the multilateral process and its incremental structures of cooperation and trust seemed naive and irrelevant.

Clinton and his team came to know that the rise of Islamic terror was destroying their peace efforts. They had no formula for fighting it, either militarily or otherwise. Clinton constructed a show gathering of regional leaders, to meet with Prime Minister Peres of Israel and with President Mubarak of Egypt. However, this collective proclamation against terrorism only helped to convince the Israeli electorate further that they needed to put aside showy peace publicity for a strong arm of the idea. What was needed was a well-designed, serious regional strategy of counterterrorism, not a statement of intentions.

The Hashemite kingdom of Jordan, under King Hussein—continued to a certain extent under his successor, King Abdullah—tried to build on the themes of cooperation, economic opening, and rule of law. They were able to take full advantage of the short American historical memory of King Hussein's break with the United States in 1990 to rebuild the Jordanian-American relationship. Of course this was completely insufficient for convincing the American government that Jordan understood anything about Iraq that should make Cheney and Bush think again about which regimes would be most damaged by its "shock and awe" in the skies over Iraq.

America never took stock of how much the defeat of Iraq in 1991 left open wounds and lingering problems for the Saudis, and for relations among Gulf Arabs, on the one hand, and Syria and Egypt on the other, once the coalition of Riyadh, Cairo, and Damascus fell apart, as all preferred to relate to Washington as the hub of the wheel. The Clinton administration was not very well focused on these issues as it turned with great attention to the Arab-Israeli issues and did not work effectively on its relations with the Saudis or with the other key Arab states. America's division of those issues has not helped it serve its own interests.

It is hard for the foreign policy community to think about Arab national consciousness as an overall factor in America's security and international relations. We focus on the nation-states and the oil issues and do not think about the identity questions and the core issue of national dignity. Because we think in state terms, we think of power in state terms. However, we need to understand the underlying power of the idea of national solidarity and the importance of collective dignity as a fundamental mode of force. Sometimes the Saudis themselves imagine that these are distant issues, and therefore it has been hard, until recently, for them to work effectively with Egypt and others on these big-picture questions, which inevitably involve the United States and Israel. The Arab Summit structure, with its irregular meetings and lack of systematic follow-up, is a very ineffective one for making these issues strongly felt and understood in the international political system. The Arab League has become a very weak organization because the individual states insist on making all the decisions themselves.

The Arab national idea no longer calls for the creation of a single unified Arab state. In this, the state system among the Arabs has succeeded in putting behind it the dominant idea that brought fear of unity to Arab leaders for decades. Pan-Arabism, it was believed, would lead to the domination of weaker states by the more powerful ones, especially Nasser's Egypt. When Egypt and Syria formed the United Arab Republic, Syrian nationalists hated the way Nasser gave all the powerful positions to Egyptians, and how Syrians, both military and civilian, were assigned subsidiary roles. This failed attempt at unity, producing great resentment and an aversion to the advocacy of Arab unity in this form, contributed to the denuding of the Arab League of any semblance of power. Now that Arab nationalism can no longer mean the creation of a single unified state, it is possible to imagine an Arab unity accepting the separate states but seeking to be a shared voice for Arab aspirations in the international community.

Still, the Arab world has not yet developed any structure that would effectively bring the Arabs a voice of collective wisdom and dialogue with the world community. What is left of Arab nationalism is a depth of popular feeling of solidarity and shared culture. However, there is no way that dealing with the states alone can give us a true comprehension of regional politics or of these intense commitments within societal subgroups. An understanding of these subgroups, not only the states, has to be integrated into our foreign policy, for they are the repositories of very strong feelings of particular identity, and often these intense commitments to a subgroup identity are what drive action agendas and can come to dominate regional politics with extremist ideology and even terrorism.

Thus the national feeling is expressed through the new mass media, through the sermons of highly politicized ulama, groups of learned preachers of Islam, and through those few intellectuals or popular opinion leaders who identify the national issues of the day and the correct patriotic approach to them. This division between state leadership and sources of patriotic fervor weakens the state only more. Thus patriotic feeling is often expressed as anger toward outside forces and growing resentment of the inability of state leadership to protect people against wounds to national pride, wounds that can come to be the most keenly felt expressions of Arab patriotism.

The Arab state system needs to develop a mechanism that can corral and channel these strong feelings. Reining in the wild horse of these resentments cannot be the policy of any one country alone. It must be taken into consideration in Arab policy discussions with the international community. The age-old theory of divide and conquer, and of treating every Arab state as a separate entity, is sometimes a useful shortcut for the United States, but often is misleading in the longer run. This simplification does not weigh adequately the powerful currents in Arab public opinion, sometimes referred to as "the Arab street," which are not well articulated in the bilateral relations with the United States, but which can have a great impact on the real behavior of the Arab leaders when they are not in conversation with American power. National pride and collective dignity can become more important than power and wealth, and these less tangible factors must be more evident in the formulation of American and Western policies.

The problem is made more intense by the new media in the Arab world, which have achieved news dominance, and have thus taken it away from the regimes. The leaders of these states want to balance popular rage with the need for their military and economic relationship with the United States. In such a context, communication can become stilted, narrowly focused, and less than authentic. Communication across loyalties can also become suspect in such an environment. It is essential to model and develop modes of dialogue that strengthen the voice of moderation in which the Islamic mainstream can at least hold its own against the extremist minorities. The formal governmental dialogue has a more rational approach, giving priority to the relationships that have so many consequences for the economic and military strength of the nation. The new media specialize in bringing the "street" view as stridently as possible to public awareness, and can often intensify suspicion of foreign powers, their actions, and their words.

The domination of public discourse by Islamic fundamentalism has reinforced the tribal political culture in which trust of outsiders is enormously difficult and even discouraged by tribal leaders. Communication does not open up the person or group to empathize with others or even to truly hear them. The rise of Islamic rejectionist intellectuals and religious ideologues only intensifies the need for a wider dialogue in which hostile expressions and waves of animosity can be responded to with alternative modes of speaking and listening and can be balanced by the voices of moderation and the Islamic mainstream. The discourse of rejection, rage, and sense of wounded identity should not be the exclusive form of communication with and about America. So far, neither the Arab League nor the Organization of the Islamic Conference has used its forums for a wider dialogue across cultures and civilizations. The call for a dialogue of civilizations by Iran has not as yet been responded to in a way that is mutually educating the parties about the need to counter the growing pattern of group hatred in the world system.

Dialogue of this kind does not replace the need for a serious political exchange between the parties. Iran and the United States are at the top of the list of those who must make a breakthrough into real dialogue of civilizations and wide-ranging political exploration and negotiation. Syria and the United States are not far behind. But all of this must be in the context of the gradual extension of dialogue beyond governments to the spectrum of opinion leaders in the cultures. We must overcome the American resistance to including religious leaders in dialogues. The United States is a more religion-centered society than most European countries, and yet it has a strong constitutional concept of separation of church and state. This is an important part of American political culture, but it does not apply to others outside of America, and cannot successfully apply to relations with the peoples and problems in the world of Islam and the Arab domain, nor to dealing with Israel.

Clinton's two terms suppressed at least temporarily the ethnic war in Yugoslavia, one region of the Ottoman Empire that had to be reorganized after World War I. The Clinton administration intensively picked up the work on Israel in the Arab world, but did not make headway in putting forward an image of how to go from cease-fires and political agreements to reconciliation of the hundred-year war between Jews and Arabs. Without success in the political approach and without the launching of any reconciliation process, it is no surprise that violence broke out again when the perfect solution was not found. Neither Bush/Baker nor Clinton could focus on the reduction of hatred as a cultural/religious/historic legacy. The outcome of the failed efforts by Clinton, the failing war of George W. Bush in Iraq, and the continuing fear of greater Islamic terrorism directed at the United States has been a sharp escalation in the severity of the Israeli-Palestinian conflict, the intensity of Arab hatred of the United States, and venom in America toward the Muslim world. Even with respect to the countries with which the United States has had a close relationship for many years—Saudi Arabia and Egypt—suspicion and distrust have outpaced shared struggle against the problems.

Moreover, these last years have consolidated a mutual contempt between Jews and Arabs that is very dangerous, not only for both of them, but also for the development of any process of reconciliation between the West and the Arab world, particularly between the United States and the Muslim world. It is not emotionally possible, and probably only marginally intellectually reasonable, to segregate this issue of tension between the Islamic peoples and the United States from the question of Israel's relationship to the Arabs. Of course this is particularly true of the Palestinian question, which is such an emotionally volatile issue for so many Arabs everywhere, and for Diaspora Muslims and Jews. It is important, moreover, to realize that these issues are deeply intertwined with the long history of complex relations among the Abrahamic faiths—Judaism, Christianity, and Islam—which are separated so much by what they share, including the sacredness of Jerusalem.

Some observers have become resigned to the notion that anything the United States does will be taken as rubbing salt in the wounded dignity of the Arab world. The history of Arab relations with the West is one that requires healing. Therefore, the idea of benign neglect is often proposed rather than recognizing the need for an activist American civil society engaged with Arab civil society so that equal status relationships can be established. To overcome despair over these relationships, which is now so common, requires the elaboration in our imagination of a best-case scenario, instead of lingering constantly on all the worst-case scenarios. America must emphasize the development of one model of success, which will show that goodwill, intelligence, and mutual respect can in fact break the vicious circle of mutual suspicion.

Focusing America's policy effort on building one good partnership will require developing contexts of honest communication and of joint planning of a shared agenda that is beneficial to both sides and feels culturally authentic for each. This is not a shortcut, but requires as many resources as we now invest in preparing for the conflicts among us.

This effort must include breaking some of the false simplifications that reify mutual hateful stereotypes between Americans and Arabs and between Orientalism and Occidentalism, the paired mutual visions of contempt. The West will have to break the perception that it is concerned only with money and has no soul or religious commitment. There must be communication about what family means in each society, so that American families will no longer be represented by the images in sitcoms, and Arab families will no longer be stereotyped by the mistreatment of women. On both sides, there are varieties of values about the nature of family and the roles of women. And so communication on these issues is very important and very complex.

Perhaps it is too much to expect American presidents to grasp the enormity of the task of creating a context of mutual respect when so much of the American legacy has been to treat the Arab world as a secondary or derivative concern of U.S. foreign policy. It is also true that American anger at the devastation and murder on September 11, 2001, has not been erased, even by the powerful but partly misplaced revenge that the American military invasion of Iraq and Afghanistan rained down on parts of the Arab and Muslim world. Talking about a turn to communication and mutual respect may seem like a bridge too far, but unless we start to build that bridge, we will come to wallow more and more in the swamp of conflict and hatred. Both Americans and Arabs, Christians, Jews, and Muslims, must speak and think more about their shared humanity and their common desire to see a world of development, education, and ethical values become the core of their communication with each other and themselves.

The economic and social development of north and south together is the concern of some international institutions, even if there is controversy over those institutions' effectiveness. However, we have no equally powerful institutions that build understanding for both science and faith as mutually reinforcing rather than as enemies in a war they both lose. We have to go beyond the economic dimensions of these international inequities and tensions to the underlying educational, cultural, and value dimensions.

Bush Sr. and Baker went quickly from war in Iraq to the Madrid Conference, which was a bold and important step to try to take hold of the spiraling Israeli-Arab and Israeli-Palestinian conflict and the widening gap between the United States and the Muslim world. Baker was brilliant in adding the multilateral dimension to the peacemaking, with its economic, environmental, and arms control elements. However, he had neither the backing of the domestic American elite nor the idea bank necessary for a sustained and long-term focus on the cultural issues, including the issue of mutual hatred. Nor did he have the time or inclination to work slowly and consistently toward the necessary breakthroughs to winding down these conflicts. Thus these efforts did not penetrate deeply enough to win sufficient respect from Jews and Muslims, in order to sustain the process when taboos had to be broken.

We can only hope that the United States will now understand that going from the war of ideas to the peace of ideas requires engaging the leading intellectual, spiritual, and cultural resources of our society and those of the Muslim and Arab world and getting beyond the stranglehold of a triangle of the conflict among the United States, the Arabs, and Israel. This enormous project must be shared by Europe and could be an opportunity for a great new cooperation between the United States and Europe. This cultural and historical reconciliation and ensuring of mutual respect is a big responsibility that must be assumed in part by Europe. Europeans make a terrible historical error in thinking they can ally themselves with the forces attacking and undermining the United States and the Jews rather than assuming the role of reconciliation and higher understanding of the issues. Europe must see that this is the ultimate step in the resolution of the conflicts that divided it for so many years. The completion of the peace that emerged after World Wars I and II has to come to include Israel and the Arab states, the Jews and the Muslims. And Europe, whose modernity coincided with the struggle for a new identity of Jews and Arabs, should understand how to approach this reconciliation challenge.

George Bush, Sr., knew that the post–cold war period demanded a new world order, as Woodrow Wilson understood that the post–World War I environment demanded a new world order very different from the Great Power competition that had led to that devastating conflict. But President Bush was too much a part of the old world order to be able to accept that a new order would require no dominance by any one state. A new world order would give a place of honor and decision-making to peoples throughout the world.

George W. Bush inadvertently went very far in undermining the notion of American dominance but not to raise the banner of an international order respecting all faiths and providing a possibility of economic and social development to as much of the world as possible. The idea of one supreme power, a Christian power with a strong Jewish element, could not be acceptable to Muslims. For Islam, there is only one supreme power, Allah, God, and America's self-aggrandizement was treading on territory that could almost be defined as sacrilegious. It is also true that the great climate crisis, which threatens the planet on which we all live, has made it ever more necessary for all states, nations, and even non-state actors to recognize and give priority to our common fate. The conflicts that have been perpetuated from World War I, almost threatening to generate World War III, must be managed and then resolved with the full energy both of the main powers of the world and of those who most avidly pursue those conflicts, whether Israelis or Palestinians, Pakistanis or Indians, in Kashmir or elsewhere. The idea of a peaceful world order has long been an American dream, but to make it into policy requires enormous energy and focus and the ability to listen to others, hear them, and speak to them from the best of shared values. It is at that level of vision that we can articulate the concepts that would be more powerful than the war of ideas by creating a peace of ideas.

CHAPTER 1: WILSON SEARCHES FOR LEADERSHIP

1. August Heckscher, *Woodrow Wilson: A Biography* (New York: Collier Books, 1991).
2. Ibid., p. 435.
3. Herbert Hoover, *The Ordeal of Woodrow Wilson* (New York: McGraw-Hill, 1958), p. 25.
4. The Fourteen Points are as follows:

I. Open covenants of peace, openly arrived at, after which there shall be no private international understandings of any kind but diplomacy shall proceed always frankly and in the public view.

II. Absolute freedom of navigation upon the seas, outside territorial waters, alike in peace and in war, except as the seas may be closed in whole or in part by international action for the enforcement of international covenants.

III. The removal, so far as possible, of all economic barriers and the establishment of an equality of trade conditions among all the nations consenting to the peace and associating themselves for its maintenance.

IV. Adequate guarantees given and taken that national armaments will be reduced to the lowest point consistent with domestic safety.

V. A free, open-minded, and absolutely impartial adjustment of all colonial claims, based upon a strict observance of the principle that in determining all such questions of sovereignty the interests of the populations concerned must have equal weight with the equitable claims of the government whose title is to be determined.

VI. The evacuation of all Russian territory and such a settlement of all questions affecting Russia as will secure the best and freest cooperation of the other nations of the world in obtaining for her an unhampered and unembarrassed opportunity for the independent determination of her own political development and national policy and assure her of a sincere welcome into the society of free nations under institutions of her own choosing; and, more than a welcome, assistance also of every kind that she may need and may herself desire. The treatment accorded Russia by her sister nations in the months to come will be the acid test of their good will, of their comprehension of her needs as distinguished from their own interests, and of their intelligent and unselfish sympathy.

VII. Belgium, the whole world will agree, must be evacuated and restored, without any attempt to limit the sovereignty which she enjoys in common with all other free nations. No other single act will serve as this will serve to restore confidence among the nations in the laws which they have themselves set and determined for the government of their relations with one another. Without this healing act the whole structure and validity of international law is forever impaired.

VIII. All French territory should be freed and the invaded portions restored, and the wrong done to France by Prussia in 1871 in the matter of Alsace-Lorraine, which has unsettled the peace of the world for nearly fifty years, should be righted, in order that peace may once more be made secure in the interest of all.

IX. A readjustment of the frontiers of Italy should be effected along clearly recognizable lines of nationality.

X. The peoples of Austria-Hungary, whose place among the nations we wish to see safeguarded and assured, should be accorded the freest opportunity of autonomous development.

XI. Rumania, Serbia, and Montenegro should be evacuated; occupied territories restored; Serbia accorded free and secure access to the sea; and the relations of the several Balkan states to one another determined by friendly counsel along historically established lines of allegiance and nationality; and international guarantees of the political and economic independence and territorial integrity of the several Balkan states should be entered into.

XII. The Turkish portions of the present Ottoman Empire should be assured a secure sovereignty, but the other nationalities which are now under Turkish rule should be assured an undoubted security of life and an absolutely unmolested opportunity of autonomous development, and the Dardanelles should be permanently opened as a free passage to the ships and commerce of all nations under international guarantees.

XIII. An independent Polish state should be erected which should include the territories inhabited by indisputably Polish populations, which should be assured a free and secure access to the sea, and whose political and economic independence and territorial integrity should be guaranteed by international covenant.

XIV. A general association of nations must be formed under specific covenants for the purpose of affording mutual guarantees of political independence and territorial integrity to great and small states alike.

5. Lawrence E. Gelfand, *The Inquiry: American Preparations for Peace, 1917–1919* (New Haven, Conn.: Yale University Press, 1963), p. xi.
6. While the intent was to constitute the Inquiry with academics and experts, there were almost no political scientists, economists, historians, or even geographers who knew much about the world outside the United States and Western Europe. Even the most elite universities had a dearth of knowledge and scholarship about Asia, the Middle East, Eastern Europe, or Africa.
7. Margaret MacMillan, *Paris 1919: Six Months That Changed the World* (New York: Random House, 2002), p. 76.
8. Westermann's expertise was on the Middle East of the pre-medieval period.
9. Italy's aspirations focused on Trieste and border areas of Italy and Greece.
10. Heckscher, *Woodrow Wilson: A Biography*, p. 519.
11. MacMillan, *Paris 1919*, p. 102.
12. In the December 30, 1918, minutes of the Imperial War Cabinet, it is noted that Wilson made it clear that the most important issue to him was the creation of the League of Nations. It also states that an arrangement between Lloyd George and Wilson could be reached since Wilson seemed to have adopted fully the ideas of General Smuts (Arthur Link, ed., *The Papers of Woodrow Wilson* [hereafter *PWW*], vol. 53 [Princeton, N.J.: Princeton University Press, 1987], p. 558). Wilson's personal physician, Dr. Grayson, noted in a diary entry that Wilson was reading the plans for the League formulated by Smuts, and that Wilson thought "it would be good politics to play the British game 'more or less' in formulating the league covenant in order that England might feel her

views were chiefly to be embodied in the final draft, thus gaining British support that would be withheld from a personal program" (*PWW*, vol. 53, p. 622). See also *PWW*, vol. 53, pp. 515–19, "The League of Nations," prepared by Jan C. Smuts.

13. Wilson's idea was that choosing countries without imperial ambitions to take responsibility for developing these underdeveloped areas would be the alternative to the stark choice between imperial ambitions and premature independence.

14. The United States under Herbert Hoover had been involved with humanitarian efforts in Armenia. Wilson agreed that it might be a good thing for the United States to take on the mandate over Armenia, but he also knew that it was up to the American people (in the form of Congress) to make this decision. In 1920, Congress rejected the mandate for Armenia. In 1921, Communist Russia invaded Armenia, and that was the end of the question of an American mandate over the area.

15. Edward House and Charles Seymour, eds., *What Really Happened at Paris: The Story of the Peace Conference, 1918–1919* (New York: Charles Scribner's Sons, 1921), p. 178.

16. Hoover, *The Ordeal of Woodrow Wilson*, p. 225.

17. Point number XII of the Fourteen Points of Woodrow Wilson. See note 4.

18. *PWW*, vol. 59, pp. 330, 632–33.

19. House and Seymour, eds., *What Really Happened at Paris*, pp. 199–200.

20. *PWW*, vol. 54, pp. 231–32, 258; vol. 55, p. 386; vol. 57, pp. 326 n3, 406. Throughout his time in Paris, Wilson was in contact with Chaim Weizmann and other Jewish leaders. He was continually supportive of national aspirations and sensitive to the abuses the Jews of Europe had suffered.

21. *PWW*, vol. 61, June 21, 1919, p. 44.

CHAPTER 2: EGYPT

1. William Roger Louis and Roger Owen, eds., *A Revolutionary Year: The Middle East in 1958* (New York: I. B. Tauris; Washington, D.C.: Woodrow Wilson Center Press, 2002), p. 3.

2. Ray Takeyh, *The Origins of the Eisenhower Doctrine: The U.S., Britain, and Nasser's Egypt, 1953–57* (New York: St. Martin's Press, 2000), p. 1.

3. Ibid., p. 53.

4. Ibid., p. 68.

5. Ibid., p. 75.

6. Anthony Gorst and Lewis Johnman, *The Suez Crisis* (New York: Routledge, 1997), p. 54.

CHAPTER 3: IRAN

1. See Benjamin Shwadran, *The Middle East, Oil, and the Great Powers* (3rd ed.) (New York: Wiley, 1974), pp. 25–27, for the details of the Armitage-Smith Agreement.
2. The country was renamed Iran in 1935.
3. Shwadran, *The Middle East, Oil, and the Great Powers*, p. 48.
4. See ibid. Reza Shah "turned for his economic needs to Germany. Not only did he see in German technical know-how, scientific knowledge, and ideology advantages for his state, but also an excellent neutralizer against British influence and economic power."
5. It is important to note that the nationalist sentiment was not the only movement in Iran during the war. The Communist-controlled Tudeh Party was active in Azerbaijan and among the Kurds.
6. James A. Bill, *The Eagle and the Lion: The Tragedy of American-Iranian Relations* (New Haven, Conn.: Yale University Press, 1988), p. 4.
7. Steven Marsh, quoted in Bill, *The Eagle and the Lion*, p. 62.
8. Ibid., pp. 50–51.
9. Ibid., pp. 69–70.
10. Bill, *The Eagle and the Lion*, p. 92.
11. This conversation with Boutros-Ghali took place at the UN on January 17, 1991, the day after the Gulf War began.

CHAPTER 4: SAUDI ARABIA

1. Anthony Cave Brown, *Oil, God, and Gold: The Story of Aramco and Saudi Kings* (Boston: Houghton Mifflin, 1999), p. 2; H. St. John B. Philby, "Report of Najd Mission, 1917–1918" (Baghdad: Government Press, 1918), in the W. E. Mulligan Papers, Special Collections, Georgetown University Library, Washington, D.C.
2. MacMillan, *Paris 1919*, p. 384.
3. David E. Long, *The United States and Saudi Arabia: Ambivalent Allies* (Boulder, Colo., and London: Westview Press, 1985), p. 13.
4. Irvine H. Anderson, *Aramco, the United States, and Saudi Arabia: A Study of the Dynamics of Foreign Oil Policy, 1933–1950* (Princeton, N.J.: Princeton University Press, 1981), p. 32.
5. Ibid., p. 37.

CHAPTER 5: SYRIA

1. Bonnie Saunders, *The United States and Arab Nationalism: The Syrian Case, 1953–1960* (Westport, Conn.: Praeger, 1996), pp. 57–58.

2. Shlomo Gazit, *The Carrot and the Stick: Israel's Policy in Judaea and Samaria, 1967–68* (Washington, D.C.: B'nai B'rith Books, 1995), p. 14.

3. Warren Bass, *Support Any Friend: Kennedy's Middle East and the Making of the U.S.-Israel Alliance* (Oxford, U.K., and New York: Oxford University Press, 2003), p. 240.

4. Henry Kissinger, *White House Years* (Boston: Little, Brown, 1979), p. 778.

CHAPTER 10: FROM THE WAR OF IDEAS TO THE PEACE OF IDEAS

1. The term *idiosyncrasy credits* was coined in 1958 by social psychologist Edwin Hollander, who explained that individuals could accumulate a group's acceptance of his deviations from their normative behavior by first demonstrating exceptional performance of the group's tasks.

BIBLIOGRAPHY

HUMAN SOURCES

My debt of gratitude to many people in the Middle East, in Washington, and elsewhere for help in my work over the last forty years is deep and extensive. This gratitude for their help, advice, and insight goes back to at least 1969, when Dean Krister Stendhal of the Harvard Divinity School was approached by a small group of his students who wanted to convene a conference on the Arab-Israeli conflict. Dean Stendhal did not want his school to be used as a site for a conference that would simply be an attack against Israel, so he insisted that these Christian and Muslim students include a Jewish Harvard graduate student in their planning group. He asked Rabbi Ben-Zion Gold, the Hillel rabbi at Harvard, to recommend a candidate. Rabbi Gold turned to me as the editor of *Mosaic*, the Jewish student magazine at Harvard. I met with these Divinity School students and we started to think through a list of invited speakers and subjects for the conference sessions.

BOOKS AND ARTICLES CONSULTED

Agha, H., S. Feldman, A. Khalidi, and Z. Schiff. *Track II Diplomacy: Lessons from the Middle East*. Cambridge and London: MIT Press, 2003.

Agha, H. J., and A. S. Khalidi. *Syria and Iran: Rivalry and Cooperation*. Great Britain: Chatham House Papers, 1995.

Ali, Tariq. *Shadows of the Pomegranate Tree*. London: Picador, 1992.

Aly, A.M.S., and S. Feldman. *Ecopolitics: Changing the Regional Context of Arab-Israeli Peacemaking*. Cambridge: Belfar Center for Science and International Affairs, 2003.

Amad, Adnan, ed. *Israeli League for Human and Civil Rights: The Shahak Papers* (Paper 46). Beirut: Palestine Research Center, 1973.

Anderson, I. H. *The United States and Saudi Arabia*. Princeton, N.J.: Princeton University Press, 1981.

Andleman, D. A. *A Shattered Peace: Versailles 1919 and the Price We Pay Today*. Hoboken, N.J.: John Wiley and Sons, 2008.

Azar, E. *The Emergence of a New Lebanon*. New York: Praeger, 1984.

Azrieli, Yehuda. *A Generation of the Knitted Kipah: The Political Revolution of the Youth of the National Religious Party* (Translated from the Hebrew). Israel: Avivim, 1990.

Barber, B. R. *Jihad vs. McWorld*. New York: Ballantine Books, 1996.

Bar-Zohar, Michael. *Ben Gurion: A Political Biography*. Vols. 1–3. Tel Aviv: Am Oved, 1977–78.

Bass, Warren. *Support Any Friend: Kennedy's Middle East and the Making of the U.S.-Israel Alliance*. Oxford, U.K., and New York: Oxford University Press, 2003.

Beilin, Yossi. *The Death of the American Uncle*. Tel Aviv: Miskal-Yedioth Ahronoth and Chemed, 1999.

————. *A Guide to an Israeli Withdrawal from Lebanon*. Israel: Hakibbutz Hameuchad, 1998.

Belof, M. *Imperial Sunset: Britain's Liberal Empire, 1897–1921*. Vol 1. London: Methuen and Co., 1969.

Ben-Ezer, Ehud. *Unease in Zion*. Tel Aviv: Am Oved, 1986.

Ben-Gurion, David. *The Restored State of Israel*. Tel Aviv: Am Oved, 1969.

Ben-Shahar, H., G. Fishelson, and S. Hirsch. *Economic Cooperation and Middle East Peace*. London: Weidenfeld and Nicolson, 1969.

Ben-Simon, Daniel. *A New Israel*. Tel Aviv: Aryeh Nir, 1997.

Benvenisti, Meron. *The Sling and the Club*. Jerusalem: Keter, 1988.

Bergman, R., and G. Meltzer. *The Yom Kippur War: Moment of Truth*. Tel Aviv: Miskal-Yedioth Ahronoth and Chemed, 2003.

Bill, James A. *The Eagle and the Lion: The Tragedy of American-Iranian Relations*. New Haven, Conn.: Yale University Press, 1988.

Bin Talal, H. *Palestinian Self-Determination: A Study of the West Bank and Gaza Strip*. London: Quartet Books, 1988.

Brecher, M. *Decisions in Israeli's Foreign Policy*. New Haven, Conn.: Yale University Press, 1975.

Brown, Antony Cave. *Oil, God, and Gold: The Story of Aramco and Saudi Kings*. Boston: Houghton Mifflin, 1999.

Burton, J. W. *Resolving Deep-Rooted Conflict: A Handbook*. Lanham: University Press of America, 1987.

Chaliand, G. *The Palestinian Resistance*. Middlesex, UK: Pelican, 1972.

Cherkaoui, M. *Morocco and the Sahara: Social Bongs and Geopolitical Issues*. Oxford, UK: Bardwell Press, 2007.

Chetrit, Nehoray-Meyer. *La terreur du rêve: Récite pique sur l'histoire Juive-Maroc*. Tel Aviv: Papyrus, 1983.

Choueiri, Y. *Islamic Fundamentalism*. Boston: Twayne, 1990.

Chubin, S. *Iran National Security Policy: Capabilities, Intentions and Impact*. Washington, D.C.: Carnegie Endowment, 1994.

Cohen, R. I., ed. *Vision and Conflict in the Holy Land*. New York: St. Martin's Press, 1985.

Cottam, R. W. *Nationalism in Iran*. Pittsburgh: University of Pittsburgh Press, 1979.

Crone, P. *God's Rule Government and Islam: Six Centuries of Medieval Islamic Political Thought*. New York: Columbia University Press, 2004.

Dankner, Amnon. *My Neighbour's Pesto Is Greener* (Translated from the Hebrew). Jerusalem: Keter, 1997.

Dodge, T. *Inventing Iran: The Failure of Nation-Building and a History Denied*. London: Hurst and Co., 2003.

Drysdale, A., and R. Hinnebusch. *Syria and the Middle East Peace Process*. New York: Council on Foreign Relations Press, 1991.

Eisenstadt, M. *Focus on Iran: Iranian Military Power Capabilities and Intentions*. Washington, D.C.: The Washington Institute for Near East Policy, 1996.

El Fadl, K. A. *Rebellion and Violence in Islamic Law*. Cambridge, UK: Cambridge University Press, 2001.

El Kenz, A. *Algerian Reflections on Arab Crises* (Translated). Austin: Center for Middle Eastern Studies, 1991.

Elon, Amos. *The Israelis: Founders and Sons*. New York: Penguin, 1981.

Enderlin, Charles. *Le rêve brisé: Histoire de l'échec du processus de paix au Proche-Orient*. Paris: Fayard, 2002.

————. *Shattered Dreams: The Failure of the Peace Process in the Middle East*. (Translated from the French). New York: Other Press, 2003.

Esposito, J. L. *The Islamic Threat: Myth or Reality?* New York: Oxford University Press, 1992.

Eyal, Yigal. *The First Intifada: The Oppression of the Arab Revolt by the British Army 1936–1939*. Tel Aviv: Ministry of Defense, 1998.

Feldman, Shai, ed. *Confidence Building and Verification: Prospects in the Middle East*. Jerusalem: Jafee Center for Strategic Studies, 1994.

Ferguson, N. *Empire: The Rise and Demise of the British World Order and the Lessons for Global Power*. London: Penguin, 2002.

Gazit, Shlomo. *The Carrot and the Stick: Israel's Policy in Judaea and Samaria, 1967–68*. Washington, D.C.: B'nai B'rith Books, 1995.

Gefland, L. E. *The Inquiry: American Preparations for Peace, 1917–1919*. New Haven, Conn., and London: Yale University Press, 1963.

Geniesse, Jane Fletcher. *Passionate Nomad: The Life of Freya Stark*. New York: Modern Library, 2001.

Ghilan, Maxim. *How Israel Lost Its Soul*. Harmondsworth, UK: Penguin, 1974.

Goode, James F. *The United States and Iran, 1946–1951*. Basingstoke, UK: Macmillan, 1989.

Gorst, A., and L. Johnman. *The Suez Crisis*. New York: Routledge, 1967.

Grabar, O. *The Dome of the Rock*. Cambridge and London: Harvard University Press, 2006.

Graham. R. *Iran: The Illusion of Power*. New York: St. Martin's Press, 1979.

Hamarneh, M., R. Hollis, and K. Shikaki. *Jordanian-Palestinian Relations: Where To? Four Scenarios for the Future*. London: The Royal Institute of International Affairs, 1997.

Hamilton, C. W. *Americans and Oil in the Middle East*. Houston: Gulf Publishing Co., 1962.

Harkabi, Y., ed. *Arab Lessons from Their Defeat*. Tel Aviv: Am Oved, 1972.

———. *Arab Strategies and Israel's Response*. New York: Free Press, 1977.

———. *Fedayeen Action and Arab Strategy*. Maarachot: Israeli Department of Defense, 1969.

Hart, A. *Arafat: A Political Biography*. Bloomington and Indianapolis: Indiana University Press, 1984.

Hart, P. T. *Saudi Arabia and the United States: The Birth of a Security Partnership*. Bloomington: Indiana University Press, 1998.

Hayerushalmi, Levy Ishak. *The Domineering Yarmulke*. Tel Aviv: Habbikutz Hameuchad, 1997.

Heckscher, A. *Woodrow Wilson: A Biography*. New York: Collier Books, 1991.

Heiss, M. *Empire and Nationhood: The United States, Great Britain, and Iranian Oil*. New York: Columbia University Press, 1997.

Hitti, P. K. *History of Syria Including Lebanon and Palestine*, Vol. 2. Piscataway, N.J.: Gorgias Press, 2002.

Hodgson, M.G.S. *The Venture of Islam: Conscience and History in a World Civilization; The Gunpowder Empires and Modern Times*, Vol. 3. Chicago: University of Chicago Press, 1974.

Hoover, H. *The Ordeal of Woodrow Wilson*. New York: McGraw-Hill, 1958.

Hourani, A. H. *Syria and Lebanon: A Political Essay*. London and New York: Oxford University Press, 1968.

House, Edward, and Charles Seymour, eds. *What Really Happened at Paris: The Story of the Peace Conference*. New York: Charles Scribner's Sons, 1921.

Husain, M. Z. *Global Islamic Politics* (2nd ed.). New York: Longman, 2003.

Ismael, T. Y. *Iraq and Iran: Roots of Conflict*. New York: Syracuse University Press, 1982.

Joyce, M. *Ruling Shaikhs and Her Majesty's Government, 1960–1969*. London and Portland, Ore.: Frank Class, 2003.

Jureidini, P. A., and R. D. McLaurin. *Beyond Camp David: Emerging Alignments and Leaders in the Middle East*. New York: Syracuse University Press, 1981.

Kedidi, A. *Islam-Occident: Un conflit millénaire . . . des croisades à la guerre du Golfe*. Paris: La Pensee Universelle, 1991.

Khadduri, M., and E. Ghareeb. *War in the Gulf: 1990–1991: The Iraq-Kuwait Conflict and Its Implications*. Oxford, UK: Oxford University Press, 1997.

Khalidi, R., L. Anderson, M. Muslih, and R. S. Simon, eds. *The Origins of Arab Nationalism*. New York: Columbia University Press, 1991.

Khalidi, W. *Conflict and Violence in Lebanon: Confrontation in the Middle East*. Cambridge, Mass.: Center for International Affairs, Harvard University, 1979.

———. *Palestine Reborn*. London and New York: I. B. Tauris and Co., 1992.

Kinzer, S. *All the Shah's Men: An American Coup and the Roots of Middle East Terror*. Hoboken, N.J.: John Wiley and Sons, 2003.

Kissinger, Henry. *White House Years*. Boston: Little, Brown, 1979.

Klieman, Aharon. *A Double-Edged Sword: Israeli Defense Exports as an Instrument of Foreign Policy*. Tel Aviv: Am Oved, 1992.

Kotler, Yair. *The Starling and the Raven: Not for Nothing Did the Starling Follow the Raven, It Is of Its Kind*. Tel Aviv: Yaron Golan, 2002.

Lacey, R. *The Kingdom*. Oxford, UK: Fontana Collins, 1981.

Laqueur, W. *Confrontation: The Middle East and World Politics*. New York: Quadrangle/The New York Times Book Co., 1974.

———. *The Road to Jerusalem*. New York: Macmillan, 1968.

Lewis, B. *The Multiple Identities of the Middle East*. London: Weidenfeld and Nicolson, 1998.

———. *What Went Wrong? Western Impact and Middle Eastern Response*. New York: Oxford University Press, 2002.

Link, A., ed. *The Papers of Woodrow Wilson*. Vols. 53–59. Princeton, N.J.: Princeton University Press, 1987.

Long, David E. *The United States and Saudi Arabia: Ambivalent Allies*. Boulder, Colo., and London: Westview Press, 1985.

Louis, William Roger, and Roger Owens, eds. *A Revolutionary Year: The Middle East in 1958*. New York: I. B. Tauris; Washington, D.C.: Woodrow Wilson Center Press, 2002.

Lunt, J. *Hussein of Jordan*. London: Macmillan, 1989.

McDonald, J. W., and D. B. Bendahmane, eds. *Conflict Resolution: Track-Two Diplomacy*. Washington, D.C.: Foreign Service Institute, U.S. Department of State, 1987.

Mackey, S. *The Iranians: Persia, Islam, and the Soul of a Nation*. New York: Penguin, 1996.

McLoughlin, L. *Ibn Saud, Founder of a Kingdom*. New York: St. Martin's Press, 1995.

MacMillan, Margaret. *Paris 1919: Six Months That Changed the World*. New York: Random House, 2001.

Malik, H. C. "Between Damascus and Jerusalem: Lebanon and Middle East Peace" (Paper 45). Washington, D.C.: The Washington Institute for Near East Policy, 1997.

Ma'oz, M. *Ottoman Reform in Syria and Palestine 1840–1861: The Impact of the Tanẓimat on Politics and Society*. Oxford, UK: Clarendon Press, 1969.

———. *The Sphinx of Damascus*. Tel Aviv: Dvir, 1988.

Marr, P. *The History of Modern Iraq* (2nd ed.). Boulder, Colo.: Westview Press, 2004.

Mattar, P. *The Mufti of Jerusalem: Al-Hajj Amin al-Husayni and the Palestinian National Movement*. New York: Columbia University Press, 1988.

Ministry of Planning. *Plan for Economic and Social Development*. Hashemite Kingdom of Jordan, 1993–1997.

Morris. B. *Righteous Victims: The History of the Zionist-Arab Conflict, 1881–1999*. New York: Alfred A. Knopf, 1999.

Mosley, L. *Power Play: Oil in the Middle East*. New York: Random House, 1973.

Nasr, V. *The Shia Revival*. New York: Norton, 2007.

Netanyahu, Benjamin. *A Place Among the Nations: Israel and the World*. New York: Bantam Books, 1993.

Noyon, J. *Islam, Politics, and Pluralism: Theory and Practice in Turkey, Jordan, Tunisia, and Algeria*. London: The Royal Institute of International Affairs, 2003.

Nusseibeh, S. *Once upon a Country: A Palestinian Life*. New York: Farrar, Straus and Giroux, 2007.

Ophir, Adi, ed. *Real Time: Al-Aqsa and the Israeli Left*. Tel Aviv: Keter, 2001.

Oz, Amos. *The Slopes of Lebanon*. Tel Aviv: Am Oved, 1987.

Paris, T. J. *Britain, the Hashemites, and Arab Rule 1920–1925: The Sherifan Solution*. London: Frank Cass, 2003.

Penkower, M. N. *Franklin D. Roosevelt and the Palestine Imbroglio*. New York: Touro College, Graduate School of Jewish Studies, 1996.

Peres, S., and A. Naor. *The New Middle East*. New York: Henry Holt, 1993.

Perl, W. R. *The Four-Front War: The Most Daring Rescue Operation of the Century*. New York: Crown, 1979.

Perthes, V. *The Political Economy of Syria Under Asad*. London and New York: I. B. Tauris, 1995.

Petran, T. *Syria*. New York: Praeger, 1972.

Philby, H. St. John B. "Report of Najd Mission, 1917–1918." Baghdad: Government Press, 1918. In the W. E. Mulligan Papers, Special Collections, Georgetown University Library, Washington, D.C.

Pillar, P. R. *Terrorism and U.S. Foreign Policy*. Washington, D.C.: Brookings Institution Press, 2002.

Rabin, Yitzhak. *The War in Lebanon*. Tel Aviv: Am Oved, 1983.

Rabinovich, I. *Waging Peace: Israel and the Arabs, 1948–2003* (rev. ed.). Princeton, N.J., and Oxford, UK: Princeton University Press, 2004.

Rabinovich, I., and H. Zamir. *War and Crisis in Lebanon, 1975–1981*. Tel Aviv: Tel Aviv University.

Rahat, Menachem. *Shas, the Spirit and the Power: How Did Shas Triumph in Israeli Politics?* Tel Aviv: Alpha Tikshoret, 1998.

Reiss, Tom. *The Orientalist: Solving the Mystery of a Strange and Dangerous Life*. New York: Random House, 2005.

Rubinstein, D. *Arafat: A Portrait*. Tel Aviv: Zmora-Bitan, 2001.

Salibi, K. *Crossroads to Civil War: Lebanon 1958–1976*. London: Ithaca Press, 1976.

———. *A House of Many Mansions: The History of Lebanon Reconsidered*. London: I. B. Tauris, 1993.

Saunders, Bonnie. *The United States and Arab Nationalism: The Syrian Case, 1953–1960*. Westport, Conn.: Praeger, 1996.

Saunders, H. H. *The Other Walls: The Politics of the Arab-Israeli Peace Process*. Washington, D.C.: American Enterprise Institute for Public Policy Research, 1985.

Savir, U. *The Process: 1,100 Days That Changed the Middle East*. New York: Random House, 1998.

Sayigh, R. *Palestinians: From Peasants to Revolutionaries*. London and Atlantic Highlands, N.J.: Zed Books Ltd., 1979.

Schiff, Z., and A. Yaari. *Intifada*. Tel Aviv: Schocken, 1990.

Segev, S. *Crossing the Jordan: Israel's Hard Road to Peace*. New York: St. Martin's Press, 1998.

Segre, D. V. *A Crisis of Identity: Israel and Zionism*. Oxford, UK, and New York: Oxford University Press, 1980.

Shapira, A. *Land and Power*. Tel Aviv: Am Oved, 1993.

Shehadeh, R. *The Third Way: A Journal in the Life in the West Bank*. London: Quartet, 1982.

Sher, Gilead. *Just Beyond Reach: The Israeli-Palestinian Peace Negotiations 1999–2001*. Vols. 1–2. Tel Aviv: Miskal-Yedioth Ahronoth and Chemed, 2001.

Shlaim, A. *Collusion Across the Jordan*. New York: Columbia University Press, 1988.

Shwadran, Benjamin. *The Middle East, Oil, and the Great Powers* (3rd ed.). New York: Wiley, 1974.

Simon, R. S., M. Laskier, and S. Reguer, eds. *The Jews of the Middle East and North Africa in Modern Times*. New York: Columbia University Press, 2003.

Sivan, Emmanuel. *Arab Political Myths*. Tel Aviv: Am Oved, 1997.

Stevens, D. G. *Challenges to Peace in the Middle East*. New York: Longman, 2003.

Stocking, G. W. *Middle East Oil: A Study in Political and Economic Controversy*. Nashville, Tenn.: Vanderbilt University Press, 1970.

Stremlau, J. J., ed. *The Foreign Policy Priorities of Third World States*. Boulder, Colo.: Westview Press, 1982.

Susser, Asher. *The PLO After the War in Lebanon: The Quest for Survival*. Tel Aviv: Tel Aviv University, 1985.

Takeyh, Ray, *The Origins of the Eisenhower Doctrine: The U.S., Britain, and Nasser's Egypt, 1953–57*. Basingstoke, U.K.: Macmillan; New York: St. Martin's Press, in association with St. Anthony's College, 2000.

Teveth, S. *Ben-Gurion and the Palestinian Arabs from Peace to War*. New York: Oxford University Press, 1985.

———. *Ben-Gurion's Spy*. New York: Columbia University Press, 1996.

———. *The Curse of the Blessing*. Tel Aviv: Schocken, 1969.

———. *The Passion of David: The Life of David Ben-Gurion*. Jerusalem and Tel Aviv: Schocken, 1980.

Tsur, Muky. *Doing It the Hard Way*. Tel Aviv: Am Oved, 1976.

Tuma, E. H. *Peacemaking and the Immoral War: Arabs and Jews in the Middle East*. New York: Harper Torchbooks, 1972.

Twite, R., and T. Hermann, eds. *The Arab-Israeli Negotiations: Political Positions and Conceptual Frameworks*. Tel Aviv: Papyrus, 2003.

Van Dam, N. *The Struggle for Power in Syria*. London: Croon Helm, 1981.

Vassiliev, A. *The History of Saudi Arabia*. London: Saqi Books, 2000.

Wasserstein, B. *Divided Jerusalem: The Struggle for the Holy City* (2nd ed.). London: Profile, 2001.

Weinbaum, M. G. *Egypt and the Politics of U.S. Economic Aid*. Boulder, Colo.: Westview Special Studies on the Middle East, 1986.

Whetten, L. L. *The Canal War: Four-Power Conflict in the Middle East*. Cambridge, Mass., and London: MIT Press, 1976.

Yaari, E., E. Haber, and Z. Schiff. *The Year of the Dove*. Tel Aviv: Zmora, Bitan, Modan, 1980.

Yale, W. *The Near East: A Modern History*. Ann Arbor: University of Michigan Press, 1958.

Yaqub, S. *Containing Arab Nationalism: The Eisenhower Doctrine and the Middle East*. Chapel Hill: University of North Carolina Press, 1994.

ACKNOWLEDGMENTS

As this book first developed, my trusted research and administrative assistant was Jennifer Goldstein Klein. Jennifer was especially helpful with the library research, poring through the stacks at New York University, Columbia, and Yale. I am grateful for her thorough work, her ongoing encouragement, and her abiding commitment to this project.

As I discussed the ideas for this book with David Flicker, a friend from Montreal, he offered to assist me with revising my work. He has a remarkable command of the English language. The many days we worked together effected a miraculous transformation of my wide-ranging ideas and long, complex sentences into a highly readable manuscript. We completed chapter after chapter with great excitement, and David's technical skills, broad knowledge, and irrepressible humor made each day a joy.

At the final stages of editing, I worked with Muriel Jorgensen, a woman of excellent skills and outstanding energy who helped develop the manuscript with me for many long evenings to make sure everything was consistent with the best practices for book manuscripts.

Working with my editor, Paul Elie, senior editor at Farrar, Straus and Giroux, helped me clarify the thesis of my book and understand the value of a concise and clearly argued manuscript.

My three daughters, Tamara, Ayelet, and Maya, all have inspired me to be my best self and to persevere in my life's commitments despite the difficulties I incurred in my constant worldwide travels. The support and love of my life partner, my wife, Elaine, was the essential element that made this work, and indeed all of my life's work, possible. Her never-flagging encouragement has propelled me through many life challenges for more than forty years. She simply refused to permit me ever to give in to the many disappointments of events in the Middle East. My journey may have been solitary at times, but with her steadfast presence it could never be lonely. She is my bedrock and my joy.

To Elaine, I dedicate this book.